MS

D0146288

First Steps
Toward
Economic Independence

First Steps Toward Economic Independence

New States of the Postcommunist World

Edited by
MICHAEL L. WYZAN

PRAEGER

Westport, Connecticut
London

Library of Congress Cataloging-in-Publication Data

First steps toward economic independence : new states of the
   postcommunist world / edited by Michael L. Wyzan.
        p.   cm.
     Includes bibliographical references and index.
     ISBN 0–275–94717–3 (alk. paper)
     1. Former Soviet republics—Economic conditions—Congresses.
   2. Europe, Eastern—Economic conditions—1989- —Congresses.
   3. Former Soviet republics—Economic policy—Congresses. 4. Europe,
   Eastern—Economic policy—1989- —Congresses. 5. Postcommunism—
   Former Soviet republics—Congresses. 6. Postcommunism—Europe,
   Eastern—Congresses. I. Wyzan, Michael Louis.
   HC336.27.F57   1995
   338.947—dc20   94–33261

British Library Cataloguing in Publication Data is available.

Library of Congress Catalog Card Number: 94–33261
ISBN: 0–275–94717–3

First published in 1995

Praeger Publishers, 88 Post Road West, Westport, CT 06881
An imprint of Greenwood Publishing Group, Inc.

Printed in the United States of America

JK

The paper used in this book complies with the
Permanent Paper Standard issued by the National
Information Standards Organization (Z39.48–1984).

10 9 8 7 6 5 4 3 2 1

To my daughter, Rebecca Ling

Contents

Figure and Tables

Preface

A project of this magnitude inevitably involves the cooperation of a large number of people. I especially wish to thank my wife, Kie Min, who graciously put up with my long hours of work on the book so soon after the birth of our baby daughter. I owe a large debt to my employer, the Stockholm Institute of East European Economics, and its former director, Anders Åslund, for funding the symposium on which this volume is based, for covering much of the publication costs, and in general facilitating my work on this project. Several members of the Institute's staff merit special mention, including Eva Sundquist, Johan Fallenius, and Eva Johansson for their work in arranging and running the symposium, and Ilze Brands, Lena Hansson, and Sten Luthman for their help with the editorial work in preparing the manuscript. Few academics have the good fortune to work for an institution that is as generous, professional, and oriented toward serious research.

This project is the outgrowth of a session held at the meetings of the American Association for the Advancement of Slavic Studies in Phoenix in November 1992. At that session, early versions of the papers contained in this volume on Estonia, Macedonia, and Slovenia were presented. The session was a success, strengthening my conviction that economic policy making in new, postcommunist states is a timely and important topic of study. I am grateful to Steven S. Rosefielde for his comments at the session.

During the first half of 1993, authors were sought to prepare studies of additional former Soviet and Yugoslav republics and of Slovakia.

Ultimately, in addition to Slovakia, Georgia, Kazakhstan, Ukraine, and Croatia were selected. Authors were chosen on the basis of having a thorough and up-to-date familiarity with the country in question, a record of substantial economic research on that country, and, where possible, knowledge of the local language. In the end, the last of these criteria was met by at least one author for all countries but one.

I have tried to encompass the diverse economic experiences of new, postcommunist economies. However, it proved impossible to fully reflect the diversity of the former Soviet republics. I was guided by the notion that a smaller number of more substantial, timely, and well-informed chapters was better than a multitude of shorter ones. At the same time, I have made no attempt to impose homogeneity on the content or the style of the contributions, other than to suggest that certain topics be covered if possible and relevant. Each chapter reflects its authors' views as to the important topics to be covered for the country in question.

In August 1993, we held a symposium in Stockholm, with papers presented on all the aforementioned nations (in addition to Latvia, the article on which for a variety of reasons was not selected for inclusion in this volume). The intention was to have at least one participant from each covered country, a goal that was realized for all nations but Georgia, for which a last-minute cancellation made this impossible. I am grateful to Judith Weibull for her excellent work in arranging and overseeing the symposium. I also wish to thank the many participants in that event who made it so stimulating, especially Vytenis Aleškaitis, Eižens Cepurnieks, Goce Petreski, and Boris Pleskovič, and the various representatives of the academic, diplomatic (both Swedish and East European based in Sweden), and business communities. The editor would also like to express his sincere appreciation for the generous financial support for the symposium provided by the Prince Bertil Foundation.

Last but not least, I would like to express my sincere appreciation to Petya Tsaneva and Lyubka Mihaylova for their expert assistance with computer hardware and software, and to my editors at Praeger, Marcy Weiner and James Ice, for their encouragement and patience.

P20

1

Book title:

Introduction

Michael L. Wyzan

The end of the 1980s and the beginning of the 1990s have witnessed the disintegration of all three formerly communist federal states — Czechoslovakia, the Soviet Union, and Yugoslavia — more or less into their constituent republics. The three cases have demonstrated three alternative scenarios as to how this might be accomplished:

(1) in a peaceful and legalistic manner, following a "divorce" precipitated by the secessionist republic but largely initiated by the formerly dominant state (Czechoslovakia);

(2) suddenly and generally peacefully, with the consent of the former central government, but with violence in certain instances and considerable regret in the formerly central republic; in the aftermath of the breakup, the formerly dominant power takes an increasingly threatening posture toward the secessionist republics, a number of which seem to wonder why they left (Soviet Union); and

(3) over the violent opposition of the formerly dominant, still communist, and ultranationalist republic, precipitating bloody civil wars in several republics; others manage to escape peacefully more because of the center's military incapability to hold them or uninterest than to its consent to their leaving (Yugoslavia).

These events have resulted in the creation of 22 new states, if one counts the formerly dominant powers of the three federations (the Czech Republic, Russia, the rump Yugoslavia[1]); assumes that all breakaway republics survive as independent nations despite, in certain instances, nearly total destruction in war (Bosnia-Herzegovina) or their own seeming disinterest in being independent (Belarus); and assumes that no new secessions take place (candidates for such being Kosovo, Montenegro, and Chechnya).

The births of this multitude of new countries have raised all sorts of interesting questions for historians, political scientists, economists, and other scholars. This volume is concerned with the first steps toward economic independence of a selection of these states — four former Soviet republics (Estonia, Kazakhstan, Ukraine, and Georgia), three former Yugoslav republics (Slovenia, Croatia, and Macedonia), and Slovakia. While the experiences of these nations vary greatly from the highly successful (e.g., Estonia, Slovenia) to the absolutely catastrophic (e.g., Georgia), it is clear that they face common problems and must make their policy selections from a fairly similar menu.

One is struck by the fact that neither economic theory nor conventional wisdom has been able to provide much useful guidance to policy makers navigating these uncharted waters. In retrospect, it is nothing short of astonishing that the International Monetary Fund (IMF) strongly advised the Baltic states against introducing their own currencies: where would Estonia or Latvia be now if they still used the Russian ruble? On another level, fears have often been expressed in the West concerning the likely exploitation of such small nations as Slovenia by larger ones ("germanization," as it is called there). That these Marxist-tinged and anachronistic views have been often expressed by representatives of EC nations[2] that had just signed the Maastricht treaty seems not to have struck anyone as ironic.

Two important aspects of the situation have often been ignored. First, the option of remaining within the former federation as it was previously constructed was in many instances unavailable (Slovakia is an exception here), so that the question of whether a state might have been better off had it not declared independence is simply irrelevant. This is especially the case when the death of the federation in question takes place in the throes of war, as in the former Yugoslavia. However, it is true in many other instances as well, generally for reasons of a noneconomic nature. At the very least, any cost-benefit analysis of the decision to secede must take into account the likely state of the relevant federal state once one or more of its constituent parts decided to head for the exits.

Second, as discussed further below, in assessing the economic viability of new states, observers have tended to neglect the question of the policy-making competence of their leaderships. Far too much attention has been paid to the natural resources and other physical attributes of the nations and not enough to the quality of their leaderships. One lesson that leaps from these pages is that Ukraine's vast territory and resources and Georgia's good climate amount to little if they are poorly led; tiny and resource-poor Estonia and Slovenia seem able to do quite well without such putative advantages. There is in fact nothing surprising about this, after a century that has witnessed the divergent fates of such countries as Japan and Singapore on the one hand, and Burma and Zaire on the other.

A number of common questions have arisen in virtually all instances considered in this volume. A sample would include the following:

(1) Should a new currency be introduced, and if so, when and how?

(2) What sort of exchange rate regime should be selected and how is that choice affected by the country's newness, the lack of foreign reserves (in most cases), and the likelihood of shocks to the foreign exchange market arising from events in the former central power and other former fellow republics?

(3) What effort should be expended in attempting to retain trade links with the former central power and other former corepublics? To what extent should the understandable desires to pursue an independent foreign policy and to rid oneself of the vestiges of "foreign" occupation (where relevant) be traded off against the need to maintain such trade ties, at least until new trading patterns are established?

(4) What should be the attitude toward ownership of assets by citizens of other former republics and how does this affect the privatization process?

(5) What should be the priorities of the parliaments of these new countries, given that these bodies are typically overwhelmed by the legislative requirements of both creating a new state and transforming the economy into one based on market principles?

There are also queries of a more academic nature, ones that policy makers are generally not asked explicitly to address, but that are worth posing if one is trying to draw general lessons from these dramatic developments. These include the following:

(6) Will the act of secession prove to have been Pareto-superior to the next best alternative political status of the country, assuming that such an alternative exists?

(7) What are the costs and benefits of secession in the short run and the long run?

(8) Is the resultant politically independent entity "economically viable"?

This book represents the first thoroughgoing examination of these pressing issues for a broad selection of new, postcommunist nations. The chapters examine some or all of the questions listed above for the countries that they cover.

The focus of this volume is on the economic decision-making process of the leaderships of these fledgling states once they were launched as independent nations. In general, less attention is devoted to the rationale of the decision to secede. This rationale is often of a noneconomic nature, and even where this is not the case, it at times reflects rather questionable reasoning. For example, in Yugoslavia both more- and less-developed republics considered themselves economically exploited (by the center, by each other, by communism, by self-management?).

For the authors of the studies contained herein, the decision to secede is taken largely as exogenous to the issues at hand. In the spotlight is the decision-making process: How are the common challenges being addressed? How do the results so far reflect on the prospects of the relevant nation to prosper on its own and to weather the transition to a market economy? The result is a panorama of extraordinarily varied experiences in dealing with largely similar problems, raising the question: Why do they find it so difficult to learn from each other? No attempt is made here to answer this last question, other than to observe that successful modes of behavior in one historical or cultural context seem extremely difficult to imitate in others. Indeed, if this were not the case there would probably be no need for social science.

Before moving on, a few words are in order on two important matters: the choice of countries covered in this study and the choice of the title of this book. With respect to the former, the first principle was to have at least one representative of each of the three federations that broke apart. The second, perhaps somewhat controversial, principle was to eschew the examination of the former central power of each federation. In the case of the former Yugoslavia, the motivation for doing so seems obvious: at least until the end of 1993 there was hardly any economic policy worthy of the name in the rump Yugoslavia, which during that year experienced what is likely the worst hyperinflation in history. Moreover, the focus of this volume is on *post*communist states and it would be difficult to classify Serbia/Montenegro as such.

Furthermore, the three formerly dominant republics of the respective federations are only "new" states in a formal sense — all three to a large extent inherited such economic institutions of those federations as the currency and the central bank, and in the Soviet case (apparently) the foreign debt and reserves as well. This continuity between the former central government and that of the newly independent, formerly dominant state is clearest in the case of the former Czechoslovakia. The Czech Republic inherited the best balanced and most competently managed macroeconomy in Central and Eastern Europe (CEE). Moreover, federalism was relatively underdeveloped in Czechoslovakia, so that the Slovaks seem to have had relatively little experience with running a macroeconomy. The exclusion of the former central powers also enables us to emphasize "new country" issues, leaving questions of the transition to a market economy somewhat in the background.

The third principle involved in selecting the countries was to examine a broad spectrum of experience within each former federation. This was a trivial task in the cases of Czechoslovakia and Yugoslavia. In the latter case there are only three breakaway republics in a condition to pursue any sort of economic policy (Bosnia-Herzegovina being consumed by civil war and Montenegro not having seceded).

With respect to the former Soviet Union, however, only a subset of the 14 possible cases could be selected. The decision was to pick one Baltic state, one case from the Transcaucasus, one from among Central Asia and Kazakhstan, and Ukraine. To some extent, the final selection was guided by the availability of knowledgeable specialists to write the chapter. The inevitable result is that a number of important cases are not considered, such as Turkmenistan, with its largely unreformed, natural gas–based, and relatively healthy economy, and the Kyrgyz Republic and Moldova, two small states that have received considerable attention from the international financial community. The Latvian experience has also in most respects been quite successful and distinctive. Unfortunately, it proved impossible to obtain an up-to-date and comprehensive examination of the relevant issues in Latvia comparable with the other studies contained in this volume.

As to the title of this collection, it is worth mentioning that *First Steps Toward Economic Independence* refers to the measures taken to create an economic system consistent with one's status as an independent state. It does not refer to an attempt to make oneself economically independent of (or autarkic relative to) one's former fellow republics or the rest of the world, even if such an attempt may be made in certain instances (such as in Gamsakhurdia's Georgia). The term *economically independent* does not even necessarily connote having one's own currency, as experience from West Africa and the Caribbean amply attests.

Economic independence as defined here refers to the establishment of sovereignty over the key macroeconomic decisions — which might well include the conscious, voluntary decision to adopt the currency of another state — consistent with political independence. It is not possible to come up with a generally accepted list of the attributes of an economically independent state. Nonetheless, the chapters contained in this volume provide considerable insight into the nature of those attributes, at least for postcommunist nations.

The remainder of this introductory chapter is organized as follows: The next section examines the importance of the introduction of one's own currency to the establishment of economic sovereignty, with the focus on the post-Soviet experience. The third section takes a critical look at the question of the "economic viability" of a (new) country. The chapter concludes with brief summaries of the country studies that follow.

MONETARY INDEPENDENCE

As noted above, it is possible for an unquestionably independent nation to employ the currency of another country (Panama comes to mind as an example). Nonetheless, for a postcommunist, breakaway republic the sine qua non for establishing itself as an economically independent state has become the successful introduction of its own monetary unit. This requires little explanation for the three post-Yugoslav republics covered here, all of which have easily displayed better macroeconomic performance than Serbia/Montenegro, with its world-record hyperinflation in 1993. This author is unaware of anyone arguing that Slovenia or Croatia should stick to the Yugoslav dinar; the outside world seemed not to be paying much attention when Macedonia[3] introduced its currency in April 1992.

However, even in Slovakia, with no obvious urgency attached to leaving the zone of the Czechoslovak koruna — characterized by the lowest inflation in CEE — the introduction of a Slovak koruna was viewed as indispensable to gaining control over macroeconomic policy. This decision was motivated largely by a desire on the part of a republic suffering from a much higher level of unemployment (than the Czech Republic) to pursue a less restrictive monetary policy. In this instance, the "gain" from establishing monetary independence may prove illusory: the space won to expand the Slovak economy is tightly constrained by its need to have relations with and obtain finance from the international financial institutions. In any case, as of the end of 1994, Slovakia continued to have one of the lowest inflation rates in the region, if somewhat higher than in the Czech Republic.

In general, there are a number of advantages to introducing one's own currency for a breakaway, postcommunist republic. National sovereignty is enhanced by having such a currency, enabling faster-reforming republics not to be hampered by slower-moving ones and to gain control over the local tax base, where the latter is defined to include seigniorage. Furthermore, the introduction of one's own monetary unit enables a republic to introduce currency convertibility, privatize its state enterprises, and reform its financial sector more rapidly than the average for its former federation.

Moreover, monetary independence contributes to economic stabilization in the sense that it enables a country to avoid the problems inherent in the functioning of a common currency area. Such areas tend to have a built-in inflationary bias (especially under postcommunist conditions) as member states run loose monetary and fiscal policies, knowing that the costs of doing so are distributed across all such states. Monetary independence also contributes to stabilization by enabling nations to depreciate (and appreciate) their currencies in response to terms-of-trade shocks that affect them disproportionately (Hansson, 1993, pp. 164–169).

The issue of monetary independence has attracted the most interest and controversy with respect to the former Soviet republics. As noted earlier, the IMF initially recommended against such republics introducing their own currencies (see IMF, 1992; Hansson, 1993, p. 164). The various republics have had a great variety of relations with the ruble zone. These range from leaving the zone at one stroke (early in the case of Estonia, later in the Kyrgyz Republic), to deciding relatively early to leave it in stages by first introducing a temporary currency in parallel with the ruble (Latvia and Lithuania), to delaying as long as possible before introducing a parallel currency in the wake of the confiscatory Russian monetary reform of July 1993 (Kazakhstan), and even to deciding (temporarily, as it turns out) to withdraw one's parallel currency and go back into monetary union with Russia (Belarus).

Although a thorough discussion of optimum currency areas is beyond the scope of this Introduction, it is useful to pause to examine whether there is a theoretical justification for retaining some form of ruble zone. The traditional theoretical literature on optimum currency areas was employed by some Western observers at an early stage to argue that the Soviet Union might indeed make such an area. Such reasoning was based on the fact that there were breaks in factor mobility at its borders and that internal trade was larger than foreign trade, especially with respect to productive inputs. It was supposed, correctly as it happens, that not employing a common currency area — and payments-clearing mechanism — would be very costly in terms of trade disruption among the republics (see Conway, 1993; Pomfret, 1993).

Any of the usual benefits of optimum currency areas, such as economizing on foreign reserves, reducing exchange rate risk, increasing credibility, and stabilizing the demand for money, might well apply in the post-Soviet case.

On the other hand, because of prevailing factor immobility and factor price rigidity within republics, flexible exchange rates between their currencies would provide a vehicle for adjustment (Mundell, 1961; McKinnon, 1963). It has long been known that countries will benefit more from the formation of a currency union the more willing they are to coordinate their fiscal and monetary policies; such a willingness is hardly likely to arise among nations with such diverse visions of economic policy as, say, Latvia and Belarus. It is possible for countries to pursue divergent fiscal policies if they can borrow from a common capital market, but the primitive financial markets of the postcommunist world make this unavailable for the foreseeable future. Moreover, recent theoretical work on optimal currency areas demonstrates that a differential desire to use the inflation tax across member countries creates a deadweight loss from employing such an area (Canzoneri and Rogers, 1990).

In reality, the ruble zone was plagued by all sorts of serious problems. An inflationary bias was built in by the free rider aspects of having a number of quasi-independent monetary authorities, each of which could issue ruble credit. Interestingly, currency unions in general, especially when the monetary authorities retain some independence, seem to suffer from such a bias (see Flandreau, 1993).

Particularly striking is the ruble zone's infamous "cash shortage," which appeared at the end of 1991 and affected the republics to varying extents. A lack of currency in the accounts of enterprises and the government made it impossible to pay wages and pensions and to buy inputs. The lack of availability of cash created a premium for this means of payment relative to account (*beznalichnyi*) rubles, the accounting entries used by Gosbank for interenterprise and enterprise-government financial flows. Inasmuch as these two types of money were formally equal in value, economic agents wanted to pay in account rubles and be paid in cash, exacerbating the cash shortage.[4]

The experience of the republics of the former USSR with attempting to form a monetary union suggests that, at least under postcommunist conditions, some additions need to be made to the standard theory of the optimum currency area. It is not just a question of nations wishing in good faith to pursue divergent fiscal and monetary policies — although this seems to apply fairly well to the Czech-Slovak split — but also of the policy competence of the monetary authorities, especially of the central one. The leadership of the Russian central bank generally displayed disinterest in the macroeconomic stability of the ruble zone, focusing its attention on keeping struggling state enterprises afloat. That leadership has also been accused of personally profiting from the provision of cash rubles to outlying republics.

Accordingly, research in a public choice vein that examines both the relative vulnerability of the monetary and fiscal authorities in member states of a currency union to interest group pressures, as well as the relative corruptibility of those authorities, seems particularly promising.

THE ECONOMIC VIABILITY OF NATIONS

An issue that inevitably arises in both popular and scholarly discussion of new nations is their "economic viability." Many of the smaller and less prepossessing new postcommunist states are frequently the object of speculation on this score. Moreover, even where this terminology is not explicitly employed, the question is frequently raised by such observers as businesspeople on visits to the Kyrgyz Republic who describe that country as of no interest because of its (apparent) lack of exploitable natural resources.

Economists have not in general paid a great deal of attention to the question of economic viability. A recent and important exception is Bookman (1993), who in her encyclopedic examination of the economics of the secession devotes considerable space to this issue. Bookman (1993, pp. 37–41) divides the process of the secession of a region into three phases — reevaluation, redefinition, and reequilibration. In the first phase, reevaluation, a feeling of economic injustice leads a region to reappraise the costs and benefits of remaining within the federation in which it currently finds itself. It is worth noting that such feelings may arise in both relatively developed and relatively underdeveloped regions, although in the postcommunist world it seems to be the former that move first to leave their federations.

The second stage, redefinition, involves the severing of current ties with the center and the establishment of new ones to both the former federation and the rest of the world. This phase, which involves what have been termed "divorce proceedings," seems in the cases discussed in this book — with the exception of the former Czechoslovakia — to be highly protracted; in the Yugoslav case, the ill will of the center may prevent them from ever taking place.

It is in the third stage, Bookman's reequilibration, that the question of economic viability comes to the fore. A number of authors have attempted to develop criteria for determining whether a breakaway piece of a former nation will be viable on its own. Deutsche Bank (1991), in its study of the former Soviet republics, cites the following yardsticks: degree of industrialization; degree of self-sufficiency; agricultural production; mineral resources; potential to earn hard currency through the export of agricultural products, raw materials, and industrial goods; business-mindedness; proximity to Europe; level of education; ethnic homogeneity; and infrastructure. In his work on former Yugoslav republics, Ding (1991, pp. 23–25) uses the following criteria: gross social product (GSP), GSP per capita, population, imports as a proportion of GSP, external exports as a proportion of GSP, regional exports as a proportion of GSP, unemployment, and enterprise losses as a proportion of GSP. Bookman's (1993, pp. 41–42) viability criteria include a region's relative income level, its absolute level of development, its trade dependency on the state, the net flows of capital and natural resources over regional frontiers, and the degree of decentralization of power concerning economic issues.

The main problem with these lists of criteria is not so much with the individual yardsticks employed — although some, such as Deutsche Bank's proximity to Europe, can certainly be questioned — but that they fail to assign any role to the (postindependence) decision-making process in nations. The studies contained in this volume of the first economic maneuvers of the leaderships of new, formerly communist states, and the visiting missions of the IMF and the World Bank (among other institutions) to these states, focus on how these leaderships deal with the problems that they face. To an important degree, the objective nature of those problems is less important than the states' ability to deal with them.

Virtually all new, postcommunist states are in need of a variety of forms of assistance from the international financial institutions and other donors: balance of payments support, technical assistance, financing for restructuring and infrastructural projects, and so on. If a state manages to alienate the international community, whether by poor economic policy or by unacceptable actions in such other spheres as human rights or its behavior toward its neighbors, it may well lose its access to these forms of assistance.

It might at first appear that these remarks are not universally applicable. In Estonia, for example, the availability of reacquired gold reserves to back the kroon and the ability to attract direct foreign investment and to attain current account surpluses seem to make large-scale international financial assistance unnecessary. However, Estonia's precarious security situation must not be forgotten. Estonia must convince the West that it is worthy of being defended — if not militarily, then diplomatically and in other ways — against the actions of its enormous, unstable, and potentially vengeful eastern neighbor.

The events of the last several years have demonstrated that, at least for former Soviet and Yugoslav republics, competence at macroeconomic management is a key desideratum for receiving pivotal financial and other support. States without significant needs for balance of payments assistance — such as Estonia and Latvia — can convince the West that it is in the latter's interest to support their positions on security issues by showing that they can manage their affairs economically. Landlocked, impoverished states, such as Macedonia, Moldova, or the Kyrgyz Republic, by demonstrating a willingness to at least entertain serious economic reform, can obviate much of the skepticism about their prospects. In this manner, they come to the attention of such important actors as the Pentagon and Jeffrey Sachs. For survival in the post–Cold War world, such considerations are far more important than the inventory of one's natural resources or one's physical location.

Another problem with Bookman's, Deutsche Bank's, and Ding's approach to the economic viability of nations is that it fails to define what it means to be "economically nonviable." The best way to define this concept is perhaps in a relative sense: a nation deeming itself nonviable may elect for combination with another nation, although not necessarily with the federation to which it formerly belonged. While there is little precedent in modern times for a nation being starved out of existence, there are instances of nations or ethnic groups electing on economic grounds not to leave their present countries: the referendum after World War I among Slovenes living in present-day Austria to remain under Vienna rather than join the new Yugoslavia is an example. Moreover, under present conditions, one cannot exclude the possibility that, for example, Belarussians may make a similar decision.

CHAPTER SUMMARIES

Former Soviet Republics

In his chapter on Estonia, Ardo H. Hansson begins by describing the environment in which that country began its economic transformation. The key factors in this regard are antipathy to such notions as international economic integration and cooperation, producing a cautious approach to economic relations with other former republics; a clear national consensus on a "return to Europe," leading to a very liberal trade regime with respect to Western countries and a willingness to bear the social costs of economic restructuring; and a large non-Estonian (mostly Russian) minority, concentrated heavily in industry and in industrial regions, which may slow reform.

Among the key steps taken by Estonia to reestablish its economic sovereignty was reform of taxation, with the goal the introduction of a system similar to those found in Western Europe. The practical steps included introducing a value-added tax, progressive personal income tax, a proportional corporate income tax, and giving local governments their own tax bases; the result was a rare fiscal system that runs surpluses.

Perhaps the best known aspect of Estonian economic reform is the fact that it employs a modified currency board system, according to which the kroon — the new currency introduced in June 1992 — is tied by law to the Deutsche mark and the central bank may issue additional reserve money only in exchange for new foreign currency receipts. Once again, the result has been highly successful, as the largely convertible kroon has quickly become the sole means of payment and foreign exchange reserves have grown considerably. The payments system is improving as insolvent commercial banks are closed.

Privatization in Estonia has, according to Hansson, been heavily influenced by the fact that it is a state whose sovereignty has been restored and finds itself with a large, nonindigenous, immigrant minority: ethnic Estonians favor restitution and voucher privatization, while non-Estonians favor free distribution to workers or tenants. Estonia's needs in terms of economic restructuring are especially great given the considerable distortion of its economy as part of the Soviet Union. In terms of external relations, breaking away from that federal state has altered the time sequence of the inevitable terms-of-trade shock faced by all transitional economies, increased the size of the fall in trade volume, and augmented the magnitude of the shift in trade orientation toward the West.

In their chapter on Ukraine, Simon Johnson and Oleg Ustenko argue that this large and seemingly promising former Soviet republic must be considered a failure from the viewpoint of economic reform. Inflation has been higher than in Russia and the decline in output has been particularly severe, largely as a result of the failure of Ukraine's government to promulgate a coherent reform strategy. These highly unfavorable developments stand in sharp contrast to its relatively advantageous starting position, abundant mineral wealth and excellent farm land, surpluses in and a relatively small dependence on interrepublic trade, and a considerable degree of energy self-sufficiency.

During the period from December 1991 to November 1992, Ukraine remained in the ruble zone, so that inflation there was quite similar to that in Russia. A new currency to circulate in parallel with the Russian ruble, the coupon-karbovanets, was introduced at the beginning of 1992; this move was followed by a few months of relatively stable prices on the heels of the large anticipatory purchases that denuded the store shelves at the end of 1991. The real budget deficit started out relatively small but grew alarmingly, largely on the strength of shrinking revenues, leading to very rapid monetary growth. On the whole, price setting continued to be on an administrative basis, so that prices in state stores grew more slowly than the overall inflation rate. In November 1992, Ukraine left the ruble zone and its government made strong statements in favor of macroeconomic stabilization; from December 1992 to May 1993, the government had special powers to make economic decisions. However, the money supply continued to grow at an extremely rapid rate, leading to virtual hyperinflation and a collapsing exchange rate.

Not surprisingly under these conditions, Ukraine has made little progress on privatization, lacking a clear privatization strategy and finding its attempts at employing the voucher method complicated and unworkable. Still, the private sector is displaying signs of growth; it is concentrated in trade, simple services, and small-scale agriculture, although there are also a substantial number of commercial banks that are not offshoots of the Gosbank system. In the end, Johnson and Ustenko attribute the failure of reform in Ukraine to a considerable degree to deficiencies in its human capital: few in the country understand the nature and necessity of economic reform.

Peter Rutland and Timur R. Isataev note that the dislocation in Kazakhstan arising from its leaving the Soviet Union includes the end of net transfers from Moscow; an economic and institutional structure unsuited to a market economy; and a need to seek Western investment in natural resource extraction in a way that does not antagonize Moscow.

They observe that despite its vast mineral wealth, Kazakhstan is relatively poor, geographically isolated, and highly integrated with the Russian economy. Kazakhstan's president, Nursultan Nazarbaev, has based his ambitious economic development programs on a hoped-for influx of direct foreign investment into natural resource exploitation, especially oil and natural gas.

Because it has not staked out an independent course in its economic policy, Kazakhstan has been vulnerable to policy shifts in Moscow; as elsewhere in the former USSR, inflation has been high and production has plummeted. The banking system has been unprepared to deal with the vicissitudes of a more liberal economy, while the budget deficit has grown alarmingly due to declining revenue and continuing subsidization of industry. Living standards have deteriorated considerably but unemployment has not (officially) risen appreciably so far. Extensive (often ineffective) government regulation of the economy persists, a fact which, according to Rutland and Isataev, is not entirely negative, since the economy is less out of control than its Russian counterpart.

The Kazakh approach to privatization has been slow and cautious; the method chosen in 1991 emphasized worker buyouts, the retention in state hands of strategic sectors, and a sharp distinction between the responsibilities of the local and central governments. In April 1993 a revised privatization program reduced worker privileges, concentrated decision-making authority at the federal level, and called for the creation of holding companies as a vehicle for industrial policy. Agricultural restructuring has not gone far, as there is no private land ownership and most state farms have simply reorganized themselves.

Kazakhstan's foreign trade activity is still closely tied to its relations with Russia, with which Kazakhstan shares an enormous border without customs posts; efforts to establish direct links with Turkey or Iran have run into increasing opposition from Moscow. As of the beginning of 1994, however, agreements with the IMF and the World Bank were beginning to yield substantial amounts of financial assistance. Rutland and Isataev conclude by briefly examining Nazarbaev's ethnic and foreign policies and by posing a number of questions the answers to which will determine whether his development strategy will succeed.

In their examination of the Georgian economy, Patrick J. Conway and Chandrashekar Pant begin by describing Georgia's starting position at independence, which was characterized by relatively high levels of social development and of economic integration with the rest of the former USSR. Georgian economic performance in the last several years has been especially poor. The authors attribute this fact partly to such union-wide factors as a contraction in production in other republics, the ineffectiveness of ministries in allocating resources, price increases toward world levels for imported inputs, and discrimination by less independent-minded republics. Internal causes of poor performance include an earthquake, political/social instability, the maintenance of export controls after price liberalization in Russia and Georgia, and large revenue shortfalls leading to enormous budget deficits.

Conway and Pant identify institutional reorganization, regulatory reform, and integration with the rest of the world as the most important steps in economic policy making for post-Soviet republics. With respect to institutional reorganization, reliance on institutions from Soviet times (e.g., the national bank, the Ministry of the Economy/former Gosplan) and sloth in creating new ones have been costly to Georgia. As to regulatory reform, price liberalization was quite thorough once finally initiated in February 1992; indeed energy prices are closer to world prices than those in other former republics. On the other hand, while it remained in the ruble zone Georgia persistently set interest rates below the levels prevailing in Russia, with predictable consequences. The failure to privatize state enterprises has meant that most firms are state-owned, unprepared to function in a market environment, and subject to unscrupulous rent-seeking behavior on the part of managers and others. However, privatization of housing and agricultural activity has been rapid.

According to Conway and Pant, the sharp decline in Georgian foreign trade is the result of autarkic, trade-hampering policies relative to the rest of the former USSR, which exacerbated the effects of the general decline in trade that attended the breakup of that federation. The economic transition in Georgia has also been marked by an attempt to pursue autarkic policies in such spheres as price-setting and in the setting of interest rates. This has led to cash shortages, financial disintermediation, out-flows of goods and capital, and a growing underground economy. Georgia's ongoing attempts to transform its economy must contend with ethnic conflict and civil unrest, a deteriorating situation in neighboring countries, and its own inclination to attempt the establishment of an autarkic economic system.

Former Yugoslav Republics

In their chapter on Slovenia, Evan Kraft, Milan Vodopivec, and Milan Cvikl note that although Slovenia was the most developed Yugoslav republic, its economic performance deteriorated markedly during the

1980s, as high inflation generated by a lack of fiscal and monetary discipline in Belgrade afflicted all such republics. However, since independence economic performance has been among the best in the postcommunist world.

In terms of monetary reform, Slovenia passed legislation on the financial system in 1991; the most important law in this regard was that which granted the Bank of Slovenia full policy independence. The tolar was introduced in October 1991 in an abrupt manner over a three-day period during which Yugoslav dinars could be exchanged for, and bank accounts converted into, tolars. The passage in early 1991 of legislation creating corporate profit and personal income taxes and reforming the system of payroll deductions has contributed to the registering of budget surpluses for each of the last several years. Monetary policy has been consistently restrictive, aided by the law granting independence to the central bank, which also forbids resort to selective credits. Due to the lack of foreign reserves and of international support at the time of the declaration of independence, the tolar, which is largely convertible, was allowed to float freely; the fruitfulness of this approach is demonstrated by the tolar's stable exchange rate since its introduction.

Slovenia is much less of a success story when it comes to privatization and restructuring. Considerable controversy and delay have accompanied attempts to pass privatization legislation. An early bill favoring internal privatization through worker buyouts was denounced by the visiting Jeffrey Sachs, under whose influence another draft law, this one based on the distribution of shares to citizens and pension funds, was promulgated. The final legislation, a compromise between the two approaches, was finally passed in November 1992. The privatization that has taken place so far has occurred through employee buyouts, direct sales and joint ventures, bankruptcy proceedings, the creation of private enterprises as subsidiaries of social sector ones, and the start-up of new firms. A special agency is operating to recapitalize the major commercial banks under a method that does not write off all bad debts and increases the state role in banking. Although laws have been passed that allow workers to be laid off, create more flexible hiring practices, institute collective bargaining, and shorten the notification period for laid-off workers, serious difficulties remain with respect to labor market policy. These include a moratorium on new bankruptcy proceedings and the suspension of incomes policy due to a breakdown in the system of collective bargaining.

Kraft, Vodopivec, and Cvikl conclude with an evaluation of the costs and benefits to Slovenia of its secession from Yugoslavia. The costs include those of reorienting trade, enhanced autarkic tendencies, the danger of unacceptably large foreign influence in the economy, heightened political risk due Slovenia's proximity to a war zone, and spillovers from war-torn republics. The benefits include exit from the bloody chaos of the former Yugoslavia, enhanced macroeconomy stability, increased capital accumulation due to the end of the subsidization of poorer Yugoslav regions, and faster entry into the EC.

In his chapter on Croatia, Ivo Bićanić begins by discussing the path to economic independence in that war-torn land. In terms of important post-independence economic reforms, the Croatian national bank immediately took on the features of a true central bank, the Croatian dinar (a temporary currency for use until the kuna is ready) abruptly replaced its Yugoslav predecessor, the fiscal system was nationalized, and an independent payments system was created. However, establishing trade relations with other former republics has not gone as smoothly, problems having arisen with respect to creating payments regimes and policing the new borders.

Bićanić goes on to detail the positive and negative features of Croatia's transition to an independent, market-based economy; there has been extensive legislative and institutional change but the larger enterprises and banks remain untouched. The chosen method of privatization is state-dominated, oriented to the generation of revenue, and prone to abuse by enterprise managers. It will create four types of enterprises: those that have been privatized according to their own privatization plans, those that have not come up with such plans and now belong to the privatization authorities, those that will remain in the state sector in deference to the "national interest," and those that will so remain because of their unclear ownership status inherited from the old economic system.

Croatia's attempts to establish its economic sovereignty under war-time conditions have been costly. The period from independence through October 1993 saw a substantial decline in production, large budget deficits, high inflation, a major fall in foreign trade volumes, a drop in real incomes (necessitating an increase in household debt), and rising inequality among regions and sectors. Croatia has made three attempts at macroeconomic stabilization. The first, in the summer of 1992, aimed at reducing public spending and inflation, increasing the autonomy of the central bank, defining a framework for financial rehabilitation, and stimulating economic growth. This plan failed to achieve its goals and was succeeded by another drafted in the fall of 1992 and calling for a balanced budget, financial discipline, strict monetary policy, and support for tourism. This program was never implemented, and was itself superseded in October 1993 by one that has enjoyed considerable success. This most recent attempt is based on devaluation of the dinar, tight monetary policy, partial internal convertibility, tax reform, attempts to increase fiscal discipline, and limitations on wage bills (replacing the previous system of collective bargaining over wages).

My chapter deals with Macedonia, Yugoslavia's poorest former republic, which now finds itself boxed in by the UN sanctions against Serbia/Montenegro and a Greek blockade. I begin by describing the country's level of development relative to other such republics: the republic was responsible for only a very small share of Yugoslav production, investment, and foreign trade activity, although it managed to become the most industrialized republic. As a relatively poor region, it was a net recipient of explicit and implicit federal transfers and ran persistent trade deficits with the rest of the world.

Macroeconomic stabilization in Macedonia can be divided into three stages. The initial stabilization program of April 1992, which coincided with the introduction of a new currency (the denar), emphasized tight monetary policy, fiscal restraint, incomes policy, and price controls on a small number of necessities. The program fell short of success as inflation and depreciation of the denar on the black market became serious problems. This failure may be traced to the maintenance of a dual exchange rate mechanism, the absence of an incomes policy, the persistence of muddled Yugoslav budgetary accounting, and the provision of selective credits to agriculture from the primary emission. In October 1992, another, less formal attempt was made to stabilize the economy, this time involving tight monetary/credit policy, incomes policy, and some price controls. Although by the middle of 1993 there were some improvements in economic performance, toward the end of the year it was clear that the results were less than satisfactory. A new, thus far more successful stabilization program, this time with financial support from the IMF, was launched in December 1993, with the emphasis on the following: restoring wage discipline, turning monetary policy into the foundation of macroeconomic stability and not the provider of selective credits to individual sectors, and fiscal sector reform to reduce the budget deficit and the pension burden and shift expenditure toward measures supporting structural reform.

Structural change has been very slow in Macedonia. Nonetheless, important legislation was passed in May 1993 on the foreign exchange market (the dual exchange rate mechanism was finally eliminated), foreign investment (a very liberal law), foreign trade, and foreign credit relations. December 1993 saw the passage of laws on the budget process and on various forms of taxation, including the personal income, corporate income, and property taxes. The most important structural issue is, of course, privatization, legislation on which was at last passed in June 1993. The privatization method, which avoids both the use of vouchers and free giveaways to workers, varies with the size of the firm; one innovation is a method that amounts to a leveraged buyout under favorable conditions. Overall, the chosen methodology is highly complex and likely to be availed of largely by enterprise insiders. The chapter ends with the observation that, despite the failure of economic policy so far to resolve the country's problems, the authorities have succeeded in demonstrating to the international community that the country is worthy of support.

Slovakia

Herta Gabrielová, Egon Hlavatý, Adela Hošková, Zora Komínková, Milan Kurucz, and Brigita Schmögnerová begin their chapter on Slovakia by discussing the country's diplomatic recognition, admission to international organizations, and relations with its neighbors. All of these matters were facilitated by the peaceful nature of the divorce with the Czech Republic. However, relations with Hungary are complicated by that country's dissatisfaction over the status of ethnic Hungarians in Slovakia, who make up the largest minority there; the authors argue that the rights of ethnic minorities are adequately protected by the constitution. A large number of treaties governing relations with the Czech Republic have been signed, but problems remain with respect to the border regime, the division of former federal property, and citizenship.

When it began life on its own, Slovakia had to prepare macroeconomic policy from scratch and set up new institutions, neither of which was necessary to the same extent in the Czech Republic. Monetary independence was achieved unexpectedly soon, as the agreement that created a monetary union at the beginning of 1993 had already fallen apart by February; monetary union was superseded by a payments agreement based on bilateral clearing. The goals of the now independent Slovak national bank are to stabilize the Slovak koruna, minimize inflation, maintain balance of payments equilibrium, and increase the foreign reserves, with the overriding objective of maintaining internal convertibility. In the fiscal sphere, although the 1993 Slovak budget was drafted in such a way as to be in balance, in fact a deficit appeared due to the steep recession, the extra expenditures involved in running a new state, and the cutoff of federal transfers; that budget also witnessed the introduction of several new forms of taxation.

One of the main motivations for wishing to leave Czechoslovakia was the desire to conduct an independent economic policy. It was believed that the burden of the federal transition program fell disproportionately on Slovakia, where economic indicators have generally been worse than those for the Czech Republic. As it turns out, however, the independent Slovak government has found little room to change course, given budget constraints, the need to obtain the support of the IMF, and the fact that many reform programs have already gone in irreversible directions. Economic indicators show the Slovak economy to be performing relatively well but worse than its Czech counterpart.

Slovakia has an especially great need for economic restructuring in view of its previous orientation toward heavy industry and military production, which brought with it high energy consumption, environmental disruption, and dependence on cheap Soviet raw materials. Slovakia participated in the first round of voucher participation overseen by the former federal government, so that much has been accomplished on this front. Nonetheless, the views of its first independent government on privatization differed somewhat from those held in Prague, especially with respect to speed, methods, and certain sectoral issues.

Turning to foreign trade, the authors argue that Slovakia has a number of disadvantages in this sphere relative to the Czech Republic — a greater import and lesser export orientation, less sophisticated export products, and a higher share in total trade of nonmarket economies. Despite these factors, Slovakia has enjoyed some success in reorienting its trade toward the West and in increasing the share of exports in GDP, although trade with the Czech Republic has fallen markedly. The authors provide various reasons why Slovakia received a disproportionately small share of foreign direct investment in Czechoslovakia, but are optimistic on the long-run attractiveness of the country in this regard.

NOTES

The author is grateful for very useful discussions with Anders Åslund, Ilze Brands, and Patrick J. Conway on some of the subjects treated in this Introduction.

1.   In this book the terms *rump Yugoslavia* and *Serbia/Montenegro* will be employed interchangeably, with no offense intended to Kosovo's long-suffering ethnic Albanians or to Vojvodina's ethnic Hungarians.

2.   Throughout this volume, the organization known, as of January 1, 1994, as the European Union (EU) is referred to as the European Community (EC), because in

virtually all instances the events described took place before the change of name.

3. The author is all too aware of the controversy concerning the appellation of this southernmost former Yugoslav republic. The practice followed in this work is to refer to it simply as "Macedonia," rather than as the "Former Yugoslav Republic of Macedonia" (FYROM) or "Skopje." It is difficult to justify rejecting a country's chosen name in favor of one suggested by a hostile neighboring country in the throes of nationalist hysteria, even if the latter has unaccountably managed to gain entry into the leading Western security and economic structures. In any case, there appears no more reason to call Macedonia "FYROM" than to refer to Estonia as "FSROE" (the "Former Soviet Republic of Estonia") or for that matter to the United States as "FBCOUSA" (the "Former British Colonies of the United States of America").

4. Many explanations for the cash shortage have been offered by monetary officials from former Soviet republics. In terms of the quantity theory of money, they can be summarized in the following manner: that P (the price level) is too high after price liberalization, that M (the money supply) has fallen too sharply due to capital flight, and that V (velocity) has fallen. In a thoughtful analysis, Conway (1993) finds these rather primitive explanations wanting and argues instead that the cash shortage is the result of financial disintermediation as holders of cash are reluctant to entrust them to the financial system.

REFERENCES

Bookman, Milica Zarkovic. *The Economics of Secession*. Basingstoke, Hampshire: Macmillan, 1993.

Canzoneri, Matthew B., and Carol Ann Rogers. "Is the European Community an Optimal Currency Area? Optimal Taxation vs. The Cost of Multiple Currencies." *American Economic Review* 80, 3 (June 1990): 419–432.

Conway, Patrick J. "Rubles, Rubles, Everywhere . . . Cash Shortages and Financial Disintermediation in the Ruble Monetary Zone." May 1993 (mimeo).

[Deutsche Bank.] *The Soviet at the Crossroads: Facts and Figures on the Soviet Republics*. Frankfurt: Deutsche Bank, 1991.

Ding, Wei. "Yugoslavia: Costs and Benefits of Union and Interdependence of Regional Economies." *Comparative Economic Studies* 33, 4 (Winter 1991): 1–26.

Flandreau, Mark. "On the Inflationary Bias of Common Currencies: The Latin Union Puzzle." *European Economic Review* 37, 2 (April 1993): 501–506.

Hansson, Ardo H. "The Trouble with the Ruble: Monetary Reform in the Former Soviet Union." In Anders Åslund and Richard Layard (eds.), *Changing the Economic System in Russia*, pp. 163–182. London: Pinter, 1993.

[IMF.] *Common Issues and Interrepublic Relations within the Former USSR*. Washington, D.C.: International Monetary Fund, April 1992.

McKinnon, Ronald I. "Optimum Currency Areas." *American Economic Review* 53, 4 (September 1963): 717–725.

Mundell, Robert A. "A Theory of Optimum Currency Areas." *American Economic Review* 51, 4 (September 1961): 657–665.

Pomfret, Richard. "The Choice of Monetary Regime in the Asian CIS Countries." July 1993 (mimeo).

I

FORMER SOVIET REPUBLICS

2

Estonia

Ar_o H. Klamer

2

Book title:

Estonia

Ardo H. Hansson

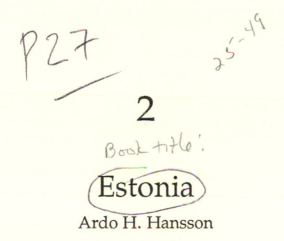

INTRODUCTION

Most Central and Eastern European countries are struggling with the daunting task of transforming their state-owned, centrally planned economies (CPEs) to a private, market-oriented basis. The newly or once again independent states emerging from the collapse of the USSR and Yugoslavia and the dissolution of Czechoslovakia face an even greater challenge. While moving from plan to market, they must at the same time restructure their often provincial economies to ones befitting a sovereign state.

For a country in the early stages of nation- and state-building, the economics of transformation are changed in two ways. First, the country faces some tasks, such as the introduction of a national currency, which are not faced by the "older" nations. Second, the precise form of steps taken by all reforming CPEs, such as privatization, can be altered by the unique constraints and needs of nation-building.

This chapter examines the specific issues faced by the "new" states during this period of "dual economic transformation," using the experience of Estonia as a case study.[1] This is done in several stages. First, the main social and political factors which have an impact on the Estonian transformation are described. This is followed by discussions of the impact of nation-building on fiscal and monetary policy, domestic liberalization, privatization, economic restructuring, and external economic relations. Finally, we conclude with a discussion of whether the Estonian experience can be generalized to other "new" states.

SOCIOPOLITICAL SETTING

The environment in which Estonia is undertaking its economic transformation is shaped by three main sociopolitical factors: the collapse of Soviet power, the desire for a return to Europe, and the ethnic dimension of economic reform.

The Collapse of Soviet Power

In the former Soviet Union (FSU), the failure of the August 1991 coup led to a discrediting of most things considered Soviet. This was especially true in the Baltic states, where Soviet rule had been more recently imposed and was viewed as particularly foreign. These perceptions both fueled the drive to restore political independence and hastened the dismantling of the main pillars of the Soviet state (communism, central planning, the ruble, and so on).

In fact, the strength of the antipathy in Estonia toward all things Soviet has been such that even concepts such as economic integration and cooperation, which are viewed positively or benignly in most countries, have been partially discredited by association with Soviet rule. For many Estonians, the term *socialist integration* conjures up images not of prosperity, but of an externally imposed and inappropriate economic structure, the forced consumption of shoddy goods, and a barely functioning currency. For these reasons, ideas which many outsiders consider appealing, such as a common Baltic currency, a Baltic customs union, or continued close cooperation with the member-states of the CIS (Commonwealth of Independent States), have so far found little real support in Estonia.

In the economic sphere, the Soviet collapse began long before the August coup. Since 1989, much of Estonian economic policy has been motivated by a desire to escape its negative effects. While the impact of real shocks, such as the rapid fall in trade volumes and the decline of certain industries, could scarcely be avoided, there were greater opportunities to escape the macroeconomic and financial chaos of the FSU.

Early Estonian attempts to counter the growing inflationary pressures in the ruble zone included the application of export controls to stem the outflow of goods to neighboring regions which were also experiencing general shortage.[2] "Protecting the internal market" was seen by much of the public as a cure for many ills of the time. In a similar fashion, the subsequent emergence of high open inflation and a cash shortage increased the pressure to introduce a national currency.

The net effect of the political and economic pressures arising from the Soviet collapse has been to encourage a cautious, at times almost autarkic approach to economic relations with "the East." In spite of its much stronger recent trade links with the FSU, Estonia has sometimes appeared less interested in maintaining these links than have the countries of Central Europe.[3] The freezing of ruble and hard currency deposits in Russian banks has been particularly instrumental in strengthening this stance, which will likely be maintained until the FSU economies are stabilized, and until Estonia feels that it is seen as equally independent as, say, Finland. As long as Russian officials continue to refer to the "near abroad," there will be domestic political pressure to place enhancement of sovereignty above the development of economic ties.[4] In this environment, and with continued financial chaos in the ex–ruble zone, little positive cooperation is possible.

Once Estonia feels secure in its nationhood and clearly sees a common interest with other states of the FSU, active cooperation will surely be pursued. Until that time, Western calls for greater cooperation among the Baltic States, or between Estonia and Russia, are simply nonstarters.[5] Western policy makers wishing to encourage long-run cooperation among these states should focus on discouraging the erection of major barriers, rather than encouraging active cooperation. This will ensure that when a real desire to cooperate emerges, it can be facilitated.

The New Goal of a "Return to Europe"

In many former Soviet republics, particularly those in Central Asia, there was no obvious wish to leave the Union, nor is there yet a clear goal of where to head as independent states.[6] In other countries, such as Ukraine, support for independence is strong, but there is little agreement on whether the future lies more with Russia or with Europe. In Estonia, there has been a clear consensus on both what to escape and where to head in the future. The latter is expressed under the general heading of the "return to Europe," a term which, while imprecise in meaning, reflects an often stated, nearly universal goal.

While this goal is also expressed in the "old" countries of Central and Eastern Europe, the difference with Estonia is a matter of degree. The simple fact that these states were already termed European makes any "return" less significant than for a country where 95 percent of trade was conducted with the other ex-Soviet republics.

The desire for a "return to Europe" has three sources. First, as in most ex-socialist economies, Europe is seen as a proven model which has delivered prosperity. Second, if large countries such as Russia cannot easily "return" to a Europe which is small by comparison, a nation of 1.5 million can be accommodated. Most importantly, while it is unclear whether Russia, being also an Asian country, can really "return" to Europe, there is no such historical and cultural ambiguity in the case of Estonia.

The consensus about this long-run goal, at least among ethnic Estonians, and the strength with which it is pursued have had two influences on the economic transformation. First, Estonia has developed a highly liberal trade regime with respect to the West. After the restoration of independence, Estonia quickly reached bilateral free trade agreements with most EFTA (European Free Trade Area) nations, and signed a GSP (generalized system of preferences) agreement with the EC. The goal of reaching a more substantial free trade agreement with the EC, which was realized in July 1994, was hardly questioned.[7] Trade with other countries is largely free as well, with only a few import duties and export quotas and licenses.[8] Finally, foreign direct investment has so far been granted highly favorable tax treatment.

Second, consensus improves the political economy of sustaining economic reforms through the phase when most of their effects are negative. As de-industrialization and the reduction of links with "the East" are seen as an integral part of the "return to Europe," the painful effects of restructuring can be presented as (and are often taken as) strong medicine which must be swallowed, rather than as a problem to be mitigated. Estonia has so far maintained social peace in the face of one of the most severe terms-of-trade shocks experienced by any former CPE, including a seventyfold increase in the nominal price of gasoline over one year.[9] The ability of the Estonian authorities to implement and maintain balanced budgets and a tight monetary policy in the face of such a shock is also founded on this broad consensus in society.

The Ethnic Dimension of Economic Reform

Problems of ethnic minorities are not confined to "new" states, as the Bulgarian and Romanian examples show. Yet, most Western discussion about (and anxiety over) minority issues has been in the context of the Soviet, Yugoslav, and Czechoslovak breakups. As non-Estonians together make up about 38 percent of its population, Estonia's ethnic relations have not surprisingly been widely discussed. While some analysts have delved into the specifics of the case (e.g., Hanson, 1993), much discussion has been based on weak analogies with other states with complex ethnic situations, for example, Azerbaijan, Bosnia-Herzegovina, or Croatia. This approach generally leads to pessimistic conclusions and tends to focus on issues which may have little actual influence on interethnic relations, especially that of citizenship rights, ignoring the potentially more important link between ethnic tensions and the impact of economic restructuring.

For Estonia, the current demographic situation creates both problems and opportunities. On the negative side, the dividing line between the short-run winners and losers from economic reform will in some cases run close to the divisions between the Estonian and non-Estonian populations. The benefits and costs of restructuring will be concentrated in certain regions, sectors, and enterprises, none of which are ethnically well integrated.[10] Non-Estonians are concentrated in Tallinn, the northeast, and towns with a strong military or railway presence (Paldiski, Tapa, Valga) and are relatively important in industry. Rural areas, and thus the agricultural sector, as well as most other cities and towns, are predominantly Estonian. Even within industry, individual enterprises are most often seen as being either Estonian or Russian.

As a whole, one group is not likely to fare much better than the other. The most dynamic regions are metropolitan Tallinn (where non-Estonians are well represented) and the west coast (where ethnic Estonians dominate). The regions faring worst are the northeast and towns linked to major Russian military bases (with a strong non-Estonian majority) and the agrarian southeast (which is almost solely Estonian). Still, this fact will not prevent residents of the harder-hit regions from ascribing their misfortune to ethnically based politics. Even when dislocation arises from objective economic factors, less fortunate non-Estonians could accuse Estonia of using economic means to drive them out of the country, while less well-off Estonians may express dismay that a supposedly nationalist government is not looking after their interests.

This segregation of society may force economic reforms to be more cautious than otherwise desired. The extreme concentration of Soviet industry means that closure of a single firm can lead to the laying off of thousands of workers. The fear that such events can quickly acquire a political dimension, especially in the Russified northeast, has at times made Estonian officials less radical in imposing market discipline than they might wish to be, even when overall recorded unemployment is still only 2.7 percent of the labor force, as it was in mid-1993 (Riigi

Statistikaamet, 1993, kuukiri no. 6, p. 71). For example, in November 1992, the government froze the tax arrears of the Kreenholm textiles enterprise in Narva, which has over 7,000 workers, almost all of them non-Estonians (Morris, 1992b). Such steps have also been discussed for other firms in politically sensitive regions.

On the positive side, the Estonian minority situation differs from that in most countries in one important way. Namely, in most other countries minority populations have resided in their current locations for generations if not centuries. As members of such historic minorities could as well go back to their ethnic homelands as Americans of Irish descent could return to Ireland, they have nowhere to go.[11] This feeling, which can lead to panic in the face of economic dislocation, largely explains why the Polish minority in Lithuania, while small in numbers, represents perhaps the most difficult case of minority relations in the Baltic region.[12]

In sharp contrast, most non-Estonians in Estonia are relatively recent immigrants. Misiunas and Taagepera have estimated that in 1945 (after war, deportations, flight to the West, and the loss of territory are taken into account) the share of ethnic Estonians in the total population was about 94 percent (Misiunas and Taagepera, 1983, p. 272). By the 1989 census, this share had fallen to 61.5 percent. More important, as the ratio of net to gross immigration during the period 1946–90 (excluding most military personnel) was 0.284 — that is, roughly three in four immigrants have subsequently re-emigrated — the non-Estonian part of the population has a strong transient element (Riigi Statistikaamet, 1991, p. 43). Immigrants were often hired to build new megaprojects, such as the oil shale mines near Narva or the new harbor at Muuga near Tallinn. After these were completed, many returned home, to be replaced by other workers as new projects were commenced.

The footloose nature of Estonia's minority populations is seen in the large increase in net emigration from Estonia in the last years. In the 1970s and 1980s, net annual immigration to Estonia averaged around 10,000 persons. In 1992, with the door to new immigration almost closed, a net of 33,700 persons (around 6 percent of the entire non-Estonian population) left Estonia (Riigi Statistikaamet, 1993, kuukiri no. 4, p. 5). As net emigration to the West was very small, this emigration was almost solely to former Soviet republics. As net emigration in the first four months of 1993 was 38 percent below that of the same period in 1992, simple extrapolation would suggest a net emigration of 21,000 in 1993. However, if economic dislocation is a factor leading to emigration, the fact that major restructuring is only now beginning makes a somewhat higher figure possible as well.

The very low volume of applications for Estonian citizenship (as nearly all residents meet the two-year residency requirement, the sole remaining hurdle is a language test) is another indicator of transience among the non-Estonian population.

This aspect of its demographic composition gives Estonia a safety valve which more homogeneous states, or ones with more entrenched minorities, do not possess. If the pace of net emigration is linked to the pace at which employment positions are lost, the net effect could be a damping of the unemployment rate in Estonia.

A continued flow of net emigration could also improve the long-run basis for establishing a liberal open economy. As ethnic Estonians begin to feel that their national survival is no longer in danger, they will be more welcoming to new foreign influences and investments. If this also eases the relations with the remaining non-Estonian population, it could further contribute to political stability.

A much smaller group which could influence developments is the Estonian diaspora. Its direct role will be minor. The net return from abroad is unlikely to exceed 1,000 persons. Unlike the overseas Chinese, for example, those remaining abroad will not be major investors in Estonia. The impact of the diaspora will be felt in some areas of technical assistance, but more importantly in the form of role models, relatives that did well in difficult conditions.

FISCAL AND MONETARY ASPECTS OF RESTORING ECONOMIC SOVEREIGNTY

A "new" state must undertake some of its most far-reaching reforms in the areas of fiscal and monetary policy. The tax base must be both nationalized and restructured to the needs of a modern market economy. In most cases, a new currency must be introduced, if for no other reason than as a manifestation of state sovereignty. Finally, fiscal, monetary, and exchange rate policies must be implemented by officials with little experience in doing so, at least in the setting of a market economy.

It is therefore surprising that perhaps the greatest successes in Estonian economic reform have so far come in these areas. The Soviet tax system has been fully nationalized and modernized. While far from perfect, it has functioned well enough to keep the budget in balance or mild surplus. The introduction of the new currency, the kroon (EEK), has been more successful than had been expected.

Tax Reform

After having won "economic independence" within the Soviet Union in November 1989, Estonia (like the other Baltic states) moved quickly to nationalize and modernize its tax system. Until the beginning of 1990, its budget had been fully integrated into the all-union budget. The two main taxes were a turnover tax and a corporate tax, neither of which is appropriate in a market economy setting. The former was highly arbitrary, with the rate for a given good simply set to sustain the chosen difference between its wholesale and retail prices. This produced a proliferation of thousands of different rates specific to particular goods.

The corporate tax was designed to appropriate all of a predetermined industry- or firm-specific profit margin in a centrally planned setting, rather than to create a neutral, stable environment in which private activity would develop.

Starting from this system, nationalization meant moving to a one-channel system in which Estonia would collect all taxes and send a single, negotiated lump-sum payment to the union government. While the removal of an assured tax base for Moscow was no way to run the union, it was a good way for Estonia to enhance its economic independence.

Modernization meant introducing a tax system akin to those found in Western market economies. The differentiated turnover tax was replaced in 1991 by a uniform 10 percent value-added tax (VAT). A progressive personal income tax based on a unified income concept was introduced. A standard corporate income tax, which was first progressive but later changed to a flat rate of 35 percent, was also implemented. Most specific excise taxes were converted to an ad valorem basis, and social security and medical taxes totaling 33 percent (to be paid by employers) were introduced. Finally, local governments were given their own tax bases.[13]

A land tax of 1 percent of assessed value and a motor fuels tax of 0.40 EEK (U.S. $0.03) per liter were added in 1993.

As a result, Estonia now has a de-Sovietized tax system which is among the most modern in the former socialist countries.[14] A tax reform now under way is focused on unifying the various taxes and strengthening sanctions against evasion and fraud. Once this is complete, future reforms should be more in the nature of calibration and rate adjustments.

Practical Implementation

Estonian and foreign specialists concur that many taxes remain unpaid and that tax administration could be improved. Still, the practical implementation of the new rules has been successful in that the Estonian government has maintained fiscal control. The 1991 and 1992 budget outcomes show consolidated surpluses equal to 5.5 percent and 1.7 percent of GDP, respectively.[15] The planned state budget for 1993 was in full balance, but the outcome for the first ten months showed a surplus of 3,000 million EEK (Riigi Statistikaamet, 1993, kuukiri no. 11, pp. 29–30), or about 1.7 percent of GDP. With local governments also producing a 179 million EEK surplus during the first five months (Riigi Statistikaamet, 1993, kuukiri no. 11, pp. 31–34), the consolidated budget showed an actual surplus of around 2.7 percent of GDP.

In the Soviet and ruble zone context, it is surprising not only that Estonia was able to maintain fiscal control, but that it chose to do so. As an unwilling member of a collapsing federation, Estonia's short-run interest would have been best served by fiscal profligacy. The resulting costs of financial instability would have been spread over the whole ruble zone, while the benefits would have been reaped locally. Instead, Estonian fiscal responsibility released some savings which were transferred at negative real interest rates to other republics. This pursuit of sensible policies, even without incentives to do so, increases the likelihood that such policies will now be continued when the incentives to do so are greater.

Money and Banking Reform

A major difference between an "old" state and a "new" state is that the latter must introduce a new currency before being able to run a monetary and exchange rate policy. Estonia was the first Soviet republic openly to discuss introduction of a separate money. An influential September 1987 proposal for economic independence included a call to make a convertible ruble the currency of Estonia.[16]

Estonia subsequently became the first ex-Soviet state to leave the ruble zone.[17] On June 17, 1992, its Monetary Reform Committee announced that as of June 20, the sole legal domestic means of payment would be the kroon (crown). The conversion from the ruble was completed over a three-day period. The exchange was nearly proportional, with most monetary values (prices, wages, assets, and so on) simply reduced by a factor of ten.[18] This was preferred to a more confiscatory reform, as open inflation had eroded any "monetary overhang" which may have existed in the past (the average resident would convert less than U.S. $12 in cash rubles).

The principle of near-proportionality has been used in all monetary reforms in the former USSR, Yugoslavia (Slovenia, Croatia, Macedonia), and Czechoslovakia.[19] In all cases, a monetary overhang had either been eliminated or never existed. Yet, while all ex-Yugoslav republics have used a one-step reform, Estonia and Kyrgyzstan have been the sole ex-Soviet republics to adopt this method.[20] In the FSU, the preferred method appears to involve two steps, between which the local currency and the ruble circulate in parallel.[21]

The main impact of the Estonian monetary reform came form the accompanying policy changes. In developing new macroeconomic policy rules, the authorities worked form the premise that Estonia is a small, "new" state undergoing a deep economic transformation. In this setting, three criteria are particularly important. First, a small, open economy should undertake policies which lead to a stable and convertible currency. Second, a country with little experience in running a monetary policy, and where fine tuning is premature, should implement simple and fail-safe policies. Third, as there will be great pressures to reflate and retreat from reforms, institutional guarantees should be created such that responsible policies will be maintained.

The Estonian strategy rests on three pillars: a balanced budget, a credibly fixed exchange rate, and a modified "currency board" rule of monetary emission. Budget balance was first strengthened by a decree (which took effect at the time of currency reform) raising the VAT from 10 to 18 percent, the previously progressive corporate income tax (with an average rate of 27 percent) to a flat rate of 35 percent, and the top personal income tax rate from 33 to 50 percent. These rates were later incorporated into the budget for the second half of 1992, and all except the upper personal income tax rate (which was returned to 33 percent) were included in the 1993 budget.

The kroon was pegged to the Deutsche mark by a law which also forbids the Bank of Estonia from devaluing it.[22] This provides a legal guarantee of exchange rate stability. By setting the initial rate at an undervalued level, the Bank of Estonia was also able to secure the kroon's initial convertibility.[23]

The key policy decision was the codification of a modified currency board rule. The Law on the Security of the Estonian Kroon, passed on May 20, 1992, required the central bank to introduce the kroon with all cash and bank deposits fully backed by gold and foreign currency reserves (these totaled around U.S. $120 million at the time of the reform). The Bank of Estonia is restricted to issuing additional kroon cash and reserve deposits (i.e., high-powered money) only in exchange for new foreign exchange receipts.

As base money must always be fully backed, present and future convertibility is nearly guaranteed. As the Bank of Estonia could redeem every kroon which it has issued without running out of reserves, a speculative run leading to devaluation is unlikely. The modified currency board rule is extremely simple to implement. Finally, the codification of such a rule creates a bulwark against pressures to run irresponsible monetary policies.

During its first year, the kroon was surprisingly successful (Hansson, 1993b). It quickly became convertible for current account purposes and for repatriating foreign direct investments, while most capital account transactions require only registration. Cash or account kroons are traded in Finland, Latvia, Lithuania, Russia, and Sweden, and convertible currency payments operate relatively smoothly.

The kroon has also been stable. The Bank of Estonia has rigidly maintained the 8 EEK/DM (Deutsche mark) parity, even through the numerous European exchange market crises of 1992 and 1993, while the Russian ruble had fallen from 75 to around 600 per DM by August 1993.

In response to its stability and convertibility, the kroon has become the actual sole means of payment within Estonia. Gone are both the ruble and the previously ubiquitous hard currency shops. One result has been greater competition in domestic trade and the wide availability of imported goods.

Contrary to initial fears, the Bank of Estonia has experienced an inflow of foreign exchange reserves, which have nearly trebled during the first year after currency reform to a level of U.S. $302 million on August 1, 1993 (*Baltic Independent*, August 13–19, 1993, p. B4).[24] Part of this may reflect reverse capital flight in response to relatively favorable interest rates.

Not all initial developments were positive. In the first three months after monetary reform, measured inflation was 56 percent, or near Russian levels. Part of this had been expected, especially as the VAT had been raised; part reflected measurement problems, but much of it did not. The result was a severe squeeze on living standards, which created pressure for increases in nominal wages. The expected results of tight monetary policies finally emerged in December 1992, six months after currency reform, when monthly consumer price index (CPI) inflation fell to 3.3 percent from 9.5 percent in November. Since then, inflation has remained in the range of 1.3–3.6 percent per month. Annual inflation for 1993 was approximately 36 percent.

Although a payments agreement was reached with Russia and several other FSU states at the time of currency reform, actual payments with these countries functioned poorly for many months. Given the high risks and the objection of the Central Bank of Russia to establishment of a ruble market in Tallinn, the Bank of Estonia has not quoted the ruble. Without an obvious market maker, the trading of ruble deposits in Russian banks was initially restricted, with high spreads and low volumes. Over time, several banks and one stock exchange began to specialize in trading former Soviet currencies, leading to a gradual reduction in spreads and improvement in payments. The main barrier to efficient ruble payments has been the slow speed at which money moves within Russia, which is beyond the influence of the Estonian authorities.

In the area of banking reform, Estonia is following the same general plan as the other ex-socialist states. The central bank has divested itself of commercial functions, creating a two-tier banking system. A recent law grants the central bank complete independence form the government. With stabilization well under way, the strengthening of the commercial banking sector has become the main focus of the central bank's activity.

The currency reform had failed to improve the functioning of the domestic payments system. When this further deteriorated in November 1992, the Bank of Estonia imposed a moratorium on three major banks with particularly severe problems (Morris, 1992a; Yu and Freibergs, 1992). In January, it closed one (with no rescue of shareholders or depositors) and merged the other two with a partial rescue of depositors. The increase of minimum bank capital from 500,000 to 6 million EEK (U.S. $500,000) on January 1, 1993, resulted in the merger of some banks and the closure of others. These steps together reduced the number of commercial banks from 45 to 23. Subsequently, two more banks were placed under moratorium, one of which was later closed. The net impact of these measures on the payments system has been positive. Most domestic payments are now made within 48 hours, and banks are more likely to complain of excess rather than insufficient liquidity. In the future, issues of bank solvency will become more important.

Political independence has changed things only by allowing Estonia to choose the pace at which it undertakes these reforms. That this has worked to accelerate the pace of banking reform is best seen in contrast with Russia, where there is an almost complete lack of effective commercial bank regulation.

DOMESTIC LIBERALIZATION

After its monetary reform, Estonia faces the same challenges as the "old" former CPEs in liberalizing its domestic economy, removing most remaining price controls, reducing remaining subsidies, and passing and implementing a competition law. These steps have largely been completed. The goods and services with remaining price controls are land; some natural resources; utility rates; precious metal; liquor; fuels and lubricants; airport, port, post, and telecommunications services; and empty bottles. Most of these are natural monopolies, giving a strong basis for price control. Subsidies remain only for public transport and residential heating. Finally, a competition law was passed in June 1993.

Before currency reform, the situation in Estonia was somewhat different. Lacking monetary and exchange rate policies, several governments attempted to stabilize the economy through the use of price policy. Until mid-1991, when inflationary pressures were still modest, some price controls were maintained in an attempt to dampen inflation.[25] Once these pressures became severe and led to extreme repressed inflation (including shortages and black markets), Estonia changed to the other tack of freeing prices in an attempt to outrun Soviet inflation. The goal of controlling inflation was subsumed to that of restoring balance between aggregate demand and supply.

The introduction of the kroon, which permitted stabilization via standard macroeconomic policies, allowed price policy to be based solely on microeconomic factors. By eliminating many of the tradeoffs which previously hampered price decontrol, currency reform indirectly speeded the process of liberalization.

PRIVATIZATION

Most issues which arise in privatizing Estonia's state-owned enterprises are the same as those in any ex-socialist economy. The actual development of privatization has also mirrored that in the "old" countries, with sale of small enterprises proceeding relatively rapidly and quietly, while large-scale privatization has been slow and controversial.[26]

One hindrance to privatization in the ex-Soviet and -Yugoslav states, which is not a direct result of nation-building, is the environment of extreme inflation and financial instability. In this milieu, accurate valuation of property is nearly impossible. Since valuation is a cornerstone of most privatization methods, this has slowed the sale of state assets.

Also, when financial assets have a highly negative expected rate of return, as has been the case in the ruble zone, there is a natural fear that real assets will be purchased not for use in production, but rather to be kept as idle stores of value. In an attempt to avoid this, privatization authorities have sometimes required new owners to make commitments as to the use of these assets. For example, purchasers of farmland might have to promise to undertake active cultivation, while purchasers of shops might be required to continue in the current general activity for a specified time period. These restrictions require sale methods which are slower and less transparent than the auctions that could safely be used in a more stable macroeconomic environment. In this respect, the financial stabilization resulting from the monetary reform could reduce these barriers and hence speed privatization.

Two influences on privatization which stem from Estonia's being a "new" state, and which complicate this process relative to the standard case, are political. First, both in formal international law and in the perception of ethnic Estonians, Estonia is not a new state but an existing state whose independence was restored de facto. Following the failure of the August coup, countries which had recognized Estonia before 1940 stressed that they were not recognizing a new state but simply restoring diplomatic relations. The first act of the new parliament elected on September 20, 1992, was also to declare that the current Republic of Estonia was legally the same state as that which existed in the interwar period.

This fact, which is well known to almost every Estonian, has had a psychological effect on the privatization process. Namely, the restoration of nationalized property to previous owners is viewed by many as the micro-level analogy to the restoration of the Estonian state.[27] While the precise strength of political support for restitution and/or compensation of such property is hard to measure, and while this level of support has changed over time, its impact on the mix of privatization methods has been undeniable. The attempt of the first Popular Front–dominated government in 1990–91 to downplay restitution simply stalled the privatization process until this method was reinstated.

Second, the debate over privatization methods is influenced by the legacy of the demographic changes which took place during Soviet rule. Different methods will differently distribute the privatized wealth among ethnic groups. At one extreme, extensive restitution or compensation of nationalized property would give relatively more property to prewar residents and their descendants, that is, largely to ethnic Estonians. At the other end, as postwar immigrants are more likely to work in industry and less likely to own their apartments, options such as free allocation of some shares to workers, or of apartments to existing tenants, would tend to favor non-Estonians.

As a result, the support for different privatization methods has varied across national lines. Estonians have been more disposed to favor restitution and voucher privatization, especially of housing, where the voucher allocation is based on years worked in Estonia.[28] Non-Estonians have favored schemes of free distribution to existing workers or tenants. As the choice of method is linked to emotional issues, such as the struggle for independence and the legacy of mass immigration during Soviet rule, debates on the choice of method have been impassioned and drawn out. This has markedly slowed the privatization process.

The model that finally emerged is a hybrid lying somewhat closer to the Estonian position. Previous owners or their descendants were able to claim restitution for property held before Soviet rule. A total of 204,000 claims were filed, of which 38,000 had been processed and judged legitimate by June 1993. Housing privatization will be completed predominantly through vouchers, the allocation of which is based on years worked in Estonia (adjusted for military service and years spent in labor camps).[29] Small- and large-scale privatization will be undertaken through sales for both cash and vouchers, with privileges for existing workers and managers in some cases.

The choice of privatization method in Estonia, as in other "new" countries, is also conditioned by a desire to ensure that most assets are initially purchased by local residents, or in some cases by reputable Western investors.[30] Methods which could lead to the dissipation of ownership over the whole FSU are frowned upon. The prospect of Latvians owning Estonian industries or vice versa meets little favor in either country. Again, these sentiments tend to favor voucher privatization based at the level of the "new" nation. Many ex-Soviet republics, including all Baltic states, are pursuing voucher privatization. Similarly, the Czechoslovak voucher privatization scheme was quickly converted to a republican basis; that is, vouchers could be used only in the republic in which they were issued, once the dissolution of the federation became certain.

ECONOMIC RESTRUCTURING

As its economy is transformed to one appropriate for an independent country operating in a market environment, Estonia will go through the same qualitative changes as other ex-socialist countries. The share of national income generated by industry will decline while the long-neglected service sector will expand. Within agriculture and industry, the relative importance of subsectors will change. The extreme concentration of the communist economy will give way to a structure with relatively more small enterprises and farms. Finally, firms will undergo internal management and organizational changes.

The difference between Estonia and most "old" states is quantitative. The required changes in Estonia will be larger, simply because its economy is more distorted. Terms-of-trade within the Soviet Union were very different from those prevailing on the world market, or even within the Council for Mutual Economic Assistance (CMEA).[31] Compared to Hungary and Poland, where some previous liberalization had taken place, Estonia's internal relative price structure was more distorted. The existence of specialized plants designed to serve the whole Soviet market means that many enterprises are too large and too concentrated in their activities. While a gravity model of foreign trade would likely predict that less than one-half of trade should be with the former Soviet Union, the actual level was around 90 percent until 1991. Finally, with less prior reform in Estonia than in most "old" CPEs, the internal organization of enterprises will have to undergo larger changes.

The area in which required changes are most obvious is physical infrastructure. Estonia's previous integration into the Soviet system means that transportation links with the East are relatively well developed. Similarly, the negligible historical trade volume with other Baltic states and with Western Europe means that north-south links and links with the West are weak.[32]

As trade with Russia becomes less significant while trade with other Baltic states and with continental Europe increases, the north-south links will need to be expanded and improved. As more east-west trade will not be Russian-Estonian trade but Russian transit trade passing through Estonia, the current east-west infrastructure within Estonia will have to be complemented with expanded port facilities. Finally, as the economy adjusts to live within its new borders, some of the infrastructure will need to be adjusted to the new domestic needs.

EXTERNAL RELATIONS

If most of the "new" states share anything in common other than their socialist heritage, it is that they are small (Russia and Ukraine are exceptions). Given that they arose form the breakup of other states, this is not surprising.

Among the "new" states, Estonia has the smallest economy and population, which naturally makes it highly dependent on foreign trade. In 1991, the average of recorded exports and imports was 45.5 percent of net material product (Riigi Statistikaamet, 1992, pp. 65, 86).

In the area of external relations more than any other, the "pure" impact of economic reform is hard to distinguish from the effects of nation-building. One way to do this is to consider how the Estonian economic transformation might have evolved had the Baltic states remained part of a unitary Soviet Union that had undertaken a radical economic reform program including largely free prices, an open economy, and an internally convertible currency. Judging from the experience of the "old" Central and Eastern European countries which have chosen this path, and of Russia, the following four things would most likely have occurred:

1. *A change in the direction of trade.* Trade with the West would have grown relative to trade with Soviet republics.[33]

2. *A change in the sectoral composition of trade.* Different sectors would have been differently affected by the net impact of economic restructuring on supply and of open borders and altered relative prices on demand.

3. *A drop in the volume of trade with Soviet republics.* The temporary disruption arising from economic reforms would in any case have broken existing links.[34]

4. *A collapse in the terms-of-trade.* A move largely to free prices in an open economy would have in the long run brought the same increase in the prices of energy and other imports which Estonia is now facing.

These changes are taking place in independent Estonia. If in 1991, about 90 percent of merchandise trade was conducted with former Soviet republics (including Latvia and Lithuania), this share fell to 47 percent in 1992 (Hansson, 1993b). Finland now accounts for over 30 percent of Estonia's trade, while Russia's share has fallen to around 15 percent. Tourism has undergone a nearly complete reorientation to the West.

The composition of trade has been influenced by the growth of transit trade between Russia and the West. Alongside several traditional sectors which continue to represent a large share of trade (agricultural and food products, timber and wood products), there has been a marked growth in the share of nonferrous metals (shipped sometimes illegally from Russia to the West) and transportation equipment (shipped from the West to Russia).

Finally, as noted above, the IMF has estimated the terms-of-trade shock in 1992 alone to be equal to a drop in GDP of around 20 percent.

Relative to the hypothetical reference point of Estonia within a reforming Soviet Union, the achievement of state sovereignty changed three things:

1. *The time sequence of the terms-of-trade shock.* As Russia has continued to keep the domestic price of key raw materials well below world market levels (the main reason for the booming transit trade in nonferrous metals), and assuming that a reforming Soviet Union would have pursued the same policy, Estonia's foreign trade has moved to world prices much faster than it would have without independence. The greater the independence which a country has achieved from Russia, the faster it has been forced to trade at world prices. Even within the CIS, countries that have left the ruble zone have faced higher prices than those that have not.

2. *The size of the trade volume decline.* The fall in Estonia's trade volume with ex-Soviet states has been increased by financial and border problems resulting from independence. Were the ruble as stable and convertible as the kroon, monetary independence need not have made much of a difference. As it turned out, payments by ruble zone enterprises have generally been cumbersome, particularly so when crossing state boundaries. One difference is that while Russian commercial banks clear payments only at the Central Bank of Russia, interstate payments also introduce the central bank of the other state. Other problems include the teething pains of learning a new payments system and the thinness of the new foreign exchange market in a small country, which reduces liquidity and increases buy-sell spreads.

    Border-related trade barriers include time delays, licenses and other quantitative restrictions, and tariffs and export taxes. These new arrangements have also been introduced in a cumbersome way.

3. *The magnitude of the direction of trade shift.* As the financial constraints have primarily dampened trade with former Soviet republics, and as Estonia has been more successful than the CIS states in signing free trade agreements with the West, the direction of trade shift toward the West has been greater under independence. This is seen clearly in the dramatic pace of trade reorientation described above.

The final dimension of external economic relations, which is by definition irrelevant in "old" states but unavoidable in "new" ones, is the eventual division of various assets, liabilities, and claims. Where the divorce is by mutual consent, as in Czechoslovakia, this settlement can be clean and rather amicable. In the Soviet and Yugoslav cases, where the breakup has been bitter and where the negative memories of (or the nostalgic longing for) empire are often strong, these issues are messy and still unresolved.

Even after several rounds of negotiations, very little can be said about the form of the final settlement. Power politics and international pressure will play major but as yet unclear roles. While the size of the net burden which one side or the other will bear is not clear, the form of some individual burdens is beginning to emerge. Estonia says it will not accept any of the external debt of the Soviet Union. As this claim is strengthened legally by the fact that most states which existed in 1940 merely restored diplomatic relations with Estonia — that is, they implicitly view the period 1940–92 as one of forced occupation — this is also a not unlikely outcome.

At the same time, the withdrawing Russian army took along or destroyed most of its equipment and buildings. As most of this will be difficult to recover, Estonia will have the new burden of outfitting its armed forces. Even though these will be minuscule in comparison to the historic size of Soviet forces in Estonia, the financial burden will be enormous relative to Estonia's economic potential. Building up even the smallest navy or air force is out of the question for the next few years.[35]

CONCLUSIONS

Estonia's dual economic transformation exhibits unique elements as well as some general features common to all "new" states undertaking economic reforms. If the analyst can commit one mistake, it is to generalize too much from the Estonian experience. After all, the collapse of the previous states reflects a desire by the "new" nations, exhausted from marching in step, to choose separate paths of development. The difference of views on economic reform strategy in the Czech Republic and Slovakia is only one example. Over time, these countries will begin to have less and less in common.

Furthermore, the recent political histories of the ex-Soviet, -Yugoslav, and -Czechoslovak states are quite different. The CIS members and the Czech and Slovak Republics are true successor states, having gained independence simultaneously and through mutual recognition. The ex-Yugoslav republics other than Serbia and Montenegro are secessionist states, having gained recognition more or less for the first time after issuing unilateral declarations of independence. In contrast, the Baltics are "restored states" which did not secede but regained their previous independence de facto.

Each type of country faces its own issues and problems. A restored state such as Estonia will more or less explicitly seek to rebuild much of what existed in the past. The desire to reduce trade links with Russia and increase them with the West (which speeds reforms) and to emphasize the restitution of nationalized property (which slows reforms) all reflect this wish to partly restore what existed in the past.

The "new" states also differ in the coherence of their future vision. The greater the social consensus on where a country should head in the future, the smoother its economic transformation will be.

Still, a summary comparison of the Estonian case with those of other "new" states that actively sought independence reveals some trends that are rather general. First, the quest for independence is partly motivated by a desire to protect against economic shocks and/or the pace of reforms in other regions of the previously unified state. Estonia sought to escape the financial chaos of the ruble zone, Slovenia the effects of a massive issuing of credits by other Yugoslav republics. Slovaks may see independence as a way to slow too-fast reforms, while Czechs may see it as a way to speed these changes further. This quest for insulation makes the "new" states unenthusiastic about economic cooperation with other regions of the previous state. If cooperation takes place, it is more out of perceived necessity than innate desire.

Second, this protective stance is only partial, as these states simultaneously and aggressively pursue new links with some neighboring regions outside the previous state. Estonia is actively building ties to Finland, Sweden, and the rest of the EC; Slovenia to Austria and the rest of the EC; and the Muslim ex-Soviet republics to Turkey and Iran. In cases where the degree of consensus about a "return to Europe" is high (Czech Republic, Estonia, Slovenia), this pursuit of new ties is particularly active.

Third, independence has exacerbated the short-run terms-of-trade shocks faced by most of these states. The reaction of the former metropolitan center may be characterized as "You asked for independence, now live with it!"

Fourth, the "new" states must undertake more restructuring than would have been required without independence. The new physical and financial boundaries have an impact on the environment in which economic activity takes place. The physical infrastructure will also need to be remade to suit the new boundaries and to foster links with newly important trading partners.

Finally, difficult ethnic relations can slow economic reforms. Slovenia and the Czech Republic, which are relatively ethnically homogeneous, can most easily focus on economic issues. At the same time, ethnic conflict is not simply linked to the physical size of ethnic groups. A small but entrenched ethnic community, such as Poles in Lithuania or Serbs in Croatia, can be the source of much greater conflict than a large but footloose community, such as Russians in Estonia.

If there is one quintessential step which the "new" states will take, it is the introduction of a national currency, as this is the vehicle for achieving most of the goals noted above. Both for symbolic and real reasons, it is an important part of nation-building. As it allows autonomous monetary and financial policies, a national currency is the vehicle for escaping the financial shocks in the previous state, be these from a too-loose or too-tight monetary policy. If it is made stable and convertible like the Estonian kroon, it becomes a vehicle for the economic "return to Europe." As it gives the "new" states an exchange rate instrument, it facilitates their absorption of the terms-of-trade shocks brought on by independence. Finally, as the "new" states tend to be unenthusiastic about close cooperation with other parts of the state from which they emerged, the conditions for a workable monetary union are unlikely to be present.

NOTES

An earlier version of this chapter was presented at the convention of the American Association for the Advancement of Slavic Studies, held in Phoenix on November 19–22, 1992. I am grateful to Toivo Raun, Steven S. Rosefielde, Erik Terk, and Michael L. Wyzan for helpful comments. Any remaining errors are my sole responsibility. The views expressed are my own and not those of the Government of Estonia or of the Bank of Estonia.

1. I use "new" and "old" in quotation marks as several of these states (including Estonia) have been politically independent at previous times in history.
2. In some other republics, this set in motion a quest for greater economic independence, even when there was no political wish to leave the Union.
3. This effect may be stronger the greater the geographic proximity of the two countries. For instance, several Estonian governments have sought to pursue better links with Ukraine, possibly as a counterweight to Russia's dominance of past trade.
4. There is a clear historical analogy with the successor states of the Austro-Hungarian Empire. The obvious longing among some Hungarian officials for a return of lost territories, especially those populated by ethnic Hungarians, merely fueled nationalist feelings and autarkic economic policies in these states. For more on this subject, see Pasvolsky (1928).
5. The different results of parliamentary elections in Estonia and Lithuania also suggest that preferred reform paths may differ so greatly that close coordination of economic policies becomes impossible. Estonia elected a distinctly right-of-center

parliament in September 1992, while the Lithuanian elections a month later were won by the renamed (pro-independence) Communist Party.

6.   For overviews of the adjustment to independence in the new Central Asian states, see Olcott (1992) and Brown (1993).

7.   There is less agreement on the desirability of full EC membership, as this is seen by some as giving up too much of the recently won political sovereignty.

8.   In the 1993 state budget, income from customs duties represented only 0.7 percent of total expected revenues (Riigi Statistikaamet, 1993, kuukiri no. 6, p. 60).

9.   The IMF (1992, p. 13) estimates the size of the terms-of-trade shock in 1992 alone to be equivalent to a drop in GNP of about 20 percent.

10.   For a discussion of regional differences in enterprise and economic development, see Raagmaa (1993).

11.   The case of the Gypsies in Europe is the clearest case of the difficulties arising when a minority truly has nowhere to go.

12.   A related problem arises if the country of ethnic origin is small. For example, Russia could relatively easily absorb all ethnic Russians returning from Estonia, where Albania would have enormous difficulties in accommodating a substantial inflow from, say, Kosovo or Macedonia.

13.   For example, the personal income tax goes to local authorities, while the corporate income tax, which had been split 65/35 between the national and local governments until 1992, now accrues fully to the national government. For an extensive discussion of Estonian tax reform, see Van Arkadie and Karlsson (1992).

14.   For example, the Czech and Slovak Republics moved to a VAT only in January 1993 (Svitek, 1992), whereas Estonia's VAT has been in place since January 1991.

15.   See IMF (1993, p. 56). This has been helped by the fact that because personal income taxes are withheld at the source, while interest and dividend income are still small, much of the assessed personal income tax can now still be collected.

16.   For an overview of the evolution of Estonian economic policy until 1991, see Van Arkadie and Karlsson (1992).

17.   For an overview of monetary reform developments in the former Soviet Union and the specifics of the Estonian reform, see Hansson and Sachs (1992) and Hansson (1993a; 1993b).

18.   The exceptions were small amounts of cash (sums above 1,500 rubles per capita) which were converted at a confiscatory rate, and some large recent transfers to bank accounts, the source of which was controlled before conversion at the 10:1 rate.

19.   For descriptions of the Slovenian reform, see Chetkovich and Chetkovich (1992) and Pleskovič and Sachs (1992). Even the chaotic August 1993 Russian attempt to invalidate certain ruble notes was close to proportional, as even the lowest of the proposed upper limits on exchanging old for new notes would have allowed almost all of the cash in circulation to be exchanged.

20.   By "one-step" we mean a case where the reform begins with an exchange of the previous union currency for some form of national currency. This includes cases where the initial new notes will subsequently be exchanged for more permanent ones, as this is usually a proportional exchange of two national moneys and hence of little if any economic importance. The 1993 Czechoslovak split is hard to classify. The exchange or stamping of large-denomination notes was accomplished quickly, but smaller Czechoslovak notes were initially left to circulate in both new countries.

21.   Latvia, Lithuania, Ukraine, Georgia, and Moldova all moved to national currencies via a parallel currency phase. Estonia's decision not to emit a parallel currency (as strongly advocated by Prime Minister Tiit Vähi in May 1992) is another case of pursuing a policy that is costly in a narrow short-run sense (coupons would have displaced some share of Russian rubles to other ex-Soviet states in exchange for real goods), but the rejection of which may raise the likelihood that future policies will be credibly tight.

22.   For a compilation of the major laws and decrees governing the currency reform, see Bank of Estonia (1992).

23.   As the German mark was then worth 70–80 rubles, the proportionality principle was used to set the kroon's external value at one-tenth of this rate, or 8 EEK/DM.

24.   Throughout this chapter unattributed items from newspapers are treated as in this citation of the *Baltic Independent*; attributed newspaper articles may be found in the list of references.

25.   For an overview of the emergence of extreme inflationary pressures in the Soviet Union, see Hansson (1992).

26.   For an overview of privatization experience in the former socialist economies, see Åslund (1992).

27.   For example, the legal scholar Paul Varul, who has worked on drafting much of Estonia's commercial and privatization legislation, recently wrote: "If no one doubts that the events of 1940 were nothing other than occupation, then one cannot make different fundamental decisions concerning previous owners. It is impossible to link two things: we recognize the fact of occupation, but legalize all resulting developments in the area of ownership" (*Postimees*, October 29, 1992, p. 5).

28.   Those who already owned their lodgings could use their vouchers to acquire small firms or shares in large enterprises.

29.   A proposal to exclude years worked in upper-level Communist party positions or in the KGB was passed by parliament but rejected by the president.

30.   Aversion to extensive foreign ownership is rather general. Nordic countries have long placed restrictions on foreign ownership of land and have required some shares sold to foreigners to have negligible voting rights.

31.   Prices for intra-CMEA trade were based on a moving average of past world prices, whereas internal Soviet prices had no clear link to world market levels.

32.   For an overview of the existing transportation infrastructure, see Van Arkadie and Karlsson (1992).

33.   Analogously, Russia's external trade is now faring much better than its economy as a whole, with export volumes to many Western European countries rising.

34.   Analogously, there is surely now a drop in the volume of trade between St. Petersburg and the rest of Russia (within the same country) arising from the restructuring of the industrial sector.

35.   If one compares only Soviet debt and Soviet military hardware, the simple arithmetic of Russia keeping both is strongly in its favor. If the Soviet external debt is around U.S. $70 billion, a simple per capita division would make Estonia's share U.S. $400 million. If one also divided the value of all Soviet military assets on a per capita basis, the value of Estonia's share would surely exceed this sum. If one instead adopted a territorial principle and remembered that several important air force bases and a major

nuclear submarine base were or still are located in Estonia, the calculation would be dramatically in Russia's favor.

REFERENCES

Åslund, Anders. *Post-Communist Economic Revolutions: How Big a Bang?* Washington: Center for Strategic and International Studies, 1992.

[Bank of Estonia.] *The Monetary Reform in Estonia 1992*. Tallinn: Bank of Estonia, 1992.

Brown, Bess. "Central Asia: The First Year of Unexpected Statehood." *RFE/RL Research Report* 2, 1 (January 1, 1993): 25–36.

Chetkovich, Sasha, and Sven Chetkovich. "Monetary Reform: The Case of Slovenia." Stockholm Institute of East European Economics, Working Paper no. 44, 1992.

Hanson, Philip. "Estonia's Narva Problem, Narva's Estonian Problem." *REF/RL Research Report* 2, 18 (April 30, 1993): 17–23.

Hansson, Ardo H. "The Emergence and Stabilization of Extreme Inflationary Pressures in the Soviet Union." In Anders Åslund (ed.), *The Post-Soviet Economy: Soviet and Western Perspectives*, pp. 67–84. London: Pinter Publishers, 1992.

Hansson, Ardo H. "The Trouble with the Ruble: Monetary Reform in the Former Soviet Union." In Anders Åslund and Richard Layard (eds.), *Reforming the Russian Economy*, pp. 163–184. London: Pinter, 1993a.

Hansson, Ardo H. "The Estonian Kroon: Experiences of the First Year." Paper presented at the CEPR Conference on the Economics of New Currencies, Frankfurt, June 1993b.

Hansson, Ardo H., and Jeffrey D. Sachs. "Crowning the Estonian Kroon." *Transition* 3, 9 (October 1992): 1–3.

[International Monetary Fund.] *Economic Review: Estonia*. Washington, D.C.: International Monetary Fund, April 1992.

[International Monetary Fund.] *Economic Review: Estonia*. Washington, D.C.: International Monetary Fund, May 1993.

Misiunas, Romuald J., and Rein Taagepera. *The Baltic States: Years of Dependence 1940–1980*. Berkeley: University of California Press, 1983.

Morris, Peter. "Black Tuesday Freeze Strikes Estonia's Commercial Banks." *Baltic Independent*, November 20–26, 1992a, pp. 1, 5.

Morris, Peter. "Government Props Up Ailing Narva Plant." *Baltic Independent*, November 20–26, 1992b, p. 4.

Olcott, Martha Brill. "Central Asian Independence." *Foreign Affairs* 71, 3 (Summer 1992): 108–130.

Pasvolsky, Leo. *Economic Nationalism of the Danubian States*. New York: Macmillan, 1928.

Pleskovič, Boris, and Jeffrey D. Sachs. "Currency Reform in Slovenia: The Tolar Standing Tall." *Transition* 3, 8 (September 1992): 6–8.

Raagmaa, Garri. "New Enterprises and Regional Development in Estonia." Paper presented at the European Summer Institute in Regional Science, Joensuu, Finland, June 1993.

[Riigi Statistikaamet.] *Statistika Aastaraamat 1991*. Tallinn: Riigi Statistikaamet, 1991.

[Riigi Statistikaamet.] *Estonia: A Statistical Profile*. Tallinn: Riigi Statistikaamet, 1992.

[Riigi Statistikaamet.] *Eesti Statistika Kuukiri 1993*. Various issues. Tallinn: Riigi Statistikaamet, 1993.

Svitek, Ivan. "The Czechoslovak Tax Reform of 1993." *RFE/RL Research Report* 1, 24 (June 12, 1992): 38–41.

Van Arkadie, Brian, and Mats Karlsson. *Economic Survey of the Baltic States*. London: Pinter Publishers, 1992.

Yu, Frank, and Karlis Freibergs. "Leading Estonian Banks Lose Control of Assets." *Baltic Observer*, November 26–December 1992, pp. 1, 9.

3

Ukraine

Simon Johnson and Oleg Ustenko

INTRODUCTION

When independence was declared in August 1991 and confirmed by a referendum that December, Ukraine was initially considered by both Ukrainians and outsiders to have relatively bright economic prospects. Ukraine's well-educated work force, large size, endowment of natural resources, and high level of industrialization appeared to confer important advantages relative to other postcommunist countries. Western Ukraine had experienced a market economy more recently than most of the former Soviet Union and there was talk of Ukraine doing better than Russia and perhaps even joining the "fast track" of economic reform exemplified by Poland, Hungary, and the former Czechoslovakia.

Two years later the situation was quite different. Ukraine had one of the highest inflation rates in the region and appeared to have moved into a phase of hyperinflation. At the same time, the fall in output was severe, there had been very little progress with privatization, and the state remained heavily involved in the economy. Key policy makers gave the impression that they would prefer a return to the planned system, but under difficult circumstances they settled for a very poorly functioning hybrid of market and intervention. Ukraine was regarded almost universally as a disappointing case of failed reform in the former Soviet Union.[1]

Some may argue that this is an unfair assessment. Certainly Ukraine has suffered both a large dislocation to its trade with other former republics and a negative terms-of-trade shock due to the higher price of imported energy. But most other newly independent countries that formerly belonged to the Soviet Union were either more involved in inter-republican trade or more dependent on energy imported from Russia. Compared to countries with similar or worse structural economic problems, Ukraine stands out as a bad performer. Why, and what really went wrong in the Ukraine?

The answer to both questions lies with inflation. Inflation was a significant and growing problem in 1991 for all parts of the Soviet Union. Ukrainian inflation during 1992 was over 1,000 percent and roughly in line with that in Russia — not surprising since Ukraine remained at least partially in the ruble zone. However, inflation accelerated dramatically after Ukraine left the ruble zone fully in November 1992. In the seven months up to November 1992, prices in Ukraine increased by 135 percent. In the seven months after November 1992, prices rose by 1,863 percent. From February to May 1993, monthly inflation was in the range of 15–23 percent. In June of that year a further acceleration of inflation pushed the monthly rate over 100 percent, although it fell back to 21 percent in July.

Data that the authors have collected on black market exchange rates reveal a matching depreciation. The Ukrainian karbovanets (Ukrainian for ruble and popularly known as the "coupon") is one of the few currencies that fell consistently against the ruble: from 1.5 to the ruble in November 1992 to 4.4 on August 4, 1993. From August 1 to August 11, 1993, the karbovanets fell by 83 percent against the dollar and by the second week of that month it was depreciating by 2–3 percent per day (see Table 3.1). By the fall of 1993, Ukraine had slipped into hyperinflation.

There was also a fall in output in almost all sectors. Real GDP in the first quarter of 1992 was about 20 percent below the level of the first quarter of 1991. Real GDP in the first quarter of 1993 showed a further fall of 10 percent compared to the same period of the previous year (Popiel, 1993b, p. 19). Such measures are not entirely reliable when inflation is so high, but the dismal picture is confirmed by physical measures of sectoral output. Measured real wages also fell and there was a particularly large decline in purchasing power over such basic goods as bread and meat. Our own surveys of state stores did not find significant improvements in the availability and quality of food. (Details on these surveys are contained in Johnson and Ustenko, 1992; 1994).

Why has Ukrainian economic performance been so bad? Certainly there were adverse initial shocks over which Ukraine had no control, particularly the disruption of inter-republican trade and the increase in

TABLE 3.1
Black Market Exchange Rates in Kiev

	Karbovanets/Dollar		Karbovanets/Ruble	
	Buying Dollars	*Selling Dollars*	*Buying Rubles*	*Selling Rubles*
1992				
January[1]	120	n.a.[2]	n.a.	n.a.
February[1]	120	n.a.	n.a.	n.a.
June 1	120	n.a.	n.a.	n.a.
July 6	200	n.a.	n.a.	n.a.
August 4	250	n.a.	n.a.	n.a.
September 4	280	n.a.	n.a.	n.a.
September 8	325	355	n.a.	n.a.
September 17	340	370	n.a.	n.a.
September 26	380	390	n.a.	n.a.
October 1	390	415	n.a.	n.a.
October 8	450 (39%)[3]	490	n.a.	n.a.
October 17	480 (41%)	500	n.a.	n.a.
October 26	530 (40%)	555	n.a.	n.a.
November 2	560 (44%)	580	n.a.	n.a.
November 8	600 (33%)	620	n.a.	n.a.
November 17	710 (48%)	740	1.55	n.a.
November 26	755 (42%)	805	1.65	n.a.
December 2	720 (29%)	n.t.[4]	1.90	n.a.
December 8	740 (23%)	n.t.	1.90	n.a.
December 17	770 (8%)	n.t.	1.85	n.a.
December 26	860 (14%)	930	1.80	1.90
1993				
January 2	1,000 (39%)	1,100	1.95	2.00
January 8	1,050 (42%)	1,150	1.95	2.00
January 17	1,200 (56%)	1,400	2.20	2.30
January 26	1,470 (71%)	1,570	2.50	2.70
February 2	1,600 (60%)	1,700	2.70	2.75
February 8	2,000 (90%)	2,150	2.80	3.00
February 17	1,900 (58%)	2,000	2.80	2.90
February 26	2,000 (36%)	2,100	2.75	2.85
March 2	2,000 (25%)	2,150	2.75	2.85
March 8	2,000 (0%)	2,200	2.60	2.80
March 17	2,200 (16%)	n.t.	2.80	2.85
March 26	2,200 (10%)	2,300	3.00	3.20
April 2	2,200 (10%)	2,300	3.00	3.20
April 8	2,800 (40%)	3,100	3.00	3.20
April 17	2,750 (25%)	3,100	3.50	3.60
April 26	3,000 (36%)	3,100	3.20	3.50

	Karbovanets/Dollar		Karbovanets/Ruble	
	Buying Dollars	Selling Dollars	Buying Rubles	Selling Rubles
May 2	3,000 (36%)	3,150	3.20	3.40
May 8	3,000 (7%)	3,150	3.10	3.30
May 17	3,050 (11%)	3,200	3.00	3.20
May 26	3,050 (2%)	3,200	2.90	3.10
June 2	3,100 (3%)	3,200	2.60	2.80
June 8	3,700 (23%)	n.t.	2.60	2.80
June 17	3,400 (12%)	3,550	2.60	2.70
June 26	3,450 (13%)	3,600	2.60	2.70
June 28	3,450	3,600	2.60	2.70
June 29	3,450	3,600	2.60	2.70
June 30	3,450	3,600	2.80	3.00
July 1	3,450	3,600	2.90	3.15
July 12	3,300	3,600	2.60	2.70
July 17	4,300 (27%)	4,100	3.40	3.60
July 21	4,450	4,700	4.10	4.20
July 26	4,500 (30%)	4,700	4.20	4.30
August 4	4,850	5,200	4.40	4.60
August 10	5,300	5,800	4.70	5.00
August 11	5,700 (33%)	6,200	4.80	5.20
August 12	6,000	6,500	4.90	5.50
August 13 a.m.	6,100	6,700	4.90	5.50
August 13 p.m.	6,200	6,900	4.90	5.50

Source: Authors' own surveys.

Notes:

[1] Approximate figures indicative of the prevailing situation in the given month.

[2] No information collected on the date in question.

[3] The number in brackets is the percentage change in the black market exchange rate compared with the same day of the previous month.

[4] No transactions of the relevant kind.

Enquiries were made in the same place at approximately the same time every day. Five people were asked their selling rates and five people their buying rates. The numbers reported are the mean prices obtained after discarding implausible outlying quotes.

energy prices. However, in large part blame must be attributed to a lack of a government strategy for economic adjustment. There were piecemeal and gradual reforms, but the evidence indicates that these measures were far from sufficient.

As a result Ukraine moved rapidly from a situation in which inflation was a result of underlying difficulties to one where it was so high, unstable, and accelerating that it threatened to become the major problem. Independent Ukraine's path toward hyperinflation is the primary subject of this chapter.

Section 2 provides background economic statistics on the Ukrainian economy and relevant comparisons with other former republics. Section 3 traces the major developments of the period of partial monetary independence, from December 1991 to November 1992. Section 4 analyzes the implications of full monetary independence after November 1992. Section 5 discusses the reasons for the disappointing pace of privatization in Ukraine. Section 6 assesses the extent of structural change in the economy. Section 7 assesses the impact of independence on real wages and living standards. Section 8 concludes with a discussion of Ukraine's likely economic prospects.

THE STARTING POINT

Ukraine definitely has economic potential.[2] In contrast to most newly independent countries in the region, Ukraine is quite large. Its population is estimated to be 51.8 million people, about 18 percent of the former Soviet total (IMF et al., 1991, p. 206). Its geographical area is 603,700 square kilometers, slightly smaller than Texas or Turkey but larger than France. Furthermore, most of Ukraine's land is well endowed with either mineral resources or good-quality soil. These facts are reflected in its relatively large share in the industrial and agricultural output of the former union.

In 1989 Ukraine accounted for 24 percent of Soviet coal production (IMF et al., 1991, p. 213), 46 percent of its iron ore production (IMF et al., 1991, p. 213), 16.2 percent of its total net output (IMF et al., 1991, p. 214), and 17.2 percent of its net agricultural output (IMF et al., 1991, p. 214). It was responsible for more than 30 percent of Soviet production of the following industrial products (IMF et al., 1991, pp. 216–217): cast iron (40.8 percent), steel (34.2 percent), rolled ferrous metal (34.5 percent), steel pipe (33.5 percent), A.C. electric motors (35.8 percent), televisions (35.9 percent), sugar (52.6 percent), and vegetable oil (33.2 percent). It also had between 20 percent and 30 percent of the all-union production of a variety of machine building and equipment products, some construction materials, shoes, and meat products. Furthermore, Ukraine also produced more than 20 percent of the total Soviet output of almost all major agricultural products, including grain (24.3 percent), potatoes (24.5 percent), vegetables (26.2 percent), meat (22.4 percent), milk (22.7 percent), and sugar beets (54.2 percent).

Before independence, Ukraine did not enjoy a high level of trade with countries outside of the Soviet Union. In 1990 its foreign exports valued at international prices were 7.829 billion rubles, about 5 percent of GDP. To put this into international perspective, France exported 23 percent of its GDP in 1989, up from 13 percent in 1965, while Turkey — which has a population of around 55 million and a land area of 779,300 square kilometers — exported 6 percent of its GDP in 1965 and 22 percent in 1989.

Ukrainian imports from abroad in 1990 were 9.301 billion rubles, implying a significant deficit. However, Western agencies estimate that the switch to international prices actually improves Ukraine's trade balance with the rest of the world. Unfortunately, moving to world prices for trade with other former republics significantly worsens Ukraine's trade balance.

Using Soviet domestic prices, Ukraine had a small inter-republican trade surplus in 1990. Its exports to other republics were 38 billion rubles, which was about 23 percent of GDP, and its imports were 39 billion rubles. Evaluated at world prices, these exports would have cost closer to 35 billion rubles and the imports would have cost over 42 billion rubles. Oil and gas combined were a substantial deficit item but were partly made up for by net exports from the ferrous metals sector, machine building, and food processing.

Most other former republics exported a far higher proportion of their production to other parts of the Soviet Union. Expressed as a percentage of net material product in 1988, Ukrainian inter-republican exports were 39.1 percent. In contrast, the Baltics exported 60–67 percent, Armenia exported 63.7 percent, Belarus exported 69.6 percent, and Central Asian countries exported 41–51 percent. Only Kazakhstan and Russia were relatively less involved in inter-republican trade — they exported 30.9 percent and 18 percent, respectively, to other republics.

One estimate puts the total terms-of-trade effect on Ukraine of the move to world prices at a loss of around 2.5 percent of GDP. However, this estimate does not take into consideration the costs of disrupting inter-republican trade. In the first nine months of 1992, inter-republican exports were around 575 billion rubles, which was about 20 percent of GDP, while foreign exports were still around 5 percent of GDP. Ukraine may have lost as much as a fifth of its exports, primarily through difficulties with exports to Russia.

The most important trade issue is how much Ukraine will pay for oil and natural gas from other former republics, and how much it will charge for the use of the gas and oil pipelines which cross its territory on the way to the more western parts of Europe. For a former Soviet republic it is unusually self-sufficient in energy, due to both its nuclear power stations and its coal. In 1990 about half of Ukraine's primary energy consumption was provided by its own resources, although this proportion had fallen from around 60 percent five years previously. In 1991 Ukraine imported about half of its energy needs, primarily from Russia.

Ukraine's most important energy problem is its almost complete reliance on imported oil, although it has its own large processing capability. There have been shortages of gasoline and aviation fuel sporadically since independence and chronically since the end of 1992. In 1993 Ukraine was paying 40–70 percent of world prices for various energy sources, but there was an agreement in principle to pay world prices for Russian oil from the beginning of 1994. As it turns out, Ukraine paid approximately 80 percent of the world price for oil in 1994, although there have been problems with nonpayment for gas deliveries.

No account of Ukraine's initial starting position would be complete without mentioning nuclear weapons. Inheriting the third largest nuclear stockpile in the world has certainly helped Ukraine grab some headlines and attain a certain strategic importance — see, for example, Mearsheimer (1993), *Economist* (1993a; 1993b), and *New York Times* (1993). Unfortunately, Ukraine's position on these weapons until late 1994 delayed rather than speeded up the building of links with the West, particularly in terms of obtaining Western economic assistance. However, as the subsequent sections make clear, at least until summer 1994, the confused macro-economic situation in Ukraine made it difficult for Western agencies to help in any meaningful way.

Ukraine may have considerable economic potential, but its performance to date has been poor. The government's GDP forecast in April 1993 was 13.658 trillion karbovantsi for calendar 1993. The exchange rates, both official and unofficial, at that time were around 3,000 karbovantsi per dollar, implying a total GDP of $4.6 billion, or about $92 per capita. This is an extraordinarily low number by any standard, but particularly considering that pre-independence purchasing power parity numbers suggested a per capita income of around $3,860.

In part the problem is an inflation-induced real appreciation of the dollar — people buy dollars as a hedge against inflation, which tends to reduce the value of everything denominated in karbovantsi. But real output has also declined unequivocally.

The numbers measured in physical units are unambiguous. From the first quarter of 1992 to the first quarter of 1993, the output of electrical energy fell by 5 percent, that of coal fell by 5 percent, that of chemicals fell by 17 percent, that of wood fell by 3 percent, that of pulp and paper fell by 15 percent, that of bread fell by 11 percent, the output of meat fell 17 percent, and that of milk fell by 35 percent. From the third quarter of 1992 to the first quarter of 1993, the output of ferrous metals fell by 15 percent, chemicals by 19 percent, and bread by 20 percent.

Official statistics indicate that output fell by relatively less in Ukraine than in other former republics. Ukraine's decline in net material product was 15 percent in 1992, which was a greater fall than in Belarus (11 percent), Uzbekistan (12.9 percent), or Kazakhstan (14.2 percent), but less than in Russia (20 percent) and the others. Ukraine's 9 percent fall in gross industrial output in 1992 was less than in all other former republics except Belarus (PlanEcon, 1993).

In contrast, inflation in Ukraine has been the highest of any ex-republic, with the possible exception of some of those that have been at war. Ukraine's retail price level rose by almost 22 times from December 1991 to December 1992, an increase which was exceeded only by Azerbaijan. Ukraine's 25-fold increase in officially measured wholesale prices was the highest of any former republic.

Output has fallen sharply in Ukraine, as it has in most other parts of the former Soviet Union, and for similar reasons. Trade between former republics has been disrupted and energy prices have risen steeply. What really sets Ukraine aside is its rapid rate of inflation, particularly from mid-1992 through mid-1993. Why has inflation risen so far and so fast?

PARTIAL MONETARY INDEPENDENCE: DECEMBER 1991 TO NOVEMBER 1992

Despite Ukraine's declaring independence in August 1991 and becoming formally independent after a referendum on December 1 of that year, the borders between Ukraine and Russia stayed almost completely open and Ukraine remained in the Russian ruble zone — using so-called non-cash (*beznalichnye* in Russian) rubles for many transactions, particularly between enterprises — until November 1992.

As a result, the two economies remained closely linked, and when the Russian government announced that state-controlled prices would be increased and "freed" at the beginning of 1992, the Ukrainian government felt the need to do likewise. However, then–prime minister Fokin and his colleagues declined to take further systematic reform measures. Ukraine during 1992 was characterized by the disintegration of state control over the economy, while the central bank provided low-interest credits to favored sectors. "Gradualism" in Ukraine has meant changing the previous structure of industry and trade as little as possible. At the same time, forms of spontaneous privatization have swept through the state enterprise sector (Johnson and Kroll, 1991).

In the fall of 1991, our surveys in Kiev showed that goods in state stores had stable prices although there were some shortages — seen in the lines for goods and in the periodic absence of some goods. For example, our data for that time period — shown in Table 3.2 — indicate that milk and bread were usually available, although subject to queueing.[3]

TABLE 3.2
Bread and Milk at State Stores in Kiev and
St. Petersburg, July 1991–June 1993

	Bread (kilo)		Milk (liter)	
	Price	Queue Length	Price	Queue Length
1991				
July 23–24	0.96	6	0.60	7
July 30	0.96	5	0.60	10
August, 4th week	0.96	3	0.60	12
September, 2nd week	0.96	7	0.60	10
September, 4th week	0.96	4	0.60	5
October, 1st week	0.96	5	0.60	5
October, 3rd week	0.96	4	0.60	3
November, 4th week	0.96	5	0.60	n.p.[1]
December, 2nd week	0.96	10	0.60	n.p.
December 4th week	0.96	n.p.	0.60	n.p.
1992				
January, 2nd week	5	15	1.95	60
January, 4th week	5	7	1.95	n.p.
February, 2nd week	5	6	1.95	n.p.
February, 4th week	5	5	1.95	n.p.
March, 2nd week	5	3	1.95	n.p.
March, 4th week	5	3	1.95	n.p.
April, 1st week	5	10	1.95	n.p.
April, 3rd week	5	5	1.95	6
May, 2nd week	5	9	1.95	n.p.
May, 4th week	5	7	1.95	n.p.
June, 2nd week	5	7	1.95	8
June, 4th week	5	9	18	10
July, 1st week	16	10	18	10
July, 3rd week	16	15	18	15

	Bread (kilo)		Milk (liter)	
	Price	Queue Length	Price	Queue Length
August, 2nd week	16	7	18	7
August, 4th week	16	15	18	15
September, 2nd week	16	n.p.	21	4
September, 4th week	16	10	12	5
October, 2nd week	16	4	n.k.[2]	n.p.
October, 4th week	16	8	n.k.	n.p.
November, 2nd week	16	4	n.k.	n.p.
November, 4th week	16	8	n.k.	n.p.
December, 2nd week	16	5	n.k.	n.p.
December, 4th week	32	4	n.k.	n.p.
1993				
January, 2nd week	40	3	n.k.	n.p.
January, 4th week	53	4	n.k.	n.p.
February, 2nd week	65	8	178	10
February, 4th week	65	7	178	5
March, 2nd week	65	4	n.k.	n.p.
March, 4th week	72	5	178	3
April, 2nd week	75	4	180	8
April, 4th week	65	40	180	15
May, 2nd week	60	30	180	17
May, 4th week	60	16	200	20
June, 1st week	60	23	217	45
June, 2nd week	180	9	440	7
June, 3rd week	200	10	325	15
June, 4th week	210	8	325	17

Source: Authors' own price surveys in Kiev and St. Petersburg.

Notes:

[1]Relevant product not in the store.

[2]Price is not known because the product was not in the store and there was not a publicly announced price.

Table 3.3 measures inflation by tracking the cost of a typical basket of goods. The basket of goods used in this calculation is the monthly ration of soldiers in the former Soviet (now Ukrainian) army. This ration comprises the following: 0.9 kilograms of butter, 1.5 kg of sugar, 4.5 kg of meat, 12.0 kg of bread, 2.0 kg of cabbage, 2.0 kg of tomatoes, 2.0 kg of cucumbers, 9.0 kg of potatoes, and 8 eggs. The ration also includes some

TABLE 3.3
Retail Food Price Index in Ukraine[1]

	Cost of Basket[2]	Cumulative Index[3]	Monthly Inflation[4]
1991			
October	198	100	n.a.
November	230	116	16
December	290	146	26
1992			
January	1,551	782	435
February	1,455	734	–6
March	1,405	708	–3
April	1,507	760	7
May	1,520	766	1
June	1,537	775	1
July	1,930	973	26
August	2,460	1,241	27
September	2,500	1,261	2
October	3,150	1,589	26
November	3,543	1,788	13
December	12,709	6,412	259
1993			
January	17,968	9,066	41
February	20,688	10,438	15
March	23,887	12,052	15
April	26,820	13,532	12
May	32,850	16,574	23
June	69,560	35,096	112
July	84,000	42,381	21
August[4]	93,000	46,969	11

Source: Authors' own price surveys.

Notes:
   [1]Based on Ukrainian Army Ration, composition of which is described in the text.
   [2]Through December 1991 in rubles, from January 1992 onward in karbovantsi.
   [3]October 1991 = 100.
   [4]Percentage monthly increase.
   [5]Applies to first week of month only.

Each month's index is computed using data from the second week of that month only. Monthly inflation is calculated by comparing the second week of the relevant month with the second week of the previous month. However, for June 1993 we also report data from the first week and fourth week.

less important goods for which we have not collected prices and excludes at least one important category of good — milk and other dairy products. In this price index, we use the state store price in all cases where a good is available in these stores, except when the queue for a good is longer than 15 people, in which case we use the price in the "peasant market" (*kolkhoznyy rynok* in Russian).[4] This provides a crude measure of the way in which shortages and waiting in line pushes up the cost of goods.

Table 3.3 shows that significant inflation already existed in November and December 1991, when the price index increased by 16 and 26 percent, respectively. These price increases were almost exclusively due to rises in the prices of goods on the peasant market. The major increases in state prices were still to come.

By the end of 1991 it was clear that the Ukrainian government intended to follow Russia at least partially and raise the prices of some goods at the beginning of January 1992. The government in Kiev also announced that it would introduce a new form of cash money, the karbovanets, at the beginning of the year.

The exchange rate of the karbovanets in its first days was high. On its first day, January 8, one karbovanets was worth eight (Russian or Soviet) rubles, but within two weeks one karbovanets could buy only two rubles and by the end of February the karbovanets and ruble were trading at one-for-one.

In effect, the government signaled clearly that prices would rise sharply in the New Year, with the predictable result that people bought all the goods that they could find. By December 23, 1991, there was no bread, milk, or eggs in any of the stores which we surveyed. In fact, none of the 22 goods on our list was available in the surveyed stores on that day. During the last two weeks of December, most goods, including bread, were absent from the seven stores surveyed, and the longest recorded line was 150 people waiting for milk.

There was a sharp anticipatory jump in market prices at the end of 1991, with a large increase in the first and second weeks of December 1991 and in the first week of January 1992. The rate of growth was highest for meat products and tomatoes, but all prices — with the curious exception of butter — increased by more than 200 percent. Table 3.3 shows that our measure of the retail price index increased by more than 400 percent in January 1992. The supply situation did not improve immediately once prices were increased: in the first two weeks of January, no surveyed store had more than 8 types of goods out of the 22 types on our list.

The price increases of January did not by themselves initiate an unstoppable inflationary spiral. From mid-January to early March 1992, prices in state stores were held constant — with the exception of eggs — and prices on the peasant market actually fell. It appears that the extent of anticipatory purchases at the end of 1991 was so great that prices on the free market actually overshot. According to our data, from the first week of January to the first week of March there was a 22 percent fall in prices in the peasant market. This is reflected in Table 3.3, which shows a 6 percent fall in the retail price index in February and a 3 percent fall in March.

This should have been a major assistance to the government in holding down prices, and Table 3.3 shows extremely good inflation results through June — for all months except April, which showed a monthly increase of 7 percent, that is, an annualized rate of 125 percent. At the same time the black market exchange rate of the karbovanets stabilized at around 120 karbovantsi to the dollar from February to June (see Table 3.1). Unfortunately, government macroeconomic policy proved inconsistent with continued price stability.

The Ukrainian government's budget deficit was quite small in the first half of 1992, although it grew steadily during the year. For the first six months the general budget deficit — for the central government plus regional authorities — was estimated at 42 billion karbovantsi, around 2 percent of GDP. For the nine months to the end of September this deficit had risen to 10 percent of GDP and for the whole year it was at least 16 percent of GDP (Popiel, 1993a, p. 16).

The government's major problem in 1992 was the shrinking of revenue in real terms, rather than an increase in real spending. Although it is difficult to measure real values correctly when inflation is so high, general government revenue in 1992 appears to have been around 27 percent of GDP and general government spending was around 43 percent. In contrast, government revenue was 33 percent of GDP in 1989, 34 percent in 1990, and 34.8 percent in 1991; government spending was 27.3 percent of GDP in 1989, 31.4 percent in 1990, and 48.3 percent in 1991. Thus, real government spending actually appears to have fallen since independence.

Even more important, of course, is that any Ukrainian government deficit is financed almost exclusively by the printing of money. Monetary emission through credits at low nominal interest rates has been used effectively to subsidize selected industrial sectors. The growth in nominal money from the end of 1991 to the end of 1992 was remarkable. The amount of currency in circulation rose 21 times; the value of M1 — currency plus demand deposits — rose by 10 times; the value of total monetary liabilities — M1 plus other deposits — rose by the same factor (Popiel, 1993c, p. 41).

Currency accounted for 13 percent of total monetary liabilities in December 1991 and 25 percent one year later. The share of household and enterprise demand deposits in total monetary liabilities fell from 27 percent to 7 percent and from 34 percent to 20 percent, respectively. Calculated as a proportion of GDP, M1 was 60 percent and total monetary liabilities were 79 percent. There may have been some monetary overhang, in the sense of money which could not buy goods in 1991, but it was almost certainly dissipated by the end of 1992. The M1/GDP ratio was down to 44 percent and the ratio of total monetary liabilities to GDP was down to 57 percent. By way of contrast, in Turkey in 1989 the ratio of broad money to GDP was 23 percent, in a country with about the same per capita income in purchasing power terms as Ukraine; 51 percent in Yugoslavia, a socialist country with high inflation; and 76 percent in France. There is still room for a further fall in the demand for real money balances in Ukraine. In a highly inflationary situation, lower real money demand usually leads directly to higher prices.

A rough indicator of broad money, without individuals' demand deposits and other deposits, indicates quarterly growth of 178 percent in the second quarter, 106 percent in the third quarter, and 95 percent in the fourth quarter of 1992 (Popiel, 1993a, p. 17). At the beginning of 1992 most monetary growth was the result of loans to state enterprises, but the relative importance of this form of money creation declined as the budget deficit worsened.

Although it is difficult to measure the real value of nominal magnitudes in a period of high inflation, the evidence suggests that the real budget deficit had risen dramatically by August 1992. Government spending was 20.2 billion karbovantsi in January and 167 billion in August. Our price index, rebased to equal 100 in January, is 159 for August 1992. This implies that real spending in August was five times higher than in January, and that the deficit was eleven times larger in real terms than in January. In nominal terms the deficit was 3.2 billion karbovantsi in January and 59 billion in August.

Published official statistics do not include any plausible numbers for monetary emission before the January–June period, so we cannot calculate, for example, monthly growth rates of money during spring 1992. However, for this period about 100 billion karbovantsi of the money growth was not due to the budget deficit, and so presumably entered the economy through low-interest loans provided to state enterprises by the

Ukrainian central bank — a practice that has been a key element of the Ukrainian government's "gradualist" economic policies.[5] This fits with anecdotal evidence obtained from our interviews with managers of industrial firms and banks (Johnson, Kroll, and Horton, 1993).

Information about inflation in our price surveys during this period must be interpreted with care, because there is strong evidence that during 1992 significant de facto price controls remained on some key goods — particularly milk and bread. The price of milk was not altered from January to June and the price of bread was held constant until July. How did this pricing policy affect the balance of supply and demand?

Although the queue length for bread remained about constant from January to June, milk was seldom available until after its price was increased in June.[6] For other less crucial goods sold in state stores, there appears to have been price regulation, but this was due mostly to the bureaucratic inertia of changing prices within state trading organizations.

For example, there were repeated changes in the price of eggs during spring 1992.[7] Interestingly, these changes are hard to correlate with the evidence on changes in availability of eggs. After the price increases in January, eggs were briefly available in state stores, although with a queue. The price cuts of February seem to have resulted in eggs disappearing from the state stores, at least until April, from which date they were available with a queue — although the price of eggs was not increased until June. The most plausible explanation for these movements is that the state trading organizations dealing with eggs were trying to achieve a rough balance in the market and had a great deal of difficulty getting the price right.

Bread and milk exhibit more price stability than most other goods sold in state stores during this period — an indication that these are viewed by the government as strategic goods. A further strong indicator of the presence of price controls is that, in spite of the gathering inflationary momentum and already significant queues, the price of milk was reduced in mid-September. As Table 3.2 shows, milk disappeared from state stores until much higher prices were introduced in February 1993.

The most important conclusion from price behavior and the availability of goods is that while price controls had been loosened, prices in state stores were not now "free." Prices continued to be set by administrators, either by the stores themselves or — more often — within the relevant state wholesale trade organization. These administrators respond to signals on prices and queue lengths only with long and variable lags.

As a result, prices in state stores exhibited considerable inertia and should be considered as lagging behind overall inflation.[8] The leading indicator of Ukrainian inflation was usually the black market exchange rate of the karbovanets against the dollar, while prices on the peasant market provided a further indicator of current and future inflation. Our retail food price index, reported in Table 3.3, provides a summary measure of monthly inflation.

The second half of 1992, particularly from August onward, was characterized by the rapidly accelerating depreciation of the Ukrainian currency. The karbovanets remained basically stable against the dollar from February to June 1992, but during the summer it began to depreciate significantly. As Table 3.1 shows, from the beginning of September 1992 the rate depreciated steadily, moving at least five karbovantsi every two days. The more rapid depreciation at the beginning of October is due to the effect on inflation of higher administered prices — particularly for gasoline — at the beginning of the month. In the last two trading days of October and the first days of November, for the first time the exchange rate depreciated five karbovantsi per day against the dollar.

The first nine months of Ukrainian independence show the effects of partially liberalizing prices while refusing to speed the privatization of trade. In Ukraine, "liberalizing" prices meant increasing state-controlled basic prices, such as those for energy, removing some subsidies at the level of intermediate goods, and decentralizing price-setting authority to the level of the bureaucrats running state trade organizations. There was some growth of private trade, particularly in nonfood products, but almost all shops and wholesale trade organizations remained as much in the state sector as before. The only exception, at least in Kiev, was a few shops which were now leased but which usually offered virtually the same goods and services as before. By early November 1992, on the verge of full monetary independence, the Ukrainian budget was out of control, credit was loose, and prices were rising sharply.

FULL MONETARY INDEPENDENCE

After January 1992 the role of Russian rubles in cash transactions in Ukraine was gradually displaced by the karbovanets. By November 1992 it was usual to use karbovantsi for almost all retail purchases, although rubles could be used in some instances at the current black market rate of exchange, and Russian coins (kopecks) were used in those increasingly rare instances when change was needed.

At the beginning of October 1992, the Russian central bank stopped honoring at least some of the payments authorized — in Russian rubles — by the Ukrainian central bank. The Russian government subsequently made it clear, most notably at the meeting of the member-states of the Commonwealth of Independent States (CIS) in Bishkek, that ex-republics should either abide by Russian monetary rules or get out of the ruble zone. In large part this was a response to the large amounts of credit issued by the Ukrainian National Bank.

On November 12, 1992, the government in Kiev reacted to this pressure by leaving the ruble zone and introducing a noncash (*beznalichnyy*) karbovanets. It also declared that the Russian ruble was no longer legal tender in Ukraine. Existing balances in Ukrainian banks were converted from noncash rubles to noncash karbovantsi at an exchange rate of one-to-one. For all new transactions, however, the *beznalichnyy* karbovanets-ruble exchange rate was fixed by the Ukrainian National Bank at one ruble to 1.45 karbovantsi.

This initial official rate was fairly close to the black market rate — from November 12 to 14 our survey showed the cash rate for buying karbovantsi to be 1.4 karbovantsi per ruble. However, the rate moved to 1.5 on November 15, held at 1.55 from November 16 to 21, and then began the fairly steady depreciation shown in Table 3.1. This was an early indication that Ukrainian monetary independence would mean more rather than less inflation compared to Russia.

The move to full monetary independence was followed by strong pro-stabilization announcements by the government. For example, on November 18, 1992, then–prime minister Kuchma addressed the parliament, with the supposed aim of establishing what anticrisis measures were required (*Golos Ukrainy*, November 19, 1992, p. 1).

On the basis of these warnings, over the next month the parliament was persuaded that the government should be granted strong anticrisis powers. From December 1992 to May 1993 the government was empowered to rule by decree on economic matters, subject to confirmation by parliament. In practice, it appears that the government had a great deal of discretion over economic policy during this period.

There were some initial signs of fiscal austerity but these soon faded. In January there was a budget surplus amounting to 48 percent of government spending, but this may have been due to the immediate effect of higher administered prices on the nominal value of state enterprise sales and thus on the corporate income taxes. In February the deficit was already 11 percent of spending and it rose to 14 percent in March and 65 percent in April. For the entire period January–April, the budget deficit was 21 percent of total government spending (Popiel, 1993c, p. 40).

Monetary emission also continued to be rapid. M3 growth was 31 percent in November 1992, 26 percent in December, 29 percent in January 1993, 17 percent in February, and 46 percent in March. The government subsequently claimed that the central bank had granted far more in credits to state enterprises than had been authorized, but it seems plausible that at least some government ministers knew what was happening. The government's emergency powers gave it greater control over the central bank than previously, but evidently this control was not exercised effectively.

Unfortunately, therefore, the government's extra powers did not result in anything approaching a coherent anti-inflationary policy; monetary emission continued unchecked. It is currently possible for outsiders to unravel the precise allocation of blame for the absence of a stabilization policy, but the outcome in terms of inflation was painfully clear.

The October and November rates of exchange rate depreciation were in the 30–40 percent range, but this fell into the mid-20 percent range in early December and below 20 percent in the last two weeks of December. However, a new round of administrative price increases in December 1992 led to more rapid depreciation through early February, peaking at 90 percent for the month to February 8. The following month showed a relative deceleration in the rate of depreciation, with 2,000–2,200 karbovantsi to the dollar appearing to be a resistance level — in the sense that traders were unwilling for a time to move beyond it. The rate moved fairly rapidly toward 3,000 karbovantsi to the dollar during April, and then again displayed relative stability — holding in the range of 3,000 to 3,100 from early May to early June.

Table 3.3 shows the dramatic surge in Ukrainian food prices in December 1992, with the index rising by more than 250 percent. The scale of Ukrainian price increases in December 1992 is quite evident. The price of bread doubled from 16 karbovantsi per kilo in the second week to 32 karbovantsi per kilo in the fourth week. This jump was followed by a steady series of increases, often followed by a couple of weeks with a stable price. Inflation fell in subsequent months, but remained in the range of 10 to 15 percent.

In the case of bread, queue length remained roughly constant and consistently less than ten persons from October 1992 through mid-April 1993. Evidence of worsening disequilibrium in the bread market is given by the very long queues at the end of April and in May. These were the longest bread queues — at least since our surveys began in the fall of 1991 — and clearly indicated that the ordinary sequence of bureaucratic price raising was not enough to clear the market. In response, bread prices tripled between the first and second weeks of June.

The supply of meat was similarly erratic in Kiev state stores. In four out of the eleven weeks in 1993 for which we have data, no meat was available. In three other weeks queue length was 15 people or more. Inflation data for goods sold in peasant markets show large fluctuations in relative prices every month and that many prices rise steeply and then fall in the aftermath of increases in administrative prices. For example, in Kiev during January–March, 5 out of 14 goods experienced price declines and another 3 had one month without any increase in price.

On June 1 the Ukrainian government announced that subsidies would shortly be withdrawn from meat, milk, and bread. The predictable result was a sharp increase in peasant market prices. Pork rose from 3,000 karbovantsi per kilo on May 30 to 7,000 on June 8, potatoes increased from 80 karbovantsi per kilo to 200, and the price of onions moved from 100 karbovantsi per kilo to 250 karbovantsi.

Also predictable was a wave of panic buying. There were big increases in the length of bread and milk queues in state stores. Milk was present in only one of the three stores that we surveyed, there was no meat in any of our surveyed stores, and the queue for eggs was the longest that it had been all year.

The announcement of official price increases at the beginning of June had a direct effect on the black market exchange rate, which fell by 19 percent from June 2 to June 8. The rate may have initially overshot its new equilibrium value — by June 11 it had risen back to 3,400 karbovantsi to the dollar. The unsettled nature of the black market is apparent in the fact that no traders were willing to sell dollars during our surveys on June 8 and 11.

Even in the absence of up-to-date monetary statistics, it is clear that a great deal of new money was created in the first eight months of 1993. A miners' strike was ended in June in part through promising extra credits and other forms of financial assistance estimated to cost between 7 and 13 trillion karbovantsi — the broad money supply was only 6.5 trillion karbovantsi in April 1993. Additional credits of around two trillion karbovantsi for agriculture and state industrial enterprises were approved in June. From May to June 1993 there was only a 4 percent increase in currency in circulation but a 73 percent increase in state enterprise deposits. M1 rose by 43 percent and M3 by 47 percent, the highest rates since monetary independence.

The acceleration of the rate of money creation presumably explains the rapid rise in the black market exchange rate from 3,300 karbovantsi to the dollar on July 12 to 4,300 on July 17. In subsequent weeks the rate rose dramatically: to 4,500 on July 26, 4,850 on August 4, 5,700 on August 11, and 6,200 in the afternoon of August 13.

In August 1993 the Ukrainian food supply situation remained approximately the same as it was just before independence. The supply of food in state stores was erratic, with frequent periods of long queues and periodic disappearance of goods. The quality of state products remained poor. At the same time, inflation had accelerated dramatically, was much higher than in Russia, and had reached hyperinflationary levels by the fall of 1993. By August 1993, the exchange rate had begun to depreciate by as much as 7 percent per day and the fundamentals of monetary and fiscal policy appeared very poor.

On top of these problems must be added the miners' strike of the summer of 1993. Miners are particularly important because they are the best organized group in the predominantly Russian area of the Donbass. This area voted overwhelmingly for independence in December 1991 — for example, both the Donets'k and Luhans'k *oblasti* (provinces) had voted 83.9 percent in favor — presumably because it thought that living standards would be higher than if it stayed under the jurisdiction of Moscow. The summer 1993 strike indicated that eastern Ukraine was very dissatisfied with the economic and political situation. If the economy continues to perform better in Russia than in Ukraine, dissatisfaction will probably grow. While open interethnic conflict or secession is unlikely in the near future, the poor economy is a destabilizing factor.

Ironically, it appears that by breaking the direct link of its currency to the ruble, the Ukrainian government eliminated the last nominal anchor in the economy. The willingness of the Russian central bank to finance Ukraine may have been a very imperfect anchor previously, but even it was now gone.

THE FAILURE OF PRIVATIZATION

In Ukraine, as in most postcommunist countries, privatization is at least nominally at the top of the political agenda (Frydman et al., 1993, pp. 83–127). The Ukrainian Privatization Program, adopted by parliament in July 1992, lays out an ambitious timetable for achieving an impressive set of goals (State Program, 1992). But so far there has been little progress.

Six criteria are commonly used to evaluate privatization proposals in postcommunist countries and to set standards according to which these programs should be deemed successful. The first four criteria are concerned with the process of privatization, while the fifth and sixth focus on the nature of the firms that privatization creates.

First, privatization should be rapid. In particular, sufficient privatization needs to take place while there is still a clear political consensus in favor of privatization. On this point Ukraine has a very disappointing record. As of mid-1993 the only privatization proceedings involved a few shops in a couple of towns along with a few initial public offerings organized by the International Finance Corporation. In contrast Russia has proceeded much faster, both with shops and with voucher privatization. Political opposition to rapid privatization has grown over time and the legislature never even passed the 1993 Privatization Program.

Second, privatization should be complete, in the sense that it results in the transfer of all de jure property rights to private persons. If privatization is initially incomplete — for example, if only leasing is allowed — there needs to be a clear procedure and timetable for private persons to acquire all de jure rights. There have been several attempts to clarify the status of leased enterprises in Ukraine, but in practice the situation remains murky.

Third, privatization should be clean, in the sense that it does not involve too much corruption. Ukraine has not yet progressed far enough for a full assessment of this point, but there are reports that up to one-half of the purchasers of privatized shops have been unable to make payment in full. If there has been any corruption of local officials it will presumably have negative repercussions on other privatization projects.

Fourth, the privatization process must allow sufficient opportunities for all interested citizens to participate. As in many other postcommunist countries, the Ukrainian government decided that a form of privatization voucher would broaden participation in the process. Unfortunately, the initial scheme adopted was rather too complicated and proved largely unworkable (Johnson and Eder, 1992). These problems have delayed mass privatization and have yet to be completely resolved.

Fifth, privatization should create firms which have effective corporate governance, so that stockholders are able to supervise managers effectively and to prevent them from taking actions not in the best interests of the stockholders. Sixth, privatized firms should be structured in a way that allows them to bring in outside capital, either in the form of debt or equity. It remains far from clear how these criteria will be met in Ukraine.

In the absence of a coherent government privatization strategy, insiders — workers and managers in state firms — have acquired some property rights for free or at very low prices. However, they do not own the firm entirely, so that privatization remains incomplete, and — even worse — there does not currently exist a clear set of rules for converting partially privatized assets into fully privatized assets. Nevertheless, insiders have obtained sufficiently strong claims to be able to minimize the property rights obtained by outsiders, ensuring that there will be only limited participation by the population as a whole.

A decree on the conversion of Ukrainian state enterprises into joint stock companies was signed by then-president Kravchuk on June 15, 1993, conferring a strong role on ministries and other state agencies. Whether these bodies can effectively control managers and the privatization process remains to be seen.

Managers and workers currently have considerable de facto property rights, but almost never exercise full de jure ownership. They have control over the property, but do not own it. Threats by the government to take this property away from them presumably reduce these actors' time horizons, making them less likely to invest and more likely to transfer assets clandestinely to the private sector. These firms lack a proper system of corporate governance and will find it very difficult to bring in outside capital.

THE BEGINNINGS OF STRUCTURAL CHANGE

Despite the poor overall performance of the Ukrainian economy, there is some evidence of positive change. Our own observations and anecdotal evidence strongly suggest that the availability and quality of nonfood goods continues to increase. However, we have not been able to develop any relevant systematic measures, primarily because many of these goods are now distributed through new retail outlets. For example, a great deal of private nonfood trade in Kiev still takes place at the republic stadium, although as traders accumulate capital, they acquire premises and usually try to specialize.

There have been two developments in nonfood trade since independence. First, in 1991 anecdotal evidence suggests that most goods on sale were purchased in the former Soviet Union — many of them at low, state-controlled prices — although there were some imports from Poland. From the fall of 1992 onward more goods cane directly from Turkey, China, Hong Kong, or Taiwan. Second, there are now more goods on sale and the range of choice is wider. Our very rough numbers on prices indicate rates of inflation in line with those given above for food products. Unfortunately, we have not been able to construct a meaningful price index for these goods.

Interestingly, while private business now appears to be quite active in nonfood trade, there has been relatively little entry by private business into wholesale food trade. The retail food trade remains as divided as in the past — products can either be bought in state stores or in the peasant market.

More broadly, the private sector has begun to show sustained growth since mid-1992. At present most of this growth is still in trade and simple services, but this is the start of significant job creation outside the state sector. In a survey of 349 people who were fired from state enterprises in the second half of 1992, we found that by December 1992, 42 percent had found work in the nonstate sector and 31 percent had found a new job in the state sector (Johnson and Ustenko, 1993b). These rates of re-employment are very high and it remains to be seen whether they can be sustained.

There has also been rapid growth in the scale and employment of new commercial banks — where *new* indicates that they were not formed out of the former Gosbank system. Based on a survey conducted in February 1993, we estimate that the approximately 130 new commercial banks in Ukraine in total have capital and deposits close to that of the four largest former state banks combined. The difference in size of operations between these two parts of the banking system is accounted for almost entirely by credits provided by the central bank to firms, because most of these pass through the former state banks.

Furthermore, we also found evidence that at least some of these new commercial banks have moved beyond being narrowly based on just one sector. In their efforts to raise more capital and to diversify their risks, successful banks are seeking more shareholders and a broader set of customers (Johnson and Ustenko, 1993a).

The evidence so far on the agricultural sector suggests that directors of state and collective farms have been quite effective in slowing down any sort of meaningful transformation. The large state farms continue to co-exist alongside the more efficient private plots of rural and urban residents. At the same time, there are now some indications of an increase in individual farming oriented toward market production rather than self-sufficiency (Johnson and Minton Beddoes, 1995).

The extent of serious adjustment within state enterprises remains unclear. In the absence of effective government-directed privatization there continues to be some spontaneous privatization, more in the form of the leaking of assets from the state sector than through complete trans-formation of legal property forms. The available evidence suggests that these steps by themselves have not significantly improved the perfor-mance of state enterprises and the outlook for jobs in the state sector remains poor (Johnson and Ustenko, 1993b; 1994).

Very high inflation usually reduces the real tax revenues of government, unless taxes have been effectively indexed. Not only is such indexation absent in Ukraine, but state enterprises are particularly suited to igniting inflation. These enterprises have no real owners (leaving aside the property rights claimed and exercised by managers and workers themselves), cannot easily go bankrupt, and have not been subject to effective supervision by the tax authorities. Loans have been available at negative real interest rates, there are few effective price controls, and real wages have fallen a great deal. As early as 1991, our interviews with managers suggested that they were beginning to find ways to reduce their real tax liabilities. Real tax revenue from enterprises fell from 11–13 percent of GDP in 1989–91 to around 6 percent in 1992.

In short, while there are some signs of structural change in the Ukrainian economy, progress so far has been limited. The three governments during the rule of President Leonid Kravchuk did not demonstrate a firm commitment to the development of the private sector, let alone a coherent strategy of promoting structural change. Furthermore, the acceleration of inflation distorted and delayed the few positive changes. The lack of privatization makes it harder to stabilize the economy because enterprise managers lobby hard for various forms of financial assistance.

WAGES AND LIVING STANDARDS

We assess the impact of economic developments in Ukraine on real wages by comparing nominal wages to the amount needed to buy the basic basket of food for which we report prices in Table 3.3. In October 1991, of the goods in the "Ukrainian Army Ration" described earlier in this chapter, only bread and sugar were available in state stores, while the rest of the goods had to be purchased on the market. The whole basket of goods would have cost 198.2 rubles. This represented 50 percent of the average wage, assuming an average wage of 400 rubles, a figure that we derive from our interviews at the time.

In contrast, in Kiev at the beginning of October 1992, the same basket of goods cost 3,067 rubles — 123 percent of the average wage, if one employs the seemingly rather high average wage of 2,500 karbovantsi that emerged from our interviews at the time. Even though there is considerable margin of error in these numbers, this is strong evidence that the average real wage fell during 1992.

People working in the state sector in November 1992 had average wages two to three times what was required to buy this basket, while the ratio in the relatively high-wage mining sector was ten times and in the relatively low-wage retail sector the ratio was unity. By March 1993 these multiples for state employees had fallen to unity for average wages, 2.0 for miners, and 0.5 for the retail sector. In late June 1993, following their strike, miners had increased their multiple to 5, while average wages had fallen to 0.6, and retail wages had dropped to 0.3.

Our assessment that average real wages fell is also strengthened if we go beyond food items and consider what people had to pay for their apartments. The basic cost of an apartment in Ukraine depends on the number of square meters in the apartment and on whether there is a telephone. One payment — referred to in Russian as "payment for the apartment" (*zaplata za kvatery*) — covers most costs, including rent, water, and gas. (Electricity is metered separately and telephone costs depend on use.) These costs rose by at least ten times during 1992 and had increased even more rapidly through the first eight months of 1993. In addition, the price of a monthly pass allowing the use of all types of municipal transport — trolleybus, tram, bus, and metro — rose massively. We estimate that apartment payments and transportation costs were no more than 6 percent of average wages in 1991 and constitute at least 10 percent in mid-1993.

In addition, for at least one section of the population living standards remained unambiguously at disastrous levels. In the fall of 1991 pensioners received 130 rubles, 66 percent of the cost of our basket of goods. At this time the living standard of pensioners had already dropped steeply and was widely regarded as too low. By the beginning of October 1992, the average pension was around 1,100 karbovantsi, 36 percent of the basket's cost. The purchasing power of pensions dropped still further in 1993.

An important caveat must be attached to this assessment because a great deal depends on the collective earnings of the family unit that shares an apartment. For example, it matters a great deal whether a pensioner lives with someone who earns at least an average salary. Unfortunately, a fuller assessment of living standards would require data on the composition of households and the intra-household sharing of income, which we do not currently have.

Overall, real living standards fell for most social groups after independence. The exception is probably the relatively few people who have managed to enter the high-paying parts of the private sector. For the vast majority of the population the march toward hyperinflation has meant steady impoverishment.

CONCLUSION

Independent Ukraine has faced significant shocks to its economy, particularly in the form of disrupted trade with Russia and higher energy prices. These shocks are smaller in magnitude for Ukraine than for most former Soviet republics, yet Ukraine's macroeconomic performance has been just as bad on most measures, its inflation has been worse, and its progress in creating a genuine private sector has been slower. The collapse of the Ukrainian karbovanets against both the dollar and the ruble after full monetary independence at the end of 1992 underlines that the major problem in Ukraine was economic policy.

The economic strategy of Ukraine after independence was a form of "gradualism," implemented by ex-communists who realized that something called economic reform was called for but who were not willing to take the decisive measures required. This same strategy was followed by both the Fokin and Kuchma governments, although the latter claimed to be in favor of radical reform. The Kuchma government did not act decisively on the budget, credit, privatization, or liberalization.

Even in comparison with the incomplete reforms that began in Russia during 1992, Ukraine fared badly. Ukraine undoubtedly fell behind Russia in terms of initiating privatization and liberalizing internal trade. Our research suggests that these measures already mean better availability of goods, particularly food, in at least some parts of Russia compared with Ukraine (Johnson and Ustenko, 1993c).

It is true that Russia has also failed to bring inflation completely under control, but during the summer and fall of 1993 there was an acceleration of inflation in Ukraine but not in Russia. During 1992 and 1993 Russia moved further in terms of reforming public finance and negotiating meaningful economic assistance from the West. The West appears willing to help Ukraine, but through 1993 Ukraine had yet to come up with an economic policy to which Western assistance would make a significant difference.

There were some positive signs in terms of new economic developments, particularly outside the state sector. However, the continuation of inflation cannot be considered helpful to these new forms of business.

High inflation tends to keep horizons short, to make it harder to build long-term relationships, and to cause a great deal of volatility in relative prices. Full-fledged hyperinflation will cause significant damage to the emergent private sector.

In an economy without long experience of inflation and without smoothly functioning indexation mechanisms, there is a tendency for very high inflation to become hyperinflation, sustained price increases over 50 percent per month. In the fall of 1993, Ukraine slipped into hyperinflation.

The required stabilization measures comprise much more than increasing some administered prices. As our evidence on the food market shows, the primary result of administered price increases is at best temporary improvements in the availability of goods. The advice of Western organizations is almost unanimous: only a set of measures that closes the budget deficit and imposes strict limits on credit can have any chance of stemming inflation at this point. Supportive measures in the form of trade liberalization and full currency convertibility would also be very helpful.

Is there any hope? In our assessment, recent experience in Eastern Europe shows three necessary conditions for economic reform: politicians who can maintain popular support to implement economic policies that inflict costs on part of the population, bureaucrats who cannot obstruct the changes, and a few operational policy makers who have sufficient economic knowledge.

The comparison with Poland in 1989 is instructive, because Poland was also facing runaway inflation due to fiscal deficits and loose credit. The situation began to improve only after the appointment of Leszek Balcerowicz as minister of finance. The key conditions for stabilization and the start of the real transformation of the economy were the abilities of Balcerowicz and his team, and the political courage of the leaders of Solidarity (Johnson and Kowalska, 1994).

Ukraine has few people with sufficient knowledge and experience to make economic policy, but it has enough. Its bureaucrats are weak and do not present the kind of obstacles encountered in Russia. Through the end of 1993, independent Ukraine had yet to find political leaders who understand why and how inflation must be controlled.

NOTES

Financial support was provided by a grant to Simon Johnson from the National Council for Soviet and East European Research and by Xerox Faculty Research Funds at the Fuqua School of Business.

1. The coal miners' strike in the summer of 1993 in the Donbass region is the leading example of Ukrainians' discontent. The scathing review of the Ukrainian economy by PlanEcon (1993) is but one example of a negative Western assessment of economic performance.

2. A detailed study of the Ukrainian economy near the end of the communist period is provided by Koropeckyj (1992). Ukraine at the time of independence is assessed by the U.S. Government (1992) and by Hogan (1991).

3. Opinions differ, but it is not uncommon to hear locals claim a real queue (*ochered*) exists only if more than ten people are waiting.

4. Since independence, as usually in the past, the peasant market has offered people a wider range and higher quality of products than are available in state stores. However, prices are almost always higher than in state stores.

5. A full explanation of the Ukrainian inflationary process would require data on the shares of the money supply of cash karbovantsi and of *beznalichnye* rubles, and some estimate of how much of these *beznalichnye* rubles was spent in Russia. During 1992 the Ukrainian central bank could and did, in effect, write checks on the Russian central bank. Also important is the time required to transfer funds from Ukraine to Russia and vice versa — in spring 1992 this was about three months, so payment orders in process probably represented a significant delayed inflationary push. Unfortunately, we do not have data on the amount of payment orders outstanding at any given moment.

6. It is strange that although bread was available with only a short queue until the summer, queue lengths actually increased after bread prices were raised in July. One possible explanation is that the general rise in food prices in the summer of 1992 pushed down real incomes such that poor people, particularly pensioners, actually bought and consumed more bread than before. It is also possible that expectations of rising inflation induced people to buy and store bread — although in warm weather the ability to store bread is limited by people's freezer capacity.

7. One significant difference between eggs and milk or bread is that when eggs disappear from state stores they can — and often do — appear in the peasant market.

8. It may also be the case that the cost of producing key goods rises while their prices are held constant and the government directly or indirectly finances the difference. While this mechanism seemed plausible even in the summer of 1993, the supportive evidence was unfortunately only anecdotal.

REFERENCES

[*Economist*.] "You'd Be Nervous Living Next to a Bear." *The Economist*, May 15, 1993, pp. 21–23.
[*Economist*.] "The Post-Cold-War War." *The Economist*, June 19, 1993, pp. 49–50.
Frydman, Roman, Andrzej Rapaczynski, John S. Earle, et al. *The Privatization Process in Russia, Ukraine and the Baltic States*. London: Central European University

Press, 1993.

Hogan, William W. "Economic Reforms in the Sovereign States of the Former Soviet Union." *Brookings Papers on Economic Activity*, no. 2, (1991): 303–319.

[IMF et al.] *A Study of the Soviet Economy*. Vol. 1. Paris: International Monetary Fund, World Bank, Organisation for Economic Co-operation and Development, and European Bank for Reconstruction and Development, February 1991.

Johnson, Simon, and Santiago Eder. "Prospects for Privatization in Ukraine." *RFE/RL Research Report* 1, 37 (September 18, 1992): 46–49.

Johnson, Simon, and Marzena Kowalska. "Poland: The Political Economy of Shock Therapy." In Steven Webb and Stephen Haggard (eds.), *Voting for Reform*, pp. 185–241. Oxford: Oxford University Press, 1994.

Johnson, Simon, and Heidi Kroll. "Managerial Strategies for Spontaneous Privatization." *Soviet Economy* 7, 4 (1991): 281–316.

Johnson, Simon, Heidi Kroll, and Mark Horton. "New Commercial Banks in the Former Soviet Union: How Do They Operate?" In Anders Åslund and Richard Layard (eds.), *Changing the Economic System in Russia*, pp. 183–209. London: Pinter Publishers, 1993.

Johnson, Simon, and Zanny Minton Beddoes. "The Acquisition of Private Property Rights in Ukrainian Agriculture." Paper presented at a conference held at University of California–San Diego in April 1993. Forthcoming as a book chapter, 1995.

Johnson, Simon, and Oleg Ustenko. "Ukraine on the Brink of Hyperinflation." *RFE/RL Research Report* 1, 50 (December 18, 1992): 51–59.

Johnson, Simon, and Oleg Ustenko. "The Role of New Banks in a Partially Reformed Economy: Ukrainian Experience." Unpublished paper, April 1993a.

Johnson, Simon, and Oleg Ustenko. "Unemployment After Communism: Five Results from Ukraine." Unpublished paper presented at the NBER summer workshop on labor economics, June 1993b.

Johnson, Simon, and Oleg Ustenko. "Ukraine Slips into Hyperinflation." *RFE/RL Research Report* 2, 26 (June 25, 1993c): 24–32.

Johnson, Simon, and Oleg Ustenko. "Corporate Control of Enterprises Before Privatization: The Effects of Spontaneous Privatization." In Horst Siebel (ed.), *Overcoming the Transformation Crisis: Lessons from Eastern Europe*, pp. 83–106. Kiel, Germany: Kiel Institute of World Economics, 1994.

Koropeckyj, Iwan S. *The Ukrainian Economy: Achievements, Problems, Challenges*. Cambridge, Mass.: Harvard University Press, 1992.

Mearsheimer, John J. "The Case for a Ukrainian Nuclear Deterrent." *Foreign Affairs* 72, 3 (Summer 1993): 50–66.

[*New York Times*.] "Belarus, A Model for Ukraine." Editorial, August 4, 1993, p. A14.

[PlanEcon.] "Ukrainian Economic Monitor." *PlanEcon Report* 9, 19/20/21 (June 10, 1993).

Popiel, Walter. "Ukraine in Numbers: Special: Year-End 1992 Edition." Monthly Economic Bulletin, Ukrainian Cabinet of Ministers, vol. 4, February 1993a.

Popiel, Walter. "Ukraine in Numbers." Monthly Economic Bulletin, Ukrainian Cabinet of Ministers. Reprinted in *Ukrainian Legal and Economic Bulletin*, vol. 1, no. 5, Kiev, May 1993b.

Popiel, Walter. "Ukraine in Numbers." Monthly Economic Bulletin, Ukrainian Cabinet of Ministers. Reprinted in *Ukrainian Legal and Economic Bulletin*, vol. 1, no.

6, Kiev, June 1993c.

[State Program.] "State Privatization Program." Kiev: Government of Ukraine, 1992 (mimeo).

[U.S. Government.] *Ukraine: An Economic Profile*. Washington, D.C.: U.S. Government Printing Office, 1992.

P27

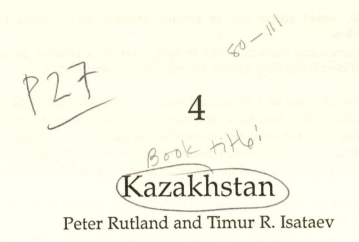

4

Book title:

Kazakhstan

Peter Rutland and Timur R. Isataev

INTRODUCTION

This chapter analyzes Kazakhstan's struggle to create the institutional and policy framework for an independent economy, and evaluates the viability of the ambitious economic development strategy propounded by President Nursultan Nazarbaev.

In the heady days of 1991, the newly born nation-states that emerged from the ruins of the USSR were very optimistic as to their prospects as independent countries. The people of each country assumed that their economy had been exploited by Moscow, and that it would blossom once freed from Russian tutelage. Alas, these assumptions proved erroneous, and independence initially brought falling output and a catastrophic decline in living standards in each of the ex-Soviet republics.

Economic science is ambiguous as to whether political independence is good or bad for economic development (Polese, 1985). In general, economists tend to argue that larger and more integrated markets are more efficient, which would argue against secession. In the Soviet case, however, nations are leaving one large, autarkic economy in order to try to integrate into the broader global economy.

Issues of scale aside, there are three ways in which political independence can be seen as aiding economic development:

- Independence may mean the end of resource transfers to the old center.
- Independence creates the opportunity to pursue economic policies tailored to the needs of a given country. The introduction of a national currency, for

example, would enable one to devalue, making one's exports more competitive.

* Independence may facilitate a shift in trade toward new partners, allowing more efficient integration into the international division of labor.

These benefits would take several years to come into effect (if they arrive at all). In the short term, one may expect considerable transition costs arising from the disruption of established patterns of activity. Over the past three years, Kazakhstan has experienced very costly dislocation while seeing precious few of the potential gains from independence:

* As a former net recipient of subsidies from Moscow, it stood to lose from a decrease in inter-republican transfers.
* The structure of economic institutions that it inherited after 70 years of central planning was totally unsuited to the implementation of market-oriented policies. Not surprisingly, Kazakhstan has been slow to stabilize and liberalize, and made little progress on large-scale privatization.
* Kazakhstan's leaders have pinned most of their hopes on the rapid expansion of trade links with its new Western partners, who are thought to be eager to develop its natural resources. While there has been some encouraging progress on this front, the success of these projects still hinges on Kazakhstan's relationship with Russia.

In practice, of course, Kazakhstan did not choose to become independent on the basis of a careful calculation of the economic costs and benefits of such a step. Independence was thrust upon it by the collapse of the Soviet empire, and political uncertainty arising from its continued dependence on Russia has dogged its efforts to pursue an independent economic policy.

THE PARADOX OF WEALTH AND DEPENDENCE

Kazakhstan was the last Soviet republic to declare independence, doing so on December 15, 1991. President Nursultan Nazarbaev still works at a desk beneath a portrait of Lenin, and most of Kazakhstan's government officials feel betrayed, rather than liberated, by the collapse of the USSR. Kazakhstan now faces the challenge of survival, both political and economic, as an independent country in the post-Soviet world. Powerful forces of ethnicity and economics are at work in Kazakhstan, and it is too early to predict whether they will undermine the country's fragile independence.

Kazakhstan is a huge country with vast natural wealth. Its 17 million inhabitants occupy a territory five times the size of France, with only 6.2 inhabitants per square kilometer. Its mineral resources include 99 of the 110 elements of the periodic chart, of which more than 60 are commercially mined (Zhigalov, 1993). It has a major share of the mineral resources of the former USSR, such as wolfram and chrome (95 percent), zinc (70 percent), lead (40 percent), and copper (30 percent). It has proven reserves of 1,600–2,100 million tons of oil, 1,600–1,800 billion cubic meters of gas, 50 billion tons of coal, and several huge hydroelectric power stations. In addition to these natural resources, it has an extensive agricultural sector (based on grain and livestock), accounting for 22 percent of GDP.

Over the past 70 years exploitation of this natural wealth took place within the framework of an integrated USSR-wide economy, with Kazakhstan serving as a source of food and natural resources. Some 40 percent of its agricultural output was exported to Russia, as were virtually 100 percent of its oil and 40 percent of its coal. Less than 20 percent of GDP involved the production of goods for final use.

Despite its huge size, Kazakhstan is geographically isolated and lacks access to world markets. It is far from any ocean, and access to the sea is barred by a ring of mountains to the east and south. Kazakhstan is nearly totally dependent on the rail and pipeline infrastructure that links it to Russia and the world beyond.

Geography dictated the close integration of the Russian and Kazakh energy sectors. The two major oil refineries in Kazakhstan are located in the east (at Pavlodar and Chimkent), while its oil deposits are in the west. There is no pipeline crossing Kazakhstan from west to east. The Kazakh refineries are supplied by a pipeline that comes down from Omsk, Siberia, while the Kazakh fields pump their oil to Samara and Orsk in the southern Urals. All the gas from the Karachaganak field in western Kazakhstan is processed in Orenburg, Russia. North and South Kazakhstan are served by separate electricity grids, connected to the Russian and Central Asian networks, respectively, with no possibility of transfer between them.

The situation in industry is no better. While Kazakhstan has large ore processing and chemical plants, its engineering industry is largely confined to tractors and agricultural machinery. Virtually everything else must be imported: cars, trucks, combine harvesters, refrigerators, televisions, and 95 percent of the equipment for the oil, gas, and coal industries. All told, imports account for 70 percent of machinery needs, 50 percent of raw materials, and 30 percent of food. In 1992 61 percent of imports came from Russia, 18 percent from Central Asia, and 7 percent from Ukraine; these regions were the destinations of exports, to the extent of 60 percent, 22 percent, and 8 percent, respectively.

Thus in the short to medium term Kazakhstan is hard-wired into the Russian energy system. Despite being self-sufficient in energy on a fuel-equivalent basis, Kazakhstan is dependent on energy trade with Russia — and will remain so for the foreseeable future.

THE ECONOMICS OF INDEPENDENCE

President Nazarbaev aims to use Kazakhstan's natural resources to launch an ambitious development program, in the hope that economic growth will assuage domestic political tensions (Lan'ko and Kuchin, 1992). A series of major projects are planned to secure Kazakhstan's economic independence and integrate Kazakhstan into the global economy. The centerpiece of his strategy is the rapid expansion of the oil and gas industry.

The World Bank predicts a 50 percent rise in oil production by 1996, with net exports rising 300 percent due to a decline in domestic consumption (see Table 4.1). (This assumes that the projects currently planned come on stream; World Bank, 1993, p. 107.)

TABLE 4.1

The Petroleum Sector in Kazakhstan

	1990	1991	1992	1993	1996	2000
Oil production[1]	25.6	26.2	25.7	29.5	36.2	45.9
Oil imports[1]	21.1	18.1	15.5	14.8	11.0	9.8
Domestic consumption[1]	19.6	18.3	15.6	14.9	11.4	12.2
Oil exports[1]	24.3	23.6	23.2	27.2	34.3	42.2
Export earnings[2]	n.a.	n.a.	2.5	3.2	4.6	5.9

Source: World Bank (1993, p. 107).

Notes:
[1]Million metric tons.
[2]U.S.$ billion.

In order to sustain this expansion the oil sector would need equipment imports of $270 million in 1993 and $400–600 million per year thereafter.

Gas production is currently 8 billion cubic meters per year, of which half is exported to Russia, while 15 billion cubic meters are imported. Gas output is projected to rise to 16 billion cubic meters by 1995 and 27 billion cubic meters by the year 2000. About 130 million tons of coal are produced per year, of which 40 percent is exported to Russia.

Nazarbaev's strategy will require an influx of foreign investment and technology on a massive scale. Among the projects being mooted are the following:

- Chevron signed a 40-year contract on April 6, 1993, for a joint venture in the Tengiz oil field, with $1.6 billion investment planned over the next five years (Zhorov, 1993a). The Tengiz deposits are deep, with high salt and sulfur content, which increases extraction costs. Chevron began negotiations six years ago: an earlier deal, concluded under Gorbachev, was renegotiated after a critical review by Yegor Gaydar in early 1991. The final deal gives Kazakhstan 80 percent of the revenues, a high share by international standards. Chevron also promised to pay $50 million over five years to the regional council — although this may be insufficient to satisfy the council's demands (Sutyagin, 1992).

- In 1992 Elf-Acquitaine signed a $380 million exploration deal for the Temirmunay field. The Elf operation was the first energy joint venture to begin operation. The project has not enjoyed easy sailing. The French managers complain of the lack of safety and environmental regulations; the absence of laws on mineral rights; and difficulties in costing local operations, because of price disputes with Kazakh suppliers (Druzenko, 1993; Syzdykov, 1993). Elf's share of the revenues will be 50 percent up to 10 million tons, falling progressively to 10 percent thereafter.

- A consortium of Agip and British Gas has been commissioned to work in the Karachaganak gas field, where there are also plans to build a new gas refinery. They plan a $6 billion investment over ten years (K. Dzhakulov, head of administration for West Kazakhstan, as interviewed in Kuznetsov, 1993).

- A Mitsui-Mitsubishi consortium will build an oil refinery in Mangystau in the west.

- Further exploration tenders are planned for Kazakhstan's 100,000 square kilometer shelf under the Caspian Sea. Seven Western firms signed such agreements on June 9, 1993.

The crucial problem will be getting this oil and gas out to hard currency markets. Several new oil pipelines are being discussed: a west-east line to supply Kazakhstan's own refineries, and one across the north Caucasus (i.e., through Russia, from Mangystau to Novorossiysk) to facilitate exports to the west. Nazarbaev has also won agreement in principle from Iran and Turkey to build a new pipeline through Turkmenistan and Iran to the Mediterranean Sea, although an alternative plan to route it across the Caspian Sea and through Turkey is also under consideration.

ECONOMIC TRENDS IN KAZAKHSTAN

Economic Performance

During the first two years of independence economic developments in Kazakhstan were driven by the abrupt shifts in economic policy emanating from Moscow. The year 1991 saw the gradual disintegration of the central planning system, with Kazakh GDP falling by 13 percent. Following the partial freeing of prices by Moscow in April 1991, prices had risen by 90 percent in Kazakhstan by December 1991. In January 1992 Yeltsin abolished price controls on 80 percent of goods — without prior consultation with the other ex-Soviet states, who had little choice but to follow suit. Prices in Kazakhstan were liberalized (except for energy, rent, bread, transport, and communications). Producers responded to their newfound freedom by cutting output and raising prices, which lurched upward by 300–500 percent within a few weeks. Kazakhstan, like Russia, plunged into a spiral of falling output and high inflation, fueled by soft credits from the central bank of Russia.

The banking system was in no fit state to provide the liquidity (e.g., working capital) that the new market economy required. Firms faced an acute shortage of cash and long delays in clearing payments with customers and suppliers. The biggest problems came in transactions with firms in other republics. Nazarbaev attributed 65 percent of the fall in production to the breakdown of links with other Soviet republics, and another 20 percent to the collapse of trade links within the former CMEA (*Kazakhstanskaya pravda*, August 17, 1992, p. 1).[1]

The stagflation of 1992 was roughly similar in each of the 15 ex-Soviet republics. In Kazakhstan in 1992 national income fell by 14.2 percent, industrial output 14.8 percent, investment 45 percent, and consumer good output 21.5 percent (*Delovoy mir*, March 10, 1993, p. 10; (*Kazakhstanskaya pravda*, April 8, 1993, p. 1). Oil and coal output were each down by 3 percent, while gas production rose by 3 percent. Retail prices rose by 1,006 percent and wholesale prices by 2,469 percent, while money incomes rose only 669 percent and retail turnover fell 48 percent in constant prices. One bright spot was the record harvest — 32 million tons of grain, 146 percent up on 1991, when drought struck and obliged Kazakhstan to import 1.5 million tons for the first time in its history. Nevertheless, because of the breakdown in the trading system, meat production in 1992 fell 31 percent, and milk by 21 percent.

The slump continued into 1993. In the first quarter of 1993 GDP fell by 14.2 percent and national income by 16.3 percent, contributing to a drop of 33 percent in the latter since 1990. Agricultural output fell by 13 percent, with meat production falling by 20 percent. State investment fell by 26 percent, and realized investment by 33 percent. For the first time prices rose faster in Kazakhstan than in Russia. By 1993 the monthly rate of inflation had risen to above 30 percent, compared to monthly rises of around 20 percent in Russia (Berkovskaya, 1993a). The cash shortage, caused by accelerating inflation and the efforts of the Gaydar government to control the money supply, led to a wave of strikes in Kazakhstan by miners and others to protest the nonpayment of wages. Unlike most other member states of the Commonwealth of Independent States (CIS), Kazakhstan did not introduce any supplementary ration coupons to ease the ruble shortage.

The heavy industrial regions of northern Kazakhstan — populated almost entirely by Russians — were hardest hit by the slump. Defense plants were devastated by a 66 percent fall in orders in 1992 (Kim, 1993). The situation was particularly critical in Pavlodar province, which provides 50 percent of the country's energy and 60 percent of its coal (Gorbunov, 1993). It is also the location of the giant Ekibastuz-2 hydroelectric station, which was finally completed in December 1993. Its 500 million kilowatt-hour capacity will help reduce Kazakhstan's dependence on electricity imports; it provided 14 billion kilowatt-hours in 1992, 20 percent of total consumption (*Kazakhstanskaya pravda*, March 20, 1993, p. 2).

Even where firms perceived a ready market, they lacked the capital to exploit it. Despite good export possibilities, one-third of ore-processing works were idle because they were unable to buy raw materials (Akava, 1993b; Zhdanov, 1993b). Kazakhstan imports 200,000 tons of steel pipe a year, which could easily be produced at the Karaganda steel works — if funds for re-equipment were available (Kurbrakov, 1993). The Pavlodar oil refinery cannot find the money to finish an additional production line, which is 80 percent complete and which will double capacity to 13 million tons a year (*Kazakhstanskaya pravda*, May 14, 1993, p. 2).

Kazakhstan has followed Russia in maintaining energy price controls, to the detriment of its energy producers. The Karaganda coal mines have found themselves in a price scissors — the price of coal was allowed to rise by only 430 percent in 1992, while machinery and steel rose 3,600 percent, and spare parts 6,700 percent (Mogal'nitskiy, 1992). Kazakh steel producers have complained about the artificially low cost of fuel throughout the CIS, because their competitive advantage (in comparison to, e.g., Ukrainian steel mills) derives from Kazakhstan's relatively abundant energy sources (Mukhin, 1993). The main beneficiary of cheap energy has been the farm sector — another powerful lobby (both Kazakh and Russian) keeping the pressure on Nazarbaev.

Nevertheless, in the course of 1992 the price of oil rose by 10,700 percent, that of coal by 8,500 percent, and that of electricity by 4,800 percent (Berkovskaya, 1993b). Under an intergovernmental agreement signed with Russia on February 4, 1993, Russia agreed to supply Kazakhstan with oil at R15,000 ($18) per ton, roughly equal to the price of domestic oil (without an export quota) on Russian commodity exchanges (*Kazakhstanskaya pravda*, February 17, 1993, p. 1). In contrast, the other republics were being asked to pay the world market price of $75–95 per ton.

Although energy is moving toward market pricing, it is still distributed to most users through nonprice channels. The monopoly refining company Kaznefteprodukt has the right to vary the price of oil by 40 percent in either direction, depending upon the profitability of the customer enterprise. As of February 1993, Russian gas was priced at R18,500 per 1,000 cubic meters — but in Kazakhstan consumers were only being charged R4,700, and farmers R2,760.

Monetary and Fiscal Policy

The budget deficit has been estimated at 8 percent of GDP in 1991 and 6 percent in 1992. Soft credits issued to firms (at a 20 percent interest rate) were R400 billion in 1992, rising to R1.5 trillion by April 1993 (Svoik and Ospanov, 1993). There was R123 billion worth of monetary emission in the first quarter of 1993, 1,900 percent up on the same period in 1992. The budget deficit for 1993 was projected to be 4 percent of GDP (R183 billion out of a GDP of R4,600 billion) — although some additional spending was shifted into off-budget funds (see Table 4.2).

TABLE 4.2
The Government Budget Plan in Kazakhstan for 1993 (billion rubles)

Income		Expenditure	
VAT	130	Economic activity	385
Duties	32	of which:	
Profit Tax	124	Bread subsidy	34
Government bonds	5	Farm subsidies	84
Rent	40	Investment	190
Resource tax	24	Sociocultural	109
Investment fund	191	Defense	69
Export/import duties	137	Law and order	62
Oil export tax	11	Aral Sea	10
Privatization	2	Semipalatinsk	10
Other	26	Other	170
Total	722	Total	1,005

Source: *Kazakhstanskaya pravda*, March 2, 1993, p. 2.

The deficit stems from a continued commitment to subsidizing industry and agriculture on the one hand, and a fall in revenues on the other. In 1992 only 60 percent of VAT was collected, and because of exemptions the average profits tax amounted to 11 percent instead of the statutory 25 percent (Tereshchenko, 1992b). Budgetary transfers from Moscow amounted to about 9 percent of GDP prior to 1991, and about 5 percent in 1991 (World Bank, 1993, p. ix). These have now ceased, although the issuance of "technical credits" by the Russian central bank in 1992–93 was a de facto subsidy.

Runaway inflation and the disruption of the banking and budgetary system have posed the most severe problems for Kazakhstan. Almaty has repeatedly found itself hostage to erratic monetary policies emanating from outside the republic — from the abrupt introduction of the som in the neighboring Kyrgyz Republic in May 1993 (which caused perhaps R15 billion worth of notes to flow into Kazakhstan), through the confiscation of pre-1993 rubles announced by the Russian central bank on July 24, 1993.

The introduction of a new national currency in Kazakhstan came to be seen as inevitable in the long term, but was delayed because of fears that it would further disrupt Russian-Kazakh trade and the absence of the hard currency reserves that would make such a currency credible. Moreover, the introduction of a new currency would be a powerful symbolic step that could trigger a crisis of loyalty among the Russians in northern Kazakhstan.

The Impact on Living Standards

The average real wage fell in the wake of the price liberalization. If the level of this variable in December 1991 were set equal to 100, it would equal 141 in January 1991, 86 in January 1992, and 77 in August 1992 (World Bank, 1993, p. 13). The deterioration in living standards continued during 1993. Nominal wages rose by 55 percent in the first quarter, but prices rose 50 percent faster. While in April the minimum budget (covering food and other necessities) for a family of four was R32,000–41,000 per month, the average family income was only R20,000 (Berkovskaya, 1993a). High inflation and radical shifts in consumption patterns make the calculation of minimum living standards extremely difficult — and politically controversial. Food was cheaper in Kazakhstan than in Russia, but more expensive than elsewhere in Central Asia (Petrovskiy, 1993c). The price range within Kazakhstan was considerable, with food costing 50 percent more in the industrial cities than in the rural south.

Despite the slump in output, factories avoided shedding labor, preferring temporary closures and wage cuts to layoffs. As in Russia, social pressure dictated that the "preservation of the work collective" was the dominant objective of factory directors. Out of a work force of 7.3 million, unemployment stood at a mere 70,000 in March 1993 — although the labor minister was predicting a rise to 500,000 by the end of 1993 (World Bank, 1993, p. 54; *Kazakhstanskaya pravda*, March 4, 1993, p. 1).

In Russia, the old system of central wage controls was abolished in December 1991. Kazakhstan followed suit, leading to a brief period when wages were free to chase prices upward. In the first half of 1992 prices rose by 680 percent and wages by 650 percent. New strict wage regulations were introduced in June 1992, which led to a storm of labor protests (Berkovskaya, 1992). The new system fixed the maximum wage at four times the minimum wage, and tied payroll increases to increases in the physical volume of production — a 1.0 percent rise in the latter would allow a 0.5 percent rise in the former. (The military industry was exempted.) The new system was, however, subject to massive evasion.

Wage differentials have widened considerably after the demise of central planning. As of April 1993 coal miners were averaging R53,000 in monthly pay, compared to R20,000–25,000 in industry and

R5,000–10,000 in such "budgetary organizations" as health and education, and a minimum wage of R2,500.

The official labor unions were preserved more or less intact, and the government tried to use them to keep labor unrest under control. The small independent labor unions also backed Nazarbaev's economic reforms. In November 1992 they signed an agreement with the government expressing their commitment to the rule of law and a market economy (Svan, 1992; L. Solomin, trade union leader, as interviewed in Cherkizov, 1993).

The Policy Process

Kazakhstan has not seen a technocratic reform team of the sort assembled in Moscow by Yegor Gaydar. Innovations in government policy were driven by exogenous shocks (the breakup of the USSR and price liberalization), rather than by any revolution within the economic policy apparatus. Policy making stayed in the hands of officials drawn from the pre-1991 elites. For example, deputy premier Erik Asanbaev, in charge of economic reforms, was a section chief in Gosplan in charge of implementing the Kosygin reforms back in 1965 (Asanbaev, 1993). In addition, the managers of state industry form a well-organized lobby with direct access to government. They maintain close ties with sister groups in the other ex-Soviet republics, putting strong pressure on Nazarbaev to work within the CIS (Zhdanov, 1993a).

Government regulation has continued to be extensive, albeit with diminishing effectiveness. Data on the scope of state orders for 1993 are not available, but the minister for natural resources argued that they had an important role to play (Turagov, 1992). Commodity exchanges accounted for less than 1 percent of turnover, and were anyway manipulated by state and parastatal agencies, and hounded by regional authorities (Akava, 1993a).

With the decline of state orders, the government turned to other instruments to influence economic behavior. Given that 33 percent of GDP consisted of trade with Russia, the role previously played by state orders was to a large extent replaced by state allocation of export and import licenses. In a cash- and capital-short economy, the allocation of cash and soft credits by the National Bank of Kazakhstan assumed central importance. Although a number of commercial banks have sprung up (reaching 115 by April 1992), the five banks formed on the basis of the old state sectoral banks still controlled 80 percent of loans and 50 percent of deposits.

Moreover, liberalization did not mean the complete withdrawal of state organs from pricing policy. A monopolist — defined as a firm with a more than 35 percent market share — faced a ceiling of 30 percent on its markup. Given the rate of inflation and the sluggish pace of post-Soviet bookkeeping, this brought many "monopolists" to the brink of bankruptcy (Dobrota, 1993).

In addition, the local authorities added new regulations of their own. For example, in February 1993 the Almaty council imposed a 20 percent payroll tax on all local firms to pay for public transportation. This came on top of the federal 37 percent social security tax, 3 percent investment tax, 2 percent employment tax, and 1 percent pension tax that firms already faced (*Kazakhstanskaya pravda*, April 15, 1993, p. 1).

The persistence of efforts at state control had many negative consequences. State interventions were ineffective and haphazard and deepened rather than alleviated the economic crisis. However, some would see a silver lining to this cloud. To the extent that Nazarbaev has managed to preserve more control over the economy than has Yeltsin in Russia, foreign investors may be more confident that a deal signed by the government of Kazakhstan would actually be brought to fruition.

Privatization and Stabilization

Structural reform of the Kazakh economy has proceeded very slowly. While Nazarbaev has committed himself to a strategy of "rapid economic development," he is not a radical market reformer. The opening to foreign capital was to take place within the framework of a "socially oriented mixed economy," with a stress on the virtues of "centrism" and "pragmatism" (Nazarbaev, 1993b).

The initial Law on Destatization and Privatization, adopted on June 22, 1991, gave priority to worker buyouts, as did the Russian law adopted at the time. Workers were offered free transfer of social facilities and a 30 percent discount on shares, with only a 20 percent down payment (World Bank, 1993, p. 72). A distinction was drawn between federal and regional property, with decision making over the latter devolved to regional councils.

Strategic sectors of the economy were to remain in state hands, with land and natural resources defined by Article 46 of the new 1993 constitution as "the exclusive property of the state." Under a decree of September 13, 1991, tenants were issued vouchers with which they could buy their apartments. By the end of 1992, 795,000 apartments had been privatized (29 percent of the total).

In April 1992 the privatization rules were revised to reduce the privileges given to work collectives. Shares were to be distributed between supplier firms (10 percent), workers (25 percent), managers (5 percent), and foreign investors (10 percent). The State Committee on Privatization (GKI) would hold onto 31 percent of the shares and devise a plan to distribute the remaining 19 percent. Survey data are scarce, although one November 1992 survey showed 85 percent of the public expressing approval for the idea of privatization, and 54 percent favoring the voucher method (which was being introduced in Russia at that time) (*Kazakhstanskaya pravda*, November 27, 1992, p. 2).

By the end of 1992, 4,500 medium and large state-owned enterprises had transformed themselves into commercially independent joint stock corporations (JSCs) (Kolchin, 1993). Of these, 698 firms had issued shares, with R41 billion in capital assets and 767,000 workers (12 percent of the work force) (Nazarbaev, 1993a). In the vast majority of cases the shares in these firms were owned by the work force and/or the GKI. By the end of 1992, 5,000 small business had been privatized — 40 percent of shops and 50 percent of service outlets — but these represented only 4.5 percent and 21 percent of turnover, respectively. Some 25 percent were sold to individuals, 57 percent to their workers, and 9 percent to other enterprises. Most of these sales were by decision of the local GKI, rather than through open auction.

The change in ownership of state enterprises does not seem to have brought about significant changes in their economic behavior. There is also little sign of a boom in private entrepreneurial activity. By April 1993 small private firms — cooperatives, leaseholds, or private firms with less than 200 workers — accounted for only 0.6 percent of industrial output, and joint ventures with foreigners another 1.1 percent (Berkovskaya, 1993a). Private entrepreneurs complained that they were shut out of the privatization process, and successful privatized ex-state firms, such as the Kustanay Dorstroy combine (one of the few privatized construction firms, albeit worker-owned), found themselves hounded by financial inspectors (Petrovskiy, 1992; Erezhepov, 1993a). A December 1992 survey of 149 private businesses in Almaty found that the chief problems that they faced were all government-related: taxation, lack of legal guarantees, red tape, the nonconvertible ruble, the breakup of the CIS, and lack of clarity in government policy (*Kazakhstanskaya pravda*, February 13, 1993).

The first phase of the privatization program was widely deemed a failure because it was seen as working to the benefit of the incumbent political and economic elites. Newspapers ran many stories of corruption and scandal in cities across the republic (Erezhepov, 1993b, 1993c; Kaleeva, 1993; Markova, 1992). For example, a military base in Zhezkazgan was sold for R522,000 to a Major Ostapchuk, who promptly resold it to a local factory for R7 million and disappeared (Nikolaev, 1993a). In Chimkent, a department store was sold to a daughter of the deputy mayor for 10 percent of the price of a neighboring store (Kaleeva, 1993). Symptomatically, the new Mercedes dealer in Almaty sold 34 cars in his first month but said that "things are worse here than in Africa" in terms of crime and bureaucracy (Erlanger, 1993).

There has been widespread criticism of the legal confusion over the division of responsibility between federal and local authorities. For example, there was a fierce dispute between the GKI and the Zhezkazgan council over the privatization of Irtyshkanalstroi, which led to asset stripping and the trust's bankruptcy (Yurchenko, 1992). Apart from disputes over jurisdiction, there has often been disagreement over whether to privatize a firm as a single unit or break it up into separate entities — for example, over the Novyy Uzen' oil construction trust (Kovalenko, 1993a). Some of these disputes went before the Arbitration Court, which on several occasions revised its judgments in the face of political pressure. This occurred, for example, in the struggle for ownership of the Almaty tourist organization, which has been waged since March 1992 between the firm's managers and the city's trade unions, in alliance with the city council (Dik, 1993a).

A Change in Approach

By fall 1992, amid mounting criticism and deepening economic crisis, the privatization program was suspended. In November 1992 Prime Minister Sergey Tereshchenko was arguing that strengthening executive power was the only way to secure economic reform (Tereshchenko, 1992a). Nazarbaev observed in March 1993 that "we made a mess of the first stage of privatization, but without doing serious harm," and he promised that in the second stage the process would be recentralized and subject to tight control (*Kazakhstanskaya pravda*, March 4, 1993, p. 1). He assured industrialists that it would be 25–30 years before the share of the state sector of the economy fell below 50 percent (*Kazakhstanskaya pravda*, February 20, 1993, p. 1.)

A revised privatization program for 5,000 firms for 1993–95 was announced in April 1993 (Natsional'naya, 1993; Kozlov, 1993). Under the revised program, decision-making authority is concentrated with the federal authorities, and there will no longer be any separation of federal from municipal property. Worker privileges are limited to the free alloca- tion of 10 percent of the shares, and the Law on Property was amended to abolish the categories of "leasehold" and "collective" ownership (which accounted for more than 50 percent of the early privatizations). The government reserves the right to hold a "golden share" in certain companies, giving it the right, for example, to impose state order.

People are allowed to use their housing coupons in auctions for small firms (up to 50 percent of the price), or sell them for cash. Additional investment coupons are being issued to be used in the privatization of large firms, with rural dwellers getting 20 percent more coupons on equity grounds. In contrast to the Russian scheme, the investment coupons must be deposited in investment funds: they do not have a face value, and cannot be resold for cash or directly used to buy shares. In the case of food processing companies, agricultural producers will be given priority in the purchase of shares, and 10 percent of shops will be given to farms free of charge. On August 7, 1993, the auctions for small privatization were restarted, and the first funds registered (Kuzmenko, 1993).

A key element in the new approach is the creation of holding companies, which will be the vehicle for the government's industrial policy (Postanovlenie, 1993). The holding companies will control networks of subsidiaries in key industrial sectors, with the state retaining a controlling packet of shares for at least five years. Thus, paradoxically, one of the aims of the second stage of the privatization program is to restore some of the state control over industry that was lost in the last years of the Soviet regime. Having won freedom from state tutelage, some directors are resisting the idea of holding companies. But Nazarbaev's parliamentary critics suggested that creating such holding companies "is the only way to stop a fire sale of natural resources, total corruption, and the hegemony of trade over production" (Svoik and Ospanov, 1993). Thus for the foreseeable future Kazakhstan's econ- omy will probably be dominated by the large, integrated industrial conglomerates forged during the Soviet era.

Alongside the new privatization program, the government announced a package of "anti-crisis measures," whose purpose was to create a "social market economy" through "further economic liberalization, although within more defined and directed borders" (Programma, 1993).

The program promised a "fairly strict" financial policy, ideally holding the deficit to 3 to 5 percent of GDP. Wage limits and price controls for energy, bread, and rent were to be maintained. It commented that "it is necessary to move immediately from . . . a policy of spontaneous privatization to a process strictly controlled by the state, as owner," and pledged "strict control" to enforce a unified policy across the regions. Section 9 of the program, dealing with measures to combat organized crime, was longer than the section on privatization.

Restructuring the Agricultural Sector

In February 1992 Nazarbaev issued a decree on agricultural privatization, which was subsequently amended in April 1993 (*Kazakhstanskaya pravda*, April 11, 1993, p. 3). All state and collective farms were to transform their ownership structure, while granting individual peasants the right to leave the farm and set themselves up as private farmers. There was no question of allowing private ownership of land — in part because of the ethnic conflicts that this could trigger (as occurred in the Osh valley in the Kyrgyz Republic in 1990).

By January 1993, 497 *sovkhozy* (state farms) had reorganized themselves (about 25 percent of the farm sector, by asset value). Some 80 percent turned themselves into "collectives" and 15 percent into leaseholders; various cooperatives, small enterprises, and peasant farms were also created within these structures. Only six *sovkhozy* broke themselves up entirely into private farms. Work collectives got 97 percent of the means of production and 69 percent of trade and catering outlets. There was considerable regional variation in the rate of transformation — ranging from 80 percent (Taldy-Kurgan) to 10 percent (Aktyubinsk, Kustanay, Mangystau) (Reutov, 1993; Naumov, 1993a, 1993b). There are also 430 *kolkhozy* (collective farms), producing 15 percent of output, who were assured by then Prime Minister Tereshchenko in March 1993 that they would not be broken up into smaller units. All of this effectively means that there has been only a cosmetic change in the management structure of the farms.

The government has tried to maintain fairly tight control over the agricultural sector. On the output side, state orders accounted for 70 percent of the 1992 grain harvest, while the commodity exchanges received government subsidies to sell grain at a loss (*Kazakhstanskaya pravda*, October 17, 1992, p. 1). However, the government could do little to close the price scissors which opened in 1992, as the price of fuel, fertilizer, and machinery ran ahead of the price of food. While the grain price on the exchanges rose from R3,000–5,000 to R30,000, the price of a truck imported from Russia rose from R70,000 to R1,000,000 (Makulbekov, 1992). Under strong pressure from the farm lobby, the government resorted to issuing soft credits to keep the farm sector afloat (Naumov, 1993c). This strategy merely fueled the inflationary spiral, while a web of patronage and corruption built up around the credit allocation process.

In 1992, 7,000 new private farms were established, bringing the total to 9,238. They had 4.5 million hectares of land, of which 400,000 were arable (about 2.2 percent of the total available land of the country) (Shevelev, 1993). In 1992 they produced 462,000 tons of grain and 12,000 tons of meat — about 2 percent of total output (Derbisov, 1993). The private farms are finding it hard to survive, in part because they remain dependent on the state and collective farms for many of their inputs. The state has channeled roughly 5 percent of the soft credits in their direction: R300 million in 1992, and perhaps R15 billion in 1993 (*Kazakhstanskaya pravda*, June 12, 1993, p. 2).

Alongside the private farms are the private plots held by each state and collective farm household. In 1992 the plots provided 31 percent of meat, 44 percent of milk, 31 percent of eggs, 54 percent of potatoes, and 35 percent of vegetables. There is, of course, a long-running controversy over the extent to which these plots are dependent upon state farms for their inputs (Naumov, 1992).

FOREIGN TRADE

Kazakhstan was heavily dependent upon foreign trade when it achieved independence. In 1992 exports and imports amounted to 47 percent and 59 percent of GDP, respectively (World Bank, 1993, p. 21). About 66 percent of trade took place with Russia, and only 9 percent of exports and 12 percent of imports went beyond the USSR. While Kazakhstan has excellent potential for growth in foreign trade with such new partners as China and Turkey, in the short run its trade activity remains enmeshed in the disintegrating structures of the CIS.

Trade Within the Commonwealth of Independent States

The Soviet economy was highly integrated, with 20 percent of GNP traded between the republics (compared to 14 percent in the European Community). At first, old trade patterns continued to operate under force of inertia. In 1992 firms continued to ship goods across state boundaries, assuming that the central bank of Russia (CBR) would cover the credits. The flow of deliveries steadily deteriorated, falling by 34 percent in 1992, as it became more difficult to clear payments through the banks, and because of price disputes due to accelerating inflation. However, trade is a two-way street. Kazakhstan's close economic ties to Russia meant that many Russian firms were in turn dependent on trade with Kazakhstan. Much of the industry in Siberia and the Urals relies upon Kazakhstan for its raw materials or to purchase its products. For example, Kazakhstan buys more than one-half of the output of the Krasnoyarsk harvester factory. These Russian firms put pressure on Moscow to release credits to Kazakhstan.

Trade mostly took the form of bilateral deals signed by individual firms or regional councils. Prices roughly reflected internal Russian prices, which meant that most prices were liberalized (and rising), while energy still sold at 20–30 percent of world market levels. In 1992 Russia gave an implicit subsidy to the other ex-Soviet states of some R15 trillion ($15 billion), equal to about 10 percent of its GDP. That same year Russia ran a trade surplus of R139 billion with Kazakhstan (exports of R284 billion and imports of R145 billion) (Bogomolov, 1993; Kon, 1993). Kazakhstan's exports to the CIS as a whole amounted to R582 billion in 1992, against imports of R787 billion (World Bank, 1993, p. 21). Total Kazakh debt to Russia rose from R250 billion in 1992 to R500 billion in 1993 — about 10 percent of GDP (*Kazakhstanskaya pravda*, June 11, 1993, p. 2).

On June 21, 1992, Yeltsin warned the other states that if they wished to stay inside the "ruble zone" they would have to accept CBR control over their credit emissions. From July 1, 1992, the CBR adopted a unified ruble-dollar exchange rate, and began keeping separate accounts for each CIS state (which meant that ruble credits granted by Russia could not be used to buy goods in a third country). In a meeting in Bishkek in October 1992, Armenia, Belarus, Kazakhstan, Uzbekistan, and the Kyrgyz Republic accepted these terms.

In 1992 Russia kept track of trade with the other republics on a clearing basis (through *korchety* — "correspondent accounts"), within the framework of annual trade agreements concluded at the beginning of the year. The government-to-government agreements were drawn up in physical quantities, and from January 1993 were denominated in dollars, in prices which in principle would move toward world market levels.

To administer these agreements in the fall of 1992 special agencies were set up in each country based around the former supply ministries

(Voloshin, 1993). The Kazakh organization, Kazkontrakt, handles about 50–75 percent of all CIS trade. It is exempt from export tariffs, and although initially confined to CIS trade, it was subsequently given the right to conduct non-CIS trade as well — which means even less hard currency will filter down to the company level (Zhorov, 1993b). In April 1993 the heads of Roskontrakt and Kazkontrakt signed a Russian-Kazakh trade agreement worth $2.1 billion for 1993. A visit from then-premier Kuchma in February 1993 failed to produce an agreement for trade with Ukraine.

This administered trade system has come under increasing strain. The Russian government has admitted that "we are not in command of the situation," as far as implementing the agreements is concerned, with Tyumen' province, for example, repudiating the intergovernmental agreements regarding oil deliveries (Berkovskaya, 1993c). Trade is supposed to be balanced with each republic on a quarterly basis, but in practice the non-Russian republics still run deficits, which continue to be covered by "technical credits" from the CBR. (For example, another R150 billion for Kazakhstan was announced in July 1993.)

There is a cumbersome and bureaucratic licensing procedure covering the export of such valuable materials as energy and metals. From February 16, 1993, the licensing of exports to the CIS was switched from the Ministry of Industry to the Ministry of Foreign Economic Relations, although some firms complained that they were not informed of the change for several months. Private trading organizations are finding it difficult to break into this system, although the parastatal Kramds organization, a brokerage company set up in 1988 that had a turnover of R20 billion by 1991, seems to be thriving (Veytsman, 1993). Complicating the picture still further are the efforts of local councils to impose their own trade restrictions. Many private brokers have still not recovered from losing the money in their dollar accounts when the old USSR Vneshekonombank collapsed. Some 600 clients in Kazakhstan lost a total of $200 million (Petrovskiy, 1993b).

Illegal, unlicensed trade is obviously extensive. There is no system of customs controls along the 6,000 km Russian-Kazakh border. Smuggling has been rife — most notably, of metals and oil. The official estimate of illegal exports to Russia in 1992 includes 23,000 tons of zinc, 212,000 tons of iron, 70,000 tons of copper, and 525,000 tons of diesel fuel (Kovalenko, 1993b). On March 20, 1992, Russia signed a unified customs agreement with Kazakhstan, Uzbekistan, the Kyrgyz Republic, Tadzhikistan, and Turkmenistan, which four others joined subsequently (but not Ukraine). Russia began building new customs posts with all the other states, first the Baltic nations, then Ukraine.

The Russian government came under increasing pressure from domestic critics to curtail its subsidies to the ruble zone. (Russians have joked that "we are the largest donor in the world.") By the end of 1992 the IMF also decided that the ruble zone was no longer viable, and in May 1993 persuaded the Kyrgyz Republic to introduce its own currency, the som. In 1993 the CBR began issuing new 1993 notes inside Russia, while pre-1993 rubles were still shipped to other states. On July 24, 1993, the CBR abruptly announced the withdrawal of all pre-1993 rubles from circulation in Russia, with the aim of separating Russian rubles from those circulating in the ruble zone (none of whose members was warned in advance). Pre-1993 rubles flooded into Kazakhstan from Russia, accelerating inflation to 30 percent in September and 45 percent in October. Meanwhile the noncash Kazakh bank account ruble fell in value to KaR2,540 to the dollar in early November (Doronin, 1993/94). As Kazakhstan's debts to Russia mounted, from September 1993 onward Russia began curtailing deliveries of oil (Zhabagin, 1993).

In September 1993 seven CIS states, including Kazakhstan, signed a treaty committing themselves to the creation of a new ruble zone, which it was hoped would pave the way to a new more integrated economic union. However, the political balance in Russia shifted with Yeltsin's crushing of the Russian parliament on October 18. From one side, market reformers such as then-finance minister Boris Fëdorov renewed their opposition to plans for a new economic union, which would probably undermine Russia's efforts to balance its budget. At the same time more conservative politicians (such as deputy prime minister Aleksandr Shokhin) became increasingly vexed at the sight of Kazakhstan and Uzbekistan signing lucrative oil and gold deals with Western corporations — with no cut for Russia.

In November Russia announced the terms for membership in the new ruble zone (Illarionov, 1993; Petrov, 1993). Members would have to deposit gold and hard currency worth 50 percent of the value of any new rubles they would receive from Moscow. The remaining 50 percent of new rubles would be exchanged at a rather confiscatory rate (2.5 or 3 to 1) for the old, pre-1993 rubles still in circulation outside Russia. Members would pledge not to introduce their own currency for at least five years. Kazakhstan and the other states rejected these terms, which they saw as unacceptably harsh. Amid considerable monetary confusion, on November 15 Kazakhstan introduced the tenge, at 1 tenge per 500 rubles. With inflation accelerating to 50 percent a month and only $723 million in hard currency reserves (of which $222 million is gold), it is doubtful whether the tenge will emerge as a stable currency, although Kazakhstan's evolving relationship with the IMF (see below) will certainly play an important role in this connection.

By December a new tough line was beginning to emerge in Russian foreign economic policy. Moscow made it clear that it would block any efforts to build new pipelines through Turkey or Iran, and Russian oil corporations began demanding equity shares in the Caspian Sea exploration projects.

Trade Outside the CIS

Kazakhstan's exports to non-CIS states rose from $774 million in 1991 to $1.546 billion in 1992, while imports fell from $1.910 billion to $1.691 billion (World Bank, 1993, p. 20). Trade with countries outside the ruble zone is clearly more profitable, given the failure to liberalize energy prices within the zone. Between January and June 1992 Kazakhstan earned R21.7 billion from oil exports to the CIS and R35.4 billion from exports to non-CIS countries. The volumes traded were 8.4 and 2.5 million tons, respectively, indicating that the price paid by non-CIS customers was five and a half times higher (World Bank, 1993, p. 116). In the first nine months of 1993 Kazakhstan's hard currency exports and imports came to $800 million and $456 million, respectively, with one-third of the trade handled by joint ventures (*Delovoy mir*, December 13, 1993, p. 13).

One obstacle to dollar trade has been the lingering question of the foreign debt of the former USSR, which amounts to $87 billion (including $11 billion incurred since January 1992) (Nadzharov, 1993). At a series of meetings with creditors, beginning in October 1991, agreements were signed dividing the debt among the CIS states in proportion to their populations and GDPs. Kazakhstan's share was 3.87 percent, which left it liable for payments of $607 million in 1992, or 38 percent of its dollar earnings. Unfortunately, apart from Russia, the new states are running large hard-currency trade deficits and have minimal reserves. Thus, of the $37 billion in payments falling due during 1992 and 1993, only $2 billion was paid in 1992 (by Russia), and $2.5 billion was paid in 1993.

In December 1992 Russia unilaterally declared that it would take over all the Soviet debts, and on February 8, 1993, Yeltsin correspondingly announced that Russia was assuming "all the rights to the real estate and movable property of the former USSR" abroad. Ten of the states, including Kazakhstan, have accepted this arrangement (the "zero variant"), although Ukraine has not.

In 1992 the major exports were metals (40 percent by value), oil (37 percent), and chemicals (16 percent). The quantities exported were as follows (in tons): oil, 4,392,000; coal, 581,000; copper, 106,000; ferrous metals, 719,000; zinc, 74,000; and lead, 56,000 (Petrovskiy, 1993a). Some 65 percent of imports were food and consumer goods, and only 21 percent machinery. As much as 38 percent of exports and 32 percent of imports went through barter deals (the main form of transaction with China) (Nikolaev, 1992).

For several years, until the major oil and gas projects come on stream, Kazakhstan will be dependent on foreign loans to cover necessary imports of machinery and consumer goods. The World Bank predicts that it will need $2.2–2.4 billion in 1993, falling to $1.7–2.0 billion in 1995 (World Bank, 1993, p. 40). Kazakhstan joined the World Bank as its 163rd member on July 23, 1992, and the IMF on July 15, 1992. Most-favored nation status with the United States was agreed to in principle during Nazarbaev's visit to Washington in May 1992, and was formally ratified on February 19, 1993. The World Bank expects direct foreign investment to account for about half of the needed capital inflow — rising from $30 million in 1992 to $380–580 million in 1993, and peaking at perhaps $875 million in 1995. The remaining funds will come under multilateral and bilateral agreements (each roughly $200–300 million per annum) and export credits ($100–200 million). Total indebtedness should level off at about $5.1 billion in 1996. The first World Bank credit, for $140 million, was awarded in October 1992, and another $214 million came in December 1993.

In July 1993 the IMF assigned $85 million under its Systemic Transformation Facility (STF). The loose conditions attached to the STF, which proved to be unrealistic, were the following:

- a budget deficit of below 6 percent of GDP;
- foreign reserves of $300 million by the end of December;
- 20 percent of credit to be allocated through auctions by the end of December;
- an end to off-budget subsidies; and
- monthly inflation of below 5 percent by the end of 1993.

After a donors' meeting in Paris on January 14, 1994, the IMF approved the use of about $255 million — $170 million under a standby arrangement and the aforementioned $85 million STF — to support the government's reform program for 1994. A total of over $1 billion in external financing for 1994 was committed, including funds from Japan, the first time that Japan has provided cofinancing for a standby arrangement. The 1994 reform program included measures to tighten monetary and fiscal policy, to liberalize trade and prices, to speed up the restructuring and privatization of enterprises, and to reform the banking system (IMF, 1994; World Bank, 1994).

Kazakhstan's efforts to expand foreign trade have not so far yielded many concrete results, beyond the oil projects discussed above. The largest acquisition is probably Philip Morris's purchase of 49 percent of the Almaty tobacco factory. In 1993 a $150 million deal was signed with a U.S.-Australian consortium to exploit the Bakirchuk gold field. In June 1993 Nazarbaev criticized what he called "the complete absence of coordination in foreign economic policy," and said that "the new national agency for foreign investment almost died before it was born" (*Kazakhstanskaya pravda*, June 8, 1993, p. 1).

Turkey's initial enthusiasm for expanding political ties in Central Asia has not been followed up on the economic front: its economy is not yet strong enough to take on such a role. However, Korea and Japan are showing interest. Samsung has established a joint venture to produce refrigerators, and later televisions, in Karaganda. Japan has pledged a $300 million credit for oil exploration. China has emerged as the leading non-CIS trade partner, accounting for 30 percent of Kazakhstan's exports in 1992 and 45 percent of its imports.

The foreign trade regime has been subject to repeated changes — and the frequent granting of exemptions. In April 1992 a 40 percent tax was introduced on export earnings. Barter trade was exempt, so there was a boom in such transactions. A system of temporary import tariffs was introduced on December 1, 1992, mostly in the range of 1–3 percent. New export tariffs, mostly ranging from 10 to 30 percent, were introduced in April 1993.

A telling example of the confusing situation in foreign trade is the case of the Balkhash copper works (Nikolaev, 1993b; Dik, 1993b). On January 25, 1992, Nazarbaev issued a decree banning Kazakh firms from settling deals with each other in dollars. However, the Balkhash firm had already received a $100 million credit from the Swiss Bank KAM to buy ore, via the Marc Rich company, and received assurances that they were exempt from the new decree. In 1992 they exported 12,000 tons of processed ore (with a license), worth $29 million, and spent $43 million abroad buying equipment — much of it for other factories, "in lieu of taxes." However, on January 17, 1993, the ministry fired the Balkhash director, claiming that the firm had hidden $7 million in foreign bank accounts. The director was supported by the regional council, and he was subsequently nominated as a parliamentary candidate by his former work force.

THE POLITICS OF INDEPENDENCE

President Nursultan Nazarbaev is playing a careful political balancing act. The basic outlines of his political position have not changed since 1990 (Nazarbaev, 1990). A native Kazakh, he is able to appeal to those of Kazakh nationality. But as a former apparatchik who prides himself on being a realist and pragmatist, and who insists on maintaining close ties with Moscow, he has also been able to command the loyalty of Kazakhstan's Russians. This explains his sweeping victory on December 1, 1991, when he was elected president with 98.76 percent of the vote. His avowed strategy since independence has been to preserve this domestic political consensus through rapid economic growth.

Nazarbaev rules through the umbrella Union of National Unity, which includes the Socialist Party, the legal successor to the banned Communist Party of Kazakhstan. The democratic movement, which grew out of the protest movement centered on the Semipalatinsk nuclear test site, is fairly weak and has remained loyal to Nazarbaev. In contrast to Uzbekistan and Turkmenistan, human rights are broadly respected in Kazakhstan. At the moment Nazarbaev seems to be firmly in control, although relations with the parliament are tense. Nazarbaev took the opportunity provided by Yeltsin's dismissal of the Russian parliament to persuade the Kazakhstan legislature to dissolve itself in December 1993, scheduling new elections for March 1994. These elections provided a landslide victory to Nazarbaev's supporters. In the meantime Nazarbaev is empowered to rule by presidential decree. However, Almaty is finding it increasingly difficult to maintain control over Kazakhstan's 19 regions, which are spread out over huge physical distances. Ironically, the state's commitment to expanding foreign trade may bolster these separatist tendencies, as the regions become less dependent on funds distributed by Almaty.

Kazakhstan's population of 18 million is about evenly divided between 6.5 million Kazakhs and 6.2 million Russians (39.7 percent and 37.8 percent, respectively), with sizable groups of Germans (5.8 percent) and Ukrainians (5.4 percent) (Asylbekov, 1991). Some 60 percent of Kazakhs live in rural areas in the south and west, where the remnants of the traditional culture have been preserved. The Russians are clustered in the large industrial cities and mining regions along the border with

Russia in the north. Thus, tough decisions over the course of economic policy are made even more difficult by the fact that they are mapped onto an ethnically divided society. (There are also quite sharp clan divisions within the Kazakh community.)

Kazakh nationalists complain that Moscow has waged a virtual genocide against the Kazakh people. There were 6 million Kazakhs in 1915, but their numbers had shrank to 2.5 million by 1945 (Smaylv, 1992). Perhaps 2 million Kazakhs died during collectivization — after which 2 million Gulag prisoners were sent to the region from elsewhere in the USSR. Kazakhs argue that in the Soviet period their culture was systematically stifled and Russified. Fully 62 percent of Kazakhs are fluent in Russian, and 30 percent speak only Russian. Only one in three schools use Kazakh as the medium of instruction.

What are the chances that the Russian-Kazakh rift will turn nasty? The unfortunate events in the Caucasus and elsewhere only too clearly illustrate the explosive potential of ethnic conflicts in the postsocialist political landscape. One should recall that the first ethnic riots of the perestroika era were launched by Kazakh students in Almaty in December 1986, protesting the replacement of First Secretary Dinmukhamed Kunaev by the Russian Gennadiy Kolbin (Kuzio, 1988). Kunaev had pursued an affirmative action policy in political and educational recruitment, favoring those of the titular nationality.

Kazakh nationalists argue that it is normal in the modern world for a state to be built around a single ethnic group, with due respect for the rights of ethnic minorities. A key bone of contention has been the new language law, introduced in September 1989 and weakened — to the annoyance of the nationalists — in September 1992. The new constitution declares Kazakh to be the official state language (and Russian the official language of "interethnic communication"); there is a vague plan to make Kazakh mandatory for certain jobs within the next ten years (Kaidarov, 1992; Molchanova, 1993). The nationalists also object to the privatization program, arguing that most of the assets being privatized are in Russified cities. Some suggest that Nazarbaev's oil-export strategy could turn Kazakhstan into a "banana republic," with few of the benefits reaching the rural population (Grozin, 1993). The nationalists want to limit contacts with Russia and re-orient Kazakhstan's foreign policy toward China, Turkey, and Iran — countries which were historically Russia's enemies.

President Nazarbaev and most of Kazakhstan's political elite see the nationalist agenda as a recipe for instability and civil war. In their view, the Kazakhs would have little to gain from such a conflict, given the dominant economic role of Russians within the country and the external dependence on Russia. Unlike elsewhere in Central Asia, secession is a feasible option for the Russian minority, given its territorial compactness and proximity to Russia.

Nazarbaev's strategy is to try to satisfy the legitimate concerns of both ethnic groups, while forging a new concept of "Kazakhstan patriotism," based on territorial identity and acceptance by Russia and the outside world (Nysanbaev and Suleymanov, 1993).

It remains to be seen whether Nazarbaev's political formula, born within the confines of the old Soviet Union, will survive the transition to political and economic independence. Will he be able to maintain the loyalty of the Kazakh and Russian communities? Will he preserve sufficient authority to push through his ambitious economic modernization program?

Relations with Moscow

Nazarbaev has consistently tried to turn the Commonwealth of Independent States into an effective institution, integrating the military and economic policies of the CIS states (Ovlev, 1993; Samoylenko, 1992). However, Russia has refused to cede any of their economic independence to the CIS — for example, by creating a CIS central bank with a governing board drawn from different states. Ukraine and several of the other states have also played a disruptive role by avoiding binding commitments.

Relations with Russia seemed to improve with the appointment of Chernomyrdin as prime minister in December 1992, with a Russian-Kazakh treaty on economic cooperation signed in Omsk on January 9, 1993. However, Russia repeatedly snubbed its Central Asian partners in the course of 1993, unilaterally pulling the plug on the ruble zone in November.

In contrast to Ukraine, Kazakhstan ratified the nuclear nonproliferation treaty on December 15, 1993, and agreed to give up all of its nuclear weapons in return for $88 million in aid from the United States to pay for their dismantling. However, the future of the Baykonur space launching complex has proved to be a contentious issue. The 100,000-strong city, populated mostly by Russians, continues to function, launching 18 satellites in the first half of 1993 (twice as many as NASA) (Zak, 1993). Kazakhstan wanted to run the base jointly with Russia (thereby sharing in any profits), but negotiations proved fruitless, and in December 1993 Kazakhstan reluctantly agreed to lease it to its northern neighbor.

Regional Cooperation

Nazarbaev has pursued an active diplomatic policy with Kazakhstan's southern neighbors, while stressing that his goal is economic cooperation rather than an anti-Russian alliance. On October 31, 1992, Turkey and five Central Asian states issued the Ankara Declaration, pledging to replace the current Cyrillic script with a Turkish-style Roman alphabet. They also agreed to promote transport links, including, for example, the construction of a 2,200-kilometer oil pipeline through Iran. The future of this endeavor is now in doubt, however, given the Russian change of heart on such projects in December 1993. In November 1992 Kazakhstan and the other Central Asian republics joined the Organization of Economic Cooperation, which unites Pakistan, Iran, and Turkey.

The ecological challenges facing Central Asia are another factor necessitating regional cooperation. Over the past 30 years the surface area of the Aral Sea has shrunk in half, leading to salt storms with devastating consequences for the health of local inhabitants (Wilkie, 1993). On February 18, 1992, the five republics occupying the Aral basin signed an agreement on water sharing and set up an Intergovernmental Coordinating Committee. However, Nazarbaev's resource-based growth strategy will only increase the environmental challenges facing Kazakhstan.

CONCLUSION

There are several questions which can be raised about Nazarbaev's ambitious economic development strategy:

1. Will Western investors come? It would be premature to offer a definitive response, but the answer is probably affirmative. British, U.S., French, and Italian companies are all showing strong interest, and are willing to gamble that Kazakhstan's political uncertainties may be more manageable than those of Russia. The World Bank expected direct foreign investment to come to $380–580 million in 1993, rising to $1 billion in 1994. Not all observers are bullish about Kazakhstan, however. *Euromoney* gave it a world ranking of 148 in early 1993 — placing it below the likes of Ukraine (*Delovoy mir*, May 12, 1993, p. 4).

2. Will political and administrative disorder disrupt the development program? So far, Nazarbaev has managed to maintain tight control over the process of approving foreign investment. This stands in sharp contrast to the situation facing investors in Russia. On the other hand, the political

situation remains fragile and Nazarbaev's hold could deteriorate very quickly if interethnic crisis were to erupt.

3. Will the development projects prove economically viable? It is one thing to have the oil and gas reserves in the ground; it is altogether more complicated to turn them into profitable assets. With margins squeezed because of the low price of oil on world markets, companies have to consider very carefully the cost and feasibility of constructing new pipelines across politically unstable regions such as the North Caucasus or Iran.

4. Will the economic take-off come in time? Nazarbaev's strategy assumes that rapid payoffs from his international growth strategy will buy domestic political tranquillity. However, it will take at least three-to-five years before significant revenues are generated — assuming everything goes according to plan. Kazakhstan will be very vulnerable to social and ethnic strife in the interim.

5. What will be the impact of the energy-export strategy on other sectors of the economy? The experience of other economies (from Nigeria to Holland) indicates that an oil boom can cause inflation and currency appreciation, making the non-oil sectors less competitive. In the case of Kazakhstan the threat of the "Dutch disease" is exacerbated by the likelihood that the oil and gas revenues will be used to keep afloat loss-making industrial plants.

6. What will Russia's policy be? Kazakhstan will remain extremely vulnerable to shifts in policy by its northern neighbor. At the end of 1993 Russia's policy appeared to be swinging in a more "selfish" direction, as indicated by an unwillingness to subsidize trade with Kazakhstan and even a certain jealousy toward Kazakhstan's dealings with Western corporations. Russian truculence, if sustained, could seriously derail Nazarbaev's economic program.

NOTES

The opinions expressed here are those of the authors and not the organizations for which they work.

1.   Throughout this chapter most unattributed items from newspapers are treated as in this citation of *Kazakhstanskaya pravda*; attributed newspaper articles and texts of government programs may be found in the list of references.

REFERENCES

Akava, A. "I snova o bar'erakh na puti reform." *Kazakhstanskaya pravda*, May 15, 1993a, p. 3.

Akava, A. "Svyazannye odnoy tsep'yu." *Kazakhstanskaya pravda*, June 4, 1993b, p. 2.

Asanbaev, Erik. "Svoë prednaznachenie." *Kazakhstanskaya pravda*, February 20, 1993, p. 2.

Asylbekov, M. "O sotsial'noy, politicheskoy i etnicheskoy strukture Kazakhstana." *Izvestiya AN KazSSSR*, Seriya obshchestvennykh nauk, no. 3, 1991, pp. 43–47.

Berkovskaya, G. "Menyaem pravili igry." *Kazakhstanskaya pravda*, November 6, 1992, p. 3.

Berkovskaya, G. "Priznakov stabilizatsiya poka ne vidno." *Kazakhstanskaya pravda*, May 1, 1993a, p. 2.

Berkovskaya, G. "Uroven' inflyatsii." *Kazakhstanskaya pravda*, May 22, 1993b, p. 2.

Berkovskaya, G. "Dorogi v zastoy uzhe net." *Kazakhstanskaya pravda*, May 29, 1993c, p. 2.

Bogomolov, Oleg. "Novye mekhanizmy torgovli i raschëtov dolzhny sozdavat'sya vnutri eks-SSSR." *Finansovye izvestiya*, April 17–23, 1993, p. 2.

Cherkizov, V. "Nezavisimye profsoyuzy podderzhivayut reformy prezidenta." *Kazakhstanskaya pravda*, April 11, 1993, p. 2.

Derbisov, Erkeshbay. "Kak rabotaet byudzhetnyy rubl' na sele." *Kazakhstanskaya pravda*, April 6, 1993, p. 3.

Dik, V. "Gruppy zakhvatki." *Kazakhstanskaya pravda*, March 20, 1993a, p. 8.

Dik, V. "Bol'shomu korablyu." *Kazakhstanskaya pravda*, April 2, 1993b, p. 1.

Dobrota, L. "O bednom monopoliste." *Kazakhstanskaya pravda*, April 16, 1993, p. 1.

Doronin, Igor'. "Respublikanskie myagkie valyuty ustupayut naporu rublya." *Finansovye izvestiya*, December 30, 1993–January 12, 1994, p. 4.

Druzenko, Yegor. "Yesli v Aktyubinske naydut neft', v eë dobychu investiruyut 5 milliardov dollarov." *Finansovye izvestiya*, April 30–May 7, 1993, p. 7.

Erezhepov, B. "Zud vlasti." *Kazakhstanskaya pravda*, March 27, 1993a, p. 2.

Erezhepov, B. "Tikhaya privatizatsiya." *Kazakhstanskaya pravda*, April 3, 1993b, p. 3.

Erezhepov, B. "O tom, kak chinovniki delayut biznes." *Kazakhstanskaya pravda*, April 5, 1993c, p. 4.

Erlanger, Steven. "Iz vsekh byvshykh sovetskikh respublik, u Kazakhstana samyy luchshiy shans na uspekh, konstantiruet N'yu-Iork Tayms." *Kazakhstanskaya pravda*, April 7, 1993, p. 3.

Gorbunov, S. "Bogach — bednyak." *Kazakhstanskaya pravda*, June 12, 1993, p. 2.

Grozin, A. "Kazakhstan mezhdu Aziey i Yevropoy." *Novoe pokolenie*, April 7, 1993, p. 3.

Illarionov, Andrey. "Vyigrayut vse." *Delovoy mir*, December 13, 1993, p. 9.

[IMF.] "Press Release no. 94/2." External Relations Department, International Monetary Fund, January 26, 1994.

Kaidarov, A. "Yesli ischeznet yazyk." *Kazakhstanskaya pravda*, October 14, 1992, p. 3.

Kaleeva, T. "Privatizatsiya metodom kollektivizatsii." *Kazakhstanskaya pravda*, April 18, 1993, p. 2.

Kim, K. "Na otlivnoy volne konversii." *Kazakhstanskaya pravda*, March 26, 1993, p. 2.

Kolchin, S. "Pyatnadtsat' pretendentov na sunduk mertvetsa." *Vek*, no. 3, 1993, p. 3.

Kon, Yu. "Dolgi gosudarstv SNG Rossii rastut." *Delovoy mir*, February 20, 1993, p. 1.

Kovalenko, O. "Lish' by shef povar ne pereborshchil." *Kazakhstanskaya pravda*, April 3, 1993a, p. 3.

Kovalenko, O. "Dostoyanie respublika pod ugrozoy." *Kazakhstanskaya pravda*, May 11, 1993b, p. 2.

Kozlov, Sergey. "Nursultan Nazarbaev: 'Khvatit kritikovat'." *Nezavisimaya gazeta*, March 4, 1993, p. 1.

Kurbrakov, N. "Chetvërtaya stupen'." *Kazakhstanskaya pravda*, March 25, 1993, p. 3.

Kuzio, Taras. "Nationalist Riots in Kazakhstan." *Central Asia Survey* 7, 4 (1988): 79–100.

Kuzmenko, Boris. "Mass privatization starts again in Kazakhstan." *Moscow News*, September 24, 1993, p. 8.

Kuznetsov, B. "Pereval uzhe blizok." *Kazakhstanskaya pravda*, May 12, 1993, p. 2.

Lan'ko, E., and I. Kuchin. "Kakoe zhe obshchestvo my sobiraemsya stroit'?" *Kazakhstanskaya pravda*, July 15, 1992, p. 1.

Makulbekov, M. "Zerno dorozhaet, no ne tak bystro." *Kazakhstanskaya pravda*, November 10, 1992, p. 3.

Markova, L. "Situatsiya s privatizatsey." *Kazakhstanskaya pravda*, December 1, 1992, p. 2.

Mogal'nitskiy, V. "Na grane bankrotstva." *Kazakhstanskaya pravda*, December 2, 1992, p. 2.

Molchanova, A. "Yazyk moy — bol' maya." *Kazakhstanskaya pravda*, April 27, 1993, p. 2.

Mukhin, Yu. "Pasynok ostaëtsya na vakhte." *Kazakhstanskaya pravda*, April 28, 1993, p. 3.

Nadzharov, Aleksandr. "Dolgi — 10,7 milliarda dollarov." *Nezavisimaya gazeta*, March 10, 1993, p. 2.

[Natsional'naya.] "Natsional'naya programma razgosudarstvleniya i privatizatsii v respublike Kazakhstana na 1993-95 g. (II etap)." *Kazakhstanskaya pravda*, April 10, 1993, p. 1.

Naumov, V. "Pravda i mif o chastnike." *Kazakhstanskaya pravda*, December 31, 1992, p. 2.

Naumov, V. "Spustya god posle ukaza." *Kazakhstanskaya pravda*, February 16, 1993a, p. 2.

Naumov, V. "Pod vozdeystviem rynka." *Kazakhstanskaya pravda*, March 19, 1993b, p. 1.

Naumov, V. "Pod gnenom tsen i nalogov." *Kazakhstanskaya pravda*, April 7, 1993c, p. 2.

Nazarbaev, Nursultan. "Za yedinstvo i konsolidatsiyu." *Kazakhstanskaya pravda*, September 12, 1990, p. 1.

Nazarbaev, Nursultan. "Nas zhdut vperedi bol'shie trudnosti." *Kazakhstanskaya pravda*, April 5, 1993a, p. 1.

Nazarbaev, Nursultan. "Nashi orientiry — konsolidatsiya, obshchestvennyy progress i sotsial'noe partnerstvo." *Kazakhstanskaya pravda*, 13 May 1993b, pp. 1–3.

Nikolaev, V. "Deshëvyy tovar." *Kazakhstanskaya pravda*, November 3, 1992, p. 2.

Nikolaev, V. "Voennye trofey." *Kazakhstanskaya pravda*, February 13, 1993a, p. 4.

Nikolaev, V. "Iz tupika vyshli. Para nakazyvat'." *Kazakhstanskaya pravda*, March 25, 1993b, p. 2.

Nysanbaev, A., and F. Suleymanov. "Obshchenatsional'naya ideologiya." *Kazakhstanskaya pravda*, May 15, 1993, p. 3.

Ovlev, Vyacheslav. "Kontinental'naya Aziya." *Nezavisimaya gazeta*, March 12, 1993, p. 3.

Petrov, Yu. "Natsional'nye valyuty." *Delovoy mir*, December 13, 1993, p. 8.

Petrovskiy, A. "Otchego grustit Yelena." *Kazakhstanskaya pravda*, December 23, 1992, p. 2.

Petrovskiy, A. "S kem i chem torguet Kazakhstan?" *Kazakhstanskaya pravda*, February 12, 1993a, p. 2.

Petrovskiy, A. "Fors-mazhor po sovetskiy." *Kazakhstanskaya pravda*, February 13, 1993b, p. 2.

Petrovskiy, A. "Tseny na produkty." *Kazakhstanskaya pravda*, March 26, 1993c, p. 3.

Polese, Michael. "Economic Integration, National Policies and the Rationality of Regional Separatism." In Ronald Rogowski and Edward A. Tiryakian (eds.), *New Nationalisms of the Developed West*, pp. 109–127. Boston: Allen and Unwin, 1985.

[Postanovlenie.] "Postanovlenie presidenta, 'O gosudarstvennykh kholdinovykh kompaniyakh'," of March 5, 1993. Published in *Kazakhstanskaya pravda*, April 12, 1993, p. 1.

[Programma.] "Programma neotlozhnykh antikrizisnykh mer i uglubleniya sotsial'no-ekonomicheskikh reform." *Kazakhstanskaya pravda*, April 8, 1993, pp. 1–4.

Reutov, A. "Neopravdannye kontrasty." *Kazakhstanskaya pravda*, February 13, 1993, p. 2.

Samoylenko, A. "'Nam nuzhen soyuz'." *Literaturnaya gazeta*, August 19, 1992, p. 2.

Shevelev, A. "Na zemle dolzhen rabotat' nastoyashchiy khozyain." *Kazakhstanskaya pravda*, February 12, 1993, p. 2.

Smaylv, K. "Radi spravedlivosti." *Kazakhstanskaya pravda*, February 8, 1992, p. 2.

Sutyagin, V. "Chto znachit' 'sedleka veka' dlya Atyraustsev?" *Kazakhstanskaya pravda*, November 4, 1992, p. 2.

Svan, T. "Nezavisimye profsoyuzy." *Kazakhstanskaya pravda*, November 3, 1992, p. 1.

Svoik, P., and M. Ospanov. "Pochemu vse khuzhe stanovit'sya zhizn' na ostrove stabilnosti?" *Kazakhstanskaya pravda*, April 20, 1993, p. 1.

Syzdykov, A. "Dogovor 'temir'." *Kazakhstanskaya pravda*, May 4, 1993, p. 2.

Tereshchenko, Sergey. "Kurs na radikal'nye ekonomicheskie preobrazovaniya." *Kazakhstanskaya pravda*, November 12, 1992a, p. 1.

Tereshchenko, Sergey. "Otchët pravitel'stva na sessii parlamenta." *Kazakhstanskaya pravda*, December 19, 1992b, p. 2.

Turagov, K. "Ot zhestkogo goszakaza." *Kazakhstanskaya pravda*, October 10, 1992, p. 2.

Veytsman, B. "A ved my — bol'shaya sila." *Kazakhstanskaya pravda*, April 30, 1993, p. 2.

Voloshin, V. "Roskontrakt — eto garantiya nadezhnosti." *Delovoy mir*, May 20, 1993, p. 11.

Wilkie, Fergus. "Disaster-Struck Sea Has Chance of Returning to Life." *Financial Times*, October 28, 1993, p. 8.

[World Bank.] "Kazakhstan: Country Economic Memorandum." World Bank, 1993.

[World Bank.] "Kazakhstan to Receive $1 Billion in 1994." *World Bank News*, January 20, 1994, p. 4.

Yurchenko, G. "Kto zakoldoval krug." *Kazakhstanskaya pravda*, December 5, 1992, p. 3.

Zak, Anatoliy. "Baykonur." *Nezavisimaya gazeta*, July 13, 1993, p. 6.

Zhabagin, Asygat. "Predvaritel'nye itogi." *Delovoy mir*, December 13, 1993, p. 13.

Zhdanov, A. "Vlast' ishchet podderzhki v delovykh krugakh." *Kazakhstanskaya pravda*, June 1, 1993a, p. 1.

Zhdanov, A. "Vopros uzhe ne v tom, kak luchshe upravlyat'." *Kazakhstanskaya pravda*, June 11, 1993b, p. 1.

Zhigalov, K. "Vliyanie ekonomicheskikh faktorov i ekonomicheskogo lobbi na vneshnepoliticheskiy kurs Kazakhstana." Almaty, February 1993 (mimeo).

Zhorov, N. "Respublika na dele pravlenie — krupnye kapitalovlozheniya." *Kazakhstanskaya pravda*, April 7, 1993a, p. 1.

Zhorov, N. "V vyigryshe budut vse." *Kazakhstanskaya pravda*, June 12, 1993b, p. 1.

5

Georgia

Patrick J. Conway and Chandrashekar Pant

INTRODUCTION

The Republic of Georgia was restored on April 9, 1991, after a seventy-year period as a constituent republic of the Soviet Union. Given that hiatus, Georgia is certainly entitled to "newborn" status, and we should expect its first steps to be tentative and sometimes misdirected. Its governments have struggled to put in place the institutions and regulatory structure of an independent nation-state, as have those of the other countries of the former Soviet Union (FSU). Institution building in Georgia has additionally been complicated by political strife stemming both from the existence of secessionist movements within the territory of Georgia and from an armed opposition movement fighting to restore a former president to power.

We have two purposes for this chapter: one descriptive, the other analytical. We present in Section 1 a description of the Georgian economy and a short summary of Georgia's recent economic performance. Here, we focus upon Georgia's historical comparative advantage and its long-standing integration with the other economies of the FSU. In Section 2 we provide a description of the policy steps that Georgia has taken in the economic sphere to reflect its new status as a nation-state.

In Section 3 we present our analysis of the economic transition in Georgia. The military and political disruptions during this period make it difficult to draw firm conclusions. However, we believe that Georgia's economic policy can be characterized by a less than complete recognition of the economic interdependence of Georgia with its neighbors and its trading partners in the FSU. Its declaration of political independence was seemingly considered a decree of economic independence as well, and for a time economic independence was taken to mean isolationism. This feature of economic policy making is important to understanding the high costs of Georgia's adjustment process.

Our primary conclusion is this: incomplete recognition of economic interdependence with trading and financial partners will have important costs for all newly independent countries. Economic interdependence is a reality, and for the relatively small countries in transition in Eastern Europe it implies strict constraints on economic policy making. These constraints are not removed or relaxed by a declaration of political independence. Policies formulated without reference to these constraints will have high costs, as we illustrate for the case of Georgia.

In Section 4 we identify three stumbling blocks for continuation of the economic transition. The first is the continuation of internal political and military warfare among the people of Georgia. The second is the continued economic decline of Georgia's traditional trading partners within the FSU. The third is drawn from our primary conclusion: if economic policies are made without full recognition of the implications of economic interdependence, they will continue to be costly and to slow the pace of economic transition.

GEORGIA'S ECONOMY AND RECENT PERFORMANCE

Georgia's economy at present is the product of two factors: its inherent economic endowment and location, and its long-standing integration in the Soviet Union. It also is greatly influenced by the tension between a nationalistic Georgian majority and traditionally separate ethnic minorities: Georgia includes the former Soviet autonomous republics of Abkhazia and Adzharia, and the former Soviet autonomous *oblast'* of South Ossetia, each of which had its own Supreme Soviet and administration. Ossetians, Abkhazi, and Adzhari were not limited to their titular territories. They take nationalist pride, however, in their distinction from the rest of Georgia.

Economic Structure

Georgia has a population of 5.5 million located in a geographical area bounded by the Black Sea, Russia, Azerbaijan, Armenia, and Turkey.

Its population was 2 percent of the total for the Soviet Union in 1990, and its land mass only 0.3 percent. Economically, Georgia is a small economy with comparative advantages in a small number of agricultural goods and in tourism. It thus exemplifies an interdependent economy, and has much to gain from open international trade.[1]

Until recently, indicators of social development in Georgia were better than elsewhere in the former Soviet Union. As Table 5.1 indicates, the life expectancy of Georgians was the highest in the FSU, and infant mortality and death rates in Georgia were below the FSU average. The number of doctors per unit of population was higher in Georgia than elsewhere. Georgia was one of the most densely populated parts of the former Soviet Union, and yet had a stock of housing space per capita unrivaled outside the Baltics. These favorable indicators appear inconsistent with measures of per capita income, according to which Georgia

TABLE 5.1

Social Indicators for the Former Soviet Republics, 1990

	Population Density[1]	Housing Space[2]	Doctor Avail.[3]	Hospital Bed Avail.[3]	Life Expectancy[4]
Armenia	113.3	15.0	42.8	89.8	71.8
Azerbaijan	82.4	12.5	39.3	102.2	71.0
Belarus	49.4	17.9	40.5	132.3	71.3
Estonia	35.1	21.6	45.7	121.0	70.0
Georgia	78.4	18.8	59.2	110.7	72.8
Kazakhstan	6.2	14.2	41.2	136.2	68.8
Kyrgyz Republic	22.3	12.1	36.7	119.8	68.8
Latvia	41.6	19.8	49.6	148.1	69.6
Lithuania	57.2	n.a.	46.1	124.4	71.5
Moldova	129.6	17.9	40.0	131.4	68.7
Russia	8.7	16.4	46.9	137.5	69.3
Tadzhikistan	37.4	9.3	27.1	105.8	69.6
Turkmenistan	7.6	11.1	35.7	113.3	66.4
Ukraine	86.0	17.8	44.0	135.5	60.5
Uzbekistan	46.3	12.1	35.8	123.7	69.5

Source: GOSKOMSTAT/SSSR (1991, pp. 67–73, 94, 194, 254, and 258).

Notes:
[1]Population per square kilometer, January 1, 1991.
[2]Square meters per capita.
[3]Per 10,000 persons.
[4]Years.

ranked among the poorer of the states of the FSU.[2] This gap between officially recorded income and observed living standards may reflect the existence of a relatively large underground economy in Georgia.

Agriculture accounts for about 30 percent of net material product (NMP), industry another 33 percent, transport and communications 21 percent, construction 8 percent, and other branches the balance. In agriculture Georgia became quite specialized: it produced nearly all the tea and citrus for the Soviet markets, and provided substantial shares of wine, fruits and vegetables, and other food products. Industry has a substantial agro-industrial base, but also includes production of aircraft, steel, wood products, locomotives, trucks, and color televisions, among other items.

The economic integration that would naturally occur between Georgia and its neighbors has been magnified greatly by the economic structures of the former Soviet Union. Productive activity in Georgia, whether agricultural or industrial, was managed by union-level ministries and integrated with upstream suppliers (for inputs of metals, oil, basic chemicals, cotton, wool, among others) and downstream consumers (for locomotives, oil-drilling tubes, tea, citrus) scattered throughout the Soviet Union. In many ways, it was among the most integrated into that system. Until recently Georgia was largely dependent on Russia (and to a lesser extent Azerbaidzhan and Turkmenistan) for its supply of oil products, natural gas, and electricity. These were provided at highly subsidized prices.[3] There was thus a continuing subsidy to Georgian consumption by participation in the union trading system.

The financial sector in Georgia was highly integrated into the financial system of the Soviet Union. All banking institutions in Georgia were branches of the Soviet national bank or of specialized state banks. Saving by households and enterprises was collected by these banks and channeled to a union-wide investment budget, which allocated some of these resources for investment in Georgia. Until the late 1980s, there were sizable transfers and capital inflows from the union budget to finance large infrastructure projects and investment in public enterprises in Georgia. Georgia shared in the use of the ruble, the common Soviet currency, printed at the central branch of the Gosbank (the Soviet national bank) in Moscow and shipped to regional offices of the national bank for emission.

Integration also took other forms important to the Georgian economy. Advanced professional training was provided by institutes in Moscow. Embassies and foreign bank representation were handled at the union level from offices in Moscow.

Recent Economic Performance

Georgia's economy is in crisis. Production fell steeply over 1991–93 (by 46 percent in 1992 alone) and price increases have bordered on hyperinflation (40 percent in May 1993). It shares these difficulties with many of the other former Soviet republics, as the economic downturn in Russia has brought about parallel contractions and inflation throughout the former Soviet Union. Georgia's first policy steps have thus been taken at a perilous time.

Georgia's economic performance was among the best in the FSU during the 1980s, especially in the first half when NMP grew by 8 percent per year. But as elsewhere in the Soviet Union, economic performance weakened considerably in 1989–90, when NMP declined by a cumulative 17 percent. When Georgia declared independence in April 1991 it was hoped that independence would allow Georgia to escape from the economic collapse facing the rest of the Soviet Union. Instead, economic performance has deteriorated, and been worse than that of many other former Soviet republics.

NMP fell by almost 21 percent in real terms in 1991 and the decline was even steeper in 1992 when NMP is estimated to have fallen another 46 percent. This contraction occurred across the board in the production of goods: industrial production fell by about 34 percent in 1992 and agricultural production by almost 50 percent. Retail sales measured in real terms fell 44.7 percent in the first five months of 1993 over the already depressed record of the same period in 1992.

Inflation accelerated. The retail price index rose by about 3 percent in 1990 and 79 percent in 1991. Inflation continued to accelerate in 1992, especially in the second half. By December 1992, the monthly inflation rate was close to 30 percent. The annual inflation rate for the period December 1991–December 1992 was about 1,500 percent. For the period May 1992–May 1993, excluding the impact of the ruble overhang, the increase in consumer prices was 831 percent.

The poor economic performance in 1991–92 was attributable in part to a number of union-wide factors. With the dissolution of the Soviet Union the union-wide ministries for coordination of production and distribution of resources became more and more ineffective, and both producers and consumers struggled to establish alternative marketing and supply channels. Demand for Georgian products was also constrained by the contraction in economic activity in partner countries, notably Russia. Further, inputs to Georgian industry and agriculture that had formerly been subsidized by the Soviet Union — fertilizers, energy, and ores — were being sold at prices closer to the world market price.[4] Finally, according to Georgian authorities, other Soviet republics discriminated against Georgia through limitations on trade in critical inputs in retaliation for Georgia's active pursuit of independence. Overall, trade between Georgia and other FSU republics and with the rest of the world fell sharply. Taking 1989 as a base, exports to FSU republics fell as a percent of GDP from 40 percent to 23 percent in 1991 and 11 percent in 1992; imports fell from 34 percent to 19 percent and 14 percent. Exports to the rest of the world fell also, albeit from a smaller base: from 2.5 percent of GDP in 1989, they fell to 0.2 percent in 1991, and 1.2 percent in 1992. Imports from the rest of the world declined similarly.

These unfavorable economic developments were also caused by factors that were internal to Georgia. Among the noneconomic factors, an earthquake that struck the northwest region of Georgia on April 29, 1991, sharply reduced agricultural output and damaged transport, communications, and other infrastructure. Later in 1991–92, volatile political and social conditions created severe disruptions in production, transportation, and trade. For example, in early 1992, oil and gas imports from Russia were almost completely disrupted due to the conflict in South Ossetia. The production and processing of tea, Georgia's main export product, was particularly hard hit by the continuing disturbance in Abkhazia where it is grown: the production of tea in 1992 was only about a third of the 1991 level.

Economic policies also contributed to the adverse economic developments. Some of these policies were inevitable following the reforms in Russia. Thus, when Russia liberalized prices and increased the prices of energy, Georgia had to follow sooner or later. The increase in prices during 1992 was directly the result of the liberalization of prices in March of that year and the significant increase in most of the prices that remained administered throughout 1992. For example, gasoline prices were increased elevenfold between March 1992 and June 1992. Milk prices rose sixfold in April and the price of bread was increased thirteenfold. The maintenance of quotas and licenses for exports, which was meant to maintain lower prices in Georgia following liberalization in Russia, contributed to the decline in trade, and to a further contraction in output.

The continuing increase in prices also reflected a loosening of financial policies, especially in the second half of 1992. The budget deficit increased from 3.5 percent of GDP in 1991 to 35 percent in 1992. This widening deficit reflected both a substantial deterioration in revenues as well as growth in expenditures. Revenues fell from about 30 percent of GDP in 1991 to 14 percent in 1992, while expenditures rose from about 32 percent of GDP to 48 percent in the same period.

The revenue shortfall was caused by several factors, including the disruption in trade, the collapse of output in the state sector, and the difficulties in tax collection in areas affected by the civil strife. Unfamiliarity with the new tax system introduced in March 1992 (when the existing turnover and sales taxes were replaced by a value-added tax) was another contributing factor. The increase in expenditures reflected the growth of subsidies resulting from the increase in import prices (for example, for energy and bread), the increase in wages and other wage related payments to compensate for inflation, the growth of other social expenditures (health, education), and increased expenditures due to the war (for example, on the growing number of refugees).

The budget deficit in 1992 was financed almost entirely through domestic bank credit creation. The growth of credit was particularly strong during the second half. Between July and December 1992, credit to the government increased from R16.6 billion to R62 billion (273 percent). Credit to nonfinancial public enterprises also increased sharply (190 percent) over the same period.[5] In 1993 the National Bank of Georgia (NBG) targeted credit emission at R140 billion for the year, but had already issued R450 billion in credits by the end of the first half.

STEPS ALONG THE TRANSITION PATH

Georgians pride themselves on their fierce independence of spirit. Starting in 1989, they were among the first to demonstrate for political independence from the Soviet Union. In a referendum held in October 1990, a large majority of the population supported secession from the Soviet Union. Georgia declared independence on April 9, 1991, and the late Zviad Gamsakhurdia, who spearheaded the independence movement, became president in May 1991. Reflecting increasing dissatisfaction with the president's rule, in December 1991 he was ousted by a military coup. Former Soviet foreign minister Eduard Shevardnadze was installed as head of state pending a general election.

Elections were held in October 1992 and Shevardnadze was elected chairman of parliament, an office tantamount to head of state. Events in 1993 were dominated by the war in Abkhazia, a territory over which Georgia effectively lost control after its capital, Sukhumi, fell to rebel forces in September. The fall of Sukhumi inspired an armed comeback bid by Gamsakhurdia and his supporters. This revolt was put down with

Russian assistance after Shevardnadze agreed to join the CIS. Gamsakhurdia's death was reported in January 1994. Whether civil strife will continue remains an open question, given the divisions in the Georgian political elite and the uncertain status of the various former autonomous territories.

Delineating the Features of the Transition

The problems of economic and political transition for the former Soviet republics are well documented elsewhere, and we summarize them only briefly in Figure 5.1. We identify three dimensions along which the former Soviet economies have evolved during the transition: (i) institutional re-organization, where the government seeks to establish new institutional structures to govern an independent nation state; (ii) regulatory reform, where the role of the market and the state in the economy are redefined; and (iii) integration with the international economy, with which closer linkages are established. The starting point and goal are shared across former Soviet republics, but their progress in transition differs. In the following sections we describe Georgia's efforts along each dimension of this transition.

Institutional Reorganization

With the restoration of independence, the legislature took final responsibility for policy making and regulation. It then delegated the responsibility for day-to-day regulation and policy formulation to the president and his ministers. Typically, these tasks were assigned to be carried out by the Georgian branches of existing Soviet ministries and organizations. Thus, the Georgian branch of Gosbank became the new National Bank of Georgia and was given responsibility for monetary policy (although the legislature retained final authority in that area). The Georgian branch of Gosplan became the new Ministry of Economy, responsible in part for the coordinated development of the different sub-sectors of the real economy. The local branch of the Ministry of Finance was charged with responsibility for fiscal matters. Branches of the Ministries of Industry and Agriculture retained their portfolios as well. This reliance on existing Soviet institutions occurred in other areas as well, for example banking, where the foreign trade bank was hived off from the Soviet Vneshekonombank, and the Savings Bank was part of a union-wide network.

Given the rapidity of change, the reliance on existing institutions was to a large extent inevitable. It may even have avoided unnecessary

FIGURE 5.1
Economic Transitions Facing Former Soviet Republics

Starting point: Soviet republic	Integrated into Soviet trading bloc	Command Economy
Transitions necessary: Redefinition of legal authority Assignment of policy-making and government regulatory functions Establishment of institutions to interact with other countries Defining political stance vis-à-vis nation-states	Definition of proper international trade incentives Encouragement of links with potential trading partners Regulation and measurement of international transactions Distribution of existing assets and liabilities	Privatization Market liberalization: —appropriate regulation —legal structure —accurate measure of activity Necessary for commodity, service, financial, and labor markets
Goal: Independent nation-state	Integration into world economy	Market economy

additional disruption, and prevented the dispersal of whatever experience and expertise there was in government. However, the reliance on existing institutions created difficulties as well. Under the command economy, these institutions and their functionaries performed functions that were very different from what they are expected to do during the transition to a market-based economy. Mostly, they implemented command economy policies that were formulated at the center. These same authorities are often reluctant to implement far-reaching market-oriented reforms. Moreover, policy-making expertise is very weak in most areas. The Ministry of Finance has very little experience in managing fiscal policy, formulating a budget, monitoring revenues and expenditures, and so on. The National Bank has little experience in running monetary policy or supervising commercial banks. The sectoral ministries have no experience in elaborating a strategic and policy framework in their areas, or in regulating the behavior of public and private entities. This experience is being developed, but it will be a slow process.

In some cases, existing institutions performed functions that are inconsistent with a market-based economy and their continued existence may thwart the transition unless the functions that they perform are radically redefined. For example, the role of the Ministry of Economy, which was born out of Gosplan, is still not very clear. The National Bank's primary function was to provide subsidized loans to enterprises at the behest of the government. This will have to change. Sectoral ministries that had in the past taken an active role in running the state enterprises in their jurisdictions will need to focus more on policy formulation and less on management of enterprises.

A new state requires new institutions, especially when it is also making the transition to a new economic system. In the economic sphere, there was a need to develop a coherent medium-term framework for systemic reforms and for coordinating these across sectors. To serve this function, the deputy prime minister's office was expanded and given the overall responsibility for policy formulation and implementa-tion. A new Ministry for Foreign Economic Relations was also created to develop foreign trade and other relations with foreign countries, a task which in the past was largely performed at the center. However, Georgia was very slow in creating a separate diplomatic or consular service. Georgia's customs activity was from the beginning coordinated through the CIS, even though it did not join the group until December 1993. A national army has evolved only slowly, although its national police force served some of these functions at an early stage. No doubt these and other institutions will develop in the future.

Regulatory Reform

As in most of the other republics of the FSU, Georgia initiated the process of market liberalization and privatization in 1992. Pricing policies for commodities still under government control were made without reference to prices in neighboring countries. For example, Georgia did not go along with mid-1991 price increases in the rest of the Soviet Union. This led to a mass outflow of goods, and trade restrictions were imposed to prevent those flows. Georgia also did not follow immediately when prices were liberalized in Russia in January 1992. This again led to renewed outflows of goods and a re-imposition of trade restrictions.

Price liberalization took place quite quickly and effectively once it was initiated in February 1992. In the first stage, the prices of all goods and services with the exception of energy products, some agricultural commodities and basic food products, and communications and transport services were liberalized. This was followed by another round of liberalization in late April when a large number of controlled prices, including some energy products, were deregulated. Prices of controlled commodities and services were also raised substantially throughout 1992, as indicated in Table 5.2. Currently, prices of bread, milk, medicines, passenger transport, communications, natural gas, liquid gas, electricity and household utilities (e.g., hot water), and housing rents are controlled at the retail level. The wholesale prices of coal, electricity, natural gas, and liquid gas are also controlled. The government has also been quite effective at removing barriers to participation in commodity markets. On May 4, 1992, for example, the government issued a decree allowing unrestricted trade among citizens.

At present, energy prices in Georgia are set well above those of the rest of CIS (and thus closer to world prices). This has led to widespread smuggling of gasoline into Georgia from neighboring countries.

Just as in the case of the market for commodities, Georgia has attempted to implement financial sector and interest rate policies independent of those in neighboring countries. Despite the use until recently of the same currency, the interest rate on refinance credits from the National Bank, which are the primary source of domestic credit, has been consistently set at a lower level than in Russia. This has reportedly led to large-scale outflows of funds from Georgia to Russia to earn the higher return.

TABLE 5.2

Evolution of Administered Prices in Georgia in 1992

		1992 Average Price (in rubles)				
	Unit	*1 Jan.*	*1 Mar.*	*% change Jan.–Mar.*	*1 July*	*% change Mar.–July*
Bread	kg	0.35	4.80	1,271	4.8	0
Milk	liter	0.79	5.30	571	5.3	0
Meat	kg	13.10	32.90	151	free[1]	n.a.
Potatoes	kg	2.00	2.00	0	free	n.a.
Salt	kg	0.08	3.00	3,650	free	n.a.
Sugar	kg	2.20	18.00	718	free[2]	n.a.
Vegetable oil	liter	2.06	7.00	240	free	n.a.
Matches	pack	0.05	1.00	1,900	free	n.a.
Medicine	n.a.	n.a.	n.a.	n.a.	n.a.	0
Gasoline (Oct. 93)	liter	0.40	4.80	1,100	free	n.a.
Diesel fuel	liter	0.07	14.00	19,900	free	n.a.
Oil	liter	0.13	6.00	4,515	free	n.a.
Coal	ton	45.00	220.00	389	set by Russia	n.a.
Industrial fuel	liter	0.07	7.00	9,900	set by Russia	n.a.
Natural gas	cubic th. m.	61.00	3,000.00	4,818	19,000	533
Liquid gas	kg	0.30	2.73	810	10.8	296
Electric power	kwh					
Private		0.04	0.12	200	0.12	0
Commercial		0.06	0.53	838	2.4	363
Passenger transport						
Taxi fare	meter unit	0.20	2.00	900	6.0	200
Subway	ride	0.05	0.60	1,100	1.0	67

Source: I. Shalamberidze, Ministry of Economy, July 6, 1992.

Notes:

[1]No longer administered.

[2]The state price of sugar was R35 per kilogram, but it was not available at that price. It was available from "Central Soyuz" for R55 per kilogram, but this was not an administered price.

To a large extent Georgia has eliminated explicit barriers to market activity. It now faces the second generation of market orientation difficulties which arise when state enterprises and other actors unmotivated by profit participate in the newly liberalized markets. One difficulty noted by government officials was the emergence of "parasites" — middle-men existing for no other reason than to redistribute the profits due a firm for its market activity. The problem of parasites surfaces especially for the activities of state-owned enterprises. These have been liberalized, but in the normal course of events the state takes any profits. Unscrupulous managers have found a way to keep these profits for themselves by encouraging a succession of unproductive middlemen. These middlemen can mark up the price while adding nothing because of scarcity in markets; the manager may be able to share in that windfall gain. One example dating from June 1992 concerned tobacco. The industry had been liberalized, but the factories had not raised prices. They continued to sell cigarettes for R3 per pack, the pre-liberalization price, despite the fact that the cigarettes sold for R7–10 per pack in the market. The difference went to a succession of middlemen. The factories came to the government that June for a R30 million subsidy because they were not profitable at a price of R3 per pack!

The instability of the present economic environment has discouraged the growth of private industrial activity. Private entrepreneurs find services more profitable than industry. Ironically, under the command regime there were many underground illegal factories that competed in bazaar markets. Now that the markets have been freed and these factories are legal, they have disappeared. Consistency of economic policy and stabilization of the political situation will right this distortion, but only in the longer term.

Georgia has moved rapidly in the privatization of housing and agricultural land. By the end of 1992 it was expected that all urban housing would be privatized, and more than 60 percent of agricultural land transferred to private farmers. Privatization of small enterprises had also been initiated and the first auctions of small assets including cars and trucks were held in March 1993. The privatization of medium and large enterprises has not yet begun, although preparations are being made to implement a voucher scheme.

Private agricultural production predates the dissolution of the Soviet Union, and private producers have historically been more productive than their state counterparts — even though the workers are the same. As Table 5.3 indicates, private-sector producers of all major agricultural crops have had higher yields than their public-sector or cooperative counterparts in the years 1989–91. This can have a large impact on aggregate output, for the 8 percent of the agricultural land in private hands last year produced 48 percent of aggregate agricultural output. In 1990 citrus crops were almost five times more productive in the private sector. Even though they had little land, private producers raised 600,000 of the 1.5 million cows.

Despite the drastic declines in output indicated by official statistics, there has been no widespread starvation or privation. Further,

TABLE 5.3

State/Collective and Private Contributions to Georgian Agriculture

	1989		1990		1991	
	S/C	Private	S/C	Private	S/C	Private
Production (thousand tons)						
Grain	332.2	151.0	519.4	173.7	417.3	113.7
Sugar beets	39.3	0.0	33.6	0.0	17.7	0.0
Sunflower seeds	2.6	0.0	8.6	0.1	0.3	0.1
Potatoes	154.2	148.1	150.6	143.2	102.2	123.5
Vegetables	238.6	276.8	183.6	259.6	130.1	196.5
Fruits	144.3	460.5	119.7	471.5	78.6	340.0
Grapes	303.3	210.3	379.0	312.0	304.5	213.7
Citrus	33.6	60.6	46.7	236.4	45.6	n.a.
Tea	462.4	35.1	465.6	36.1	400.4	n.a.
Beef	174.6	104.0	136.4	125.7	77.4	125.3
Eggs	600.1	260.7	505.8	263.4	354.0	262.9
Milk	300.0	411.4	256.9	402.5	179.3	406.2
Yields (centners per hectare)						
Grain	19.8	28.3	24.3	30.9	18.8	20.6
Sugar beets	284.8	n.a.	252.0	n.a.	153.0	n.a.
Sunflower seeds	1.9	2.3	6.5	7.9	8.7	10.3
Potatoes	114.5	148.6	100.9	1111.0	95.8	98.0
Vegetables	102.9	155.5	85.7	142.8	86.4	128.0
Fruits	34.9	77.3	28.8	77.7	n.a.	n.a.
Grapes	44.3	58.5	57.7	83.6	n.a.	n.a.
Citrus	38.5	70.6	57.2	275.4	50.0	n.a.
Tea	86.8	99.7	89.2	102.5	74.0	n.a.

Source: Chairman Dzandgava, Committee on Social and Economic Indicators, July 3, 1992.

information sampled directly at the bazaar markets paints a picture of a more moderate downturn, especially in agricultural products. Ratios of the real value of selected agricultural products sold in the bazaar market for the first five months of 1991 and 1992 indicate that the availability of foodstuffs in the market has declined, but not to the extent implied by other official statistics. What has declined is the state's share of agricultural production.

It does not take away from the seriousness of Georgia's economic situation to note that part of the free fall in the production statistics in 1992 may be due to nonreporting by private producers or underreporting by state enterprises. It is in the interest of all these to underreport for tax purposes, given the production base of the new tax system. For state enterprises, underreporting would further provide a means to redirect profits from the state to managers or employees. New statistical methods must evolve along with the market economy. Data must be sampled from both private and public production and consumption. Although the economic crisis is real, it may be less severe than indicated by statistics gathered from the state-dominated sector, as individual producers and consumers participate in the private and parallel markets.

Integration with the Rest of the World

The late President Gamsakhurdia and the legislature decided soon after declaring independence not to sign the Union Treaty. At the time, this was a gesture of defiance of the center. But this attitude has carried over until very recently. Georgia remained outside the CIS until the autumn of 1993, despite the demise of the center as it then existed. Georgia's relations with Russia have been troubled, in part because of the perceived support of Russia for secessionist forces in Abkhazia and Ossetia, despite Russian logistical support in putting down the Gamsakhurdia revolt. Georgia was the last of the former Soviet states to establish diplomatic relations with Russia, and the last to sign an economic agreement.

Georgia is also among the last to reach agreement with Russia on its share of the external assets and liabilities of the FSU. When the Soviet Union was dissolved, Georgia inherited claims on both the assets and liabilities of the Soviet Union. The most visible external liability of the Soviet Union was the international debt (said to total $87 billion), while the external assets included diplomatic missions, international banking operations, and foreign exchange reserves. Russia made a "zero option" proposal to the other republics: it would accept responsibility for all international liabilities if it were given undisputed claim to the external assets of the Soviet Union. All former Soviet republics except Ukraine and Georgia accepted the "zero option" quickly. Georgia hesitated for a long time before making the same decision.

The Georgian authorities decided at independence to maintain the use of the ruble as the national currency and maintained this resolve for some time. In April 1993 they introduced a coupon as a supplement to the currency. Only in August 1993 did they break with the ruble zone completely, and then only in response to the Russian central bank's currency reform of July 24, 1993.

The shortage of foreign exchange to use in defense of the new currency has been severe, although by late 1994, Georgia began to receive funds for this purpose from the international financial community. At independence the National Bank of Georgia had no foreign exchange reserves. The local branch of the Foreign Trade Bank had little as well — all foreign exchange transactions under the Soviet Union were undertaken from Moscow. Since independence, few reserves have been accumulated. The Central Bank of Russia in mid-1992 excluded Georgia (and other republics) from access to foreign exchange, despite the nominal existence of the ruble zone. Foreign exchange reserves remained quite low in March 1993, with the bulk of those coming from a foreign exchange tax on visitors to Georgia. The government has introduced a surrender requirement on foreign exchange earnings, but little foreign exchange is collected because of underreporting of export revenues.

Since independence in 1991 trade has slumped. This decline in trade was partly due to the policies of the Georgian government. First, Georgia was the first of the republics to separate unilaterally from the Union in April 1991. This action invited economic retaliation from the rest of the FSU. Second, the Gamsakhurdia government adopted autarkic policies, which further inhibited trade relations in the second half of 1991. Third, shortages of essential imported inputs (such as energy and fertilizers) and disruptions due to the civil conflict (for example, in freight transport) reduced the production and sale of exportables.[6] Fourth, exports were hampered by the imposition of export quotas and licenses that sought to prevent the outflow of goods in response to higher prices outside Georgia. Among factors common across countries, the recession in the neighboring markets reduced demand for Georgian exports. The breakdown in traditional trade and payments arrangements throughout the region was another factor. Georgia's imports also suffered from a severe terms of trade shock as imported energy prices rose manifold during 1992.

The shortfall in imports of energy and the volatility in energy prices during 1991–92 served as a strong inducement to Georgian policy makers to diversify Georgia's sources of imports. Throughout 1992–93, efforts were made to identify alternative sources for supply of oil and gas. Trade agreements were reached with Turkmenistan and Iran for the supply of natural gas. Fuel oil and diesel fuel were imported from Azerbaijan, and electricity from Turkey. Reliance on imports of wheat from Russia was also lessened and alternative suppliers in the EC, Turkey, and Eastern Europe were identified.

DEFINING THE ECONOMIC TRANSITION PROCESS

Georgia began its economic transition as a constituent part of the Soviet Union, functioning within the framework of a command economy and well integrated with the rest of the FSU but very little integrated with the rest of the world. The goal is to emerge as an independent nation-state with a market-based economy that is well integrated into the world trading system. Georgia has made some progress in the transition along each dimension. However, the transition process has been complicated, and sometimes undermined, by the lack of a coherent policy with respect to economic relations with the rest of the world. This, we argue, was due to the apparent belief (in the early months after independence) that political and economic independence meant autarky. Later, even when this narrow notion of independence was abandoned, the exercise of independent economic policies sometimes failed to recognize the interdependence between policies in Georgia and elsewhere, especially in Russia. This provoked a combative approach to international transactions that has led to increased suffering and an isolation from world markets.

We discussed in the preceding section the details of the transition in Georgia. In the institutional transition, Georgia has used the Russian example in establishing the legal structures of a new nation-state. It has also assigned policy making and government regulatory functions to the local offices that were occupied with that policy or regulation within the Soviet system.

In the regulatory transition, Georgia has been more successful than other republics in its privatization of housing and agricultural land, but has proceeded roughly on pace with other former republics in other privatization efforts. The relaxing of market restrictions has also occurred roughly apace with other republics: the salient point here has been the constraint imposed upon the desired autonomy of the Georgian government in this area by market integration with Russia and other former Soviet republics. The policy of price liberalization provides a case in point. The liberalization of prices in Georgia was delayed in the apparent belief within the government of the time that political independence would allow Georgia to follow an independent pricing policy and insulate itself from the price liberalization policy in Russia. This proved not to be the case in practice. When Georgia did not go along with the mid-1991 price increases in the rest of the Soviet Union, this led to a mass outflow of goods, and trade restrictions were imposed to prevent those flows. Then Vice President Tengiz Sigua was highly critical of this strategy. He stated that "Georgia's economic self-blockade — an action that was purely political and unfounded even as a political move — brought 400 million rubles of direct losses in one month. And as for indirect losses, those are in the billions" (Tengiz Sigua, as interviewed in Malkina, 1991). While we can disagree that the action was purely political, the costs (in current rubles of that time) of the assumption of price-setting autonomy are evident. More recently we observe the same goods arbitrage in reverse in the gasoline market, as gasoline flows into Georgia illicitly to earn the higher price set there.

Just as in the case of the market for commodities, Georgia has attempted to implement financial sector and interest rate regulations independently of those in neighboring countries. In an effort to maintain economic activity in Georgia, the NBG has consistently announced interest rates on refinancing credits below the rates charged by the central bank of Russia. Domestic credit also expanded strongly starting in the second half of 1992, based largely on refinance loans from the NBG. These policies were only partly effective due to the interdependence of Georgia and Russia: the low interest rates contributed to financial disintermediation and capital flight, with their attendant costs.

As can be seen from Table 5.4, there is clear indication of a process of disintermediation underway in Georgia.

TABLE 5.4

Financial Disintermediation in Georgia

	12/31/90	12/31/91	5/31/92	11/30/92
Nominal saving deposits[1]	7.65	12.58	13.39	26.77
Nominal time deposits[1]	2.68	6.78	8.65	34.17
Real saving deposits[2]	7.65	5.64	1.13	1.04
Real time deposits[2]	2.68	3.04	0.73	1.33
Saving deposits as % of NMP[3]	70.4	62.2	19.4	18.0
Time deposits as % of NMP[3]	25.0	33.5	22.5	22.9

Source: National Bank of Georgia.

Notes:

[1]Billions of current rubles.

[2]Billions of December 1990 rubles.

[3]NMP (net material product) figures reported by Committee for Social and Economic Information are assumed to reflect the average price index for the year in question. In estimating NMP on the relevant dates, the monthly retail price index is used to deflate the values of NMP reported by the Committee.

The interest rates offered on savings deposits and certificates (of deposit) have been as follows: 4.5 percent in nominal terms in 1991, rising to roughly from 5 to 25 percent in nominal terms by mid-1993. Given the inflation of over 1,500 percent in 1991–1993, the returns on such deposits are strongly negative.[7] In July 1992, the government announced that the value of all accounts held in the savings bank would be doubled in two weeks. The response was dramatic: there was an inflow of cash equivalent to R5 billion, nearly equivalent to the existing stock of deposits. Currency and other savings outflows have apparently occurred to countries with higher interest rates on ruble deposits. This has caused both cash shortages and credit rationing at the controlled rates specified by the government. Restrictions on savings withdrawals designed to conserve currency only increased the speed of this disintermediation and reinforced ruble flight; these restrictions have since been lifted.[8]

In summary, the regulatory transition has occurred in fits and starts, with liberalization followed by imposition of tight controls, because the policy makers ignored the economic interdependence of Georgia with its neighbors. The only way to support independent price and interest rate setting for Georgia is through closure of the economy — and the trade restrictions were evidence that the policy makers were willing to do just that.

The dimension of international orientation has seen the least progress. For the Gamsakhurdia regime, political independence appeared to mean the right (and even the obligation) to contest every international transaction. The decisions taken at that time not to participate in union trading agreements were political in nature, but appeared to have large economic costs. The short-lived decision to reject the "zero option" left unresolved Georgia's relations with international financial institutions and contributed for a time to a reluctance by these institutions to enter into long-term agreements with Georgia. These may have demonstrated Georgia's political clout, but at the cost of disrupting economic activity.

Georgia's relations with its neighbors and the rest of the world have improved considerably under the new regime of Mr. Shevardnadze, and there is a greater recognition of interdependence and the need for cooperation. However, economic policies continue to reflect a tension between the desire for greater autonomy in economic policy making and the constraints on implementing such policies.

This tension is most evident in the question of the currency. Georgia reacted to the distress in the ruble area in an ambivalent way. On the one hand, it recognized its dependence on Russia by choosing not to introduce its own currency. Foreign exchange reserves were almost nonexistent, and the institutions and instruments necessary to manage a new currency were lacking. Although the dependence on the ruble effectively circumscribed Georgia's autonomy in monetary policy, there was a tendency to implement policies that did not fully recognize these constraints. Thus, in an effort to maintain economic activity in Georgia, the NBG announced interest rates on refinancing credits that were consistently below the rates charged by the Central Bank of Russia. There was also the tendency later in the period for Georgia (as did many former Soviet republics) to attempt to manipulate the ruble zone by inflating credit more rapidly than Russia and using the excess to purchase Russian goods. The Russian central bank in response halted its further accumulation of clearing balances in mid-1992; this resulted in trade interruptions, a de facto flexible exchange rate for non-cash rubles, and an unnecessarily sharp contraction in Georgian economic activity.

Georgia's problems with currency shortages have been a symptom of the inconsistency of monetary and credit policies given the international constraints of the monetary regime. Cash has been in short supply to the government because citizens were unwilling to deposit cash in the savings accounts that provide the cash inflow to the banking system. Thus, the disintermediation noted earlier is the mirror image of the cash shortage. Restrictions on savings withdrawals designed to conserve currency only increase the speed of this disintermediation because savings accounts become less liquid.[9] A common monetary system also makes commodity and credit purchases in neighboring countries much easier and this further restricts the supply of cash in circulation.

The National Bank of Georgia chose to solve the currency shortage problem through the issuance of coupons: these were first put into circulation in April 1993. After an initial period of success the coupon rapidly lost value — from an initial parity with the ruble, the coupon by the end of June 1993 traded at five to the ruble on unofficial markets. This creates severe strains on the financial sector. On August 2, 1993, the NBG authorities responded to the currency reform in Russia by breaking the official parity between the ruble and the Georgian coupon — thereafter the exchange rate regime would be flexible for both cash and non-cash transactions.

National Bank authorities had in the past forecast that by mid-summer 1993 the National Bank would introduce a Georgian currency known as the lari; this step is now set to occur in summer 1995. They recognize that international constraints make the introduction of the lari useless until the Georgian fiscal and monetary imbalances have been eliminated.

Premature introduction would be another failure to gauge the constraints due to economic interdependence.

Thus, even as interdependence with other economies was recognized, policies sometimes failed to recognize adequately the constraints imposed by interdependence. Moreover, these policies were at odds with the fundamental economic structure of Georgia, and this has led to costs greater than would otherwise have been incurred. These costs take two forms. First, the inconsistency has led to an outflow of goods and capital from Georgia. This has resulted in shortages (of goods and cash) and led to rationing, with adverse consequences for efficiency. Second, in response to government's efforts to stop this outflow, the private sector has tended to bypass the regulatory and institutional structure of the government entirely. This has led to growth in an underground economy which the government cannot regulate, tax, or even measure. The government's regulatory and institutional structure so recently put in place has become more and more irrelevant, with adverse consequences for the government's ability to implement social and infrastructural policies.

THE STUMBLING BLOCKS FOR
THE REMAINING TRANSITION

We identify three potential stumbling blocks for the next steps in the transition. First, intermittent ethnic conflict and civil unrest in Georgia have contributed to macroeconomic instability and absorbed scarce resources necessary for modernization of the economy. Second, the unstable economic and political situation among neighboring countries will dampen Georgia's economic prospects: the interlinkages are simply too strong. Finally, the transition may be slowed by policies that continue to ignore Georgia's appropriate place in the world trading system.

Domestic conflicts, whether ethnic or political, have imposed various costs on Georgia. First, resources have been used directly in the fighting. These resources (fuel, manpower, transport) could be used more productively in the absence of the conflict. Second, conflict disrupts economic activity where it occurs. One example is the aforementioned fall by one-third in tea production in 1992 compared to 1991, which resulted from the conflict in Abkhazia. The citrus crop was also substantially reduced. Tourism was badly affected in the Black Sea region, depriving Georgia of much-needed foreign exchange. Third, the conflicts disrupted transportation of goods and factors of production. Rail and road transport through Abkhazia and Ossetia were subject to periodic blockades, and port services were disrupted. This affected production in the rest of the country and its capacity to export. Fifth, there are the costs of reconstruction. For example, in 1992 about 8 percent of total planned public investment went toward repairing the buildings in Tbilisi damaged in the fighting in December 1991. The reconstruction of damaged infrastructure such as roads, rail, and ports, constitutes a significant burden. Finally, there is the growing financial burden of refugee resettlement. For example, as early as mid-1992, it was estimated that about $5.5 million would be required to provide for the most elementary needs of the refugees.

The Georgian economy remains highly integrated with that of Russia. Until the Russian economy gets on its feet, those stresses will be transmitted to Georgia as well. Political independence does not shelter the Georgian economy from such strains. Weak economic recovery in Russia would adversely affect Georgia in at least two ways. First, Russia has traditionally been the largest market for Georgian products. In 1991, almost 67 percent of Georgia's exports to the FSU went to Russia alone. If the Russian economy stagnates, the demand for Georgian products will remain low and thwart export-led recovery in Georgia. Second, Georgia relies heavily on Russia for imports of critical inputs such as energy and fertilizers. Until 1992, virtually all crude oil and oil products as well as natural gas were imported from Russia. Although Georgia has succeeded to some extent in diversifying its energy suppliers, its access to critical imports will be adversely affected if the Russian economy continues to perform poorly. Shortfalls in imported inputs will slow output recovery in Georgia.

Developments in Russia are likely to affect Georgia in other ways as well. Just as a favorable climate for market-oriented transformation within Russia will have a strong positive demonstration effect in Georgia, a shift to conservative policies could slow down the momentum for reforms in Georgia. Moreover, political developments in Russia influence Russia's support for separatist factions within Georgia and thus have a direct bearing on the continuation of ethnic conflict.

Georgia is a small country, suitably located for trade, and blessed with old trading traditions. Under these conditions, there are costs to a repudiation of Georgia's comparative advantage. These costs include the foregone gains from trade in Georgia's comparative-advantage goods; but they also include the costs in terms of resource outflows due to policies undertaken that are inconsistent with the policies of larger neighbors. The pricing controls of 1991 and 1992 are illustrative of the dislocations possible when such international constraints are ignored. Political and economic independence need not imply economic insularity: the European Community is a good example of a meshing of the two.

NOTES

The views presented here are those of the authors and do not imply any policy or judgment on the part of the World Bank. The statistical information contained in this report is drawn from the authors' research on and visits to Georgia. If not otherwise cited, it can be found in Conway (1993) and World Bank (1993). Figures from mid-1993 are drawn from periodic reports of the Committee on Social and Economic Information of the Republic of Georgia.

1. Alexander Rondeli of Tbilisi State University put it well: "Georgia is condemned to be an open economy" (from private discussions, March 11, 1993, Tbilisi).

2. According to preliminary estimates of the World Bank, Georgia's per capita GDP in 1991 exceeded only that of the Kyrgyz Republic, Uzbekistan, and Tadzhikistan among the FSU republics.

3. According to some estimates, Georgia's terms of trade would deteriorate by more than 20 percent if its imports and exports were valued at international prices.

4. The import price of crude oil had increased from R82 per ton in 1990 to R4,000 by mid-1992. That for natural gas had increased from R42 per thousand cubic meters to R1,710 in the same period. Retail prices had increased by 14 times over the same period.

5. In contrast, in the period January–June 1992, domestic credit to the government rose marginally, from R13.9 billion to R16.2 billion. Credit to the nonfinancial public enterprises increased by 97 percent.

6. For example, imports of natural gas were reduced from 5.5 billion cubic meters in 1990 to 4.6 billion in 1991 due to a blockade of gas to Georgia. Imports of fuel oil from Russia also fell from 2,743 million tons in 1990, to 1,652 million tons in 1991, and to only 300,000 tons in 1992.

7. Given the shortage of consumer goods, however, the proper comparison may be with the return on holding currency — which is even more negative in real terms. However, savings accounts are much less liquid than currency.

8. NBG issued its first directive to limit cash withdrawals on September 1, 1991. Another issued June 1, 1992, allowed cooperatives and nongovernmental enterprises to withdraw in currency only that component of their accounts deposited in currency after April 1. There were no NBG limits on withdrawals in currency by state enterprises; the ministries police those withdrawals themselves. Citizens with accounts at the savings bank could withdraw from their accounts only the portion due to current wage and pension payments deposited directly at the bank by the employer.

9. This disintermediation may in fact cause ruble flight if other countries (e.g., Russia) have more attractive financial instruments for savers.

REFERENCES

Conway, Patrick J. "Rubles, Rubles Everywhere: Cash Shortages and Financial Disintermediation in the Ruble Monetary Union." 1993 (mimeo).

GOSKOMSTAT/SSSR. *Narodnoe khozyaystvo SSSR v 1990 g.* Moscow: Finansy i statistika, 1991.

Malkina, Tatyana. *Nezavisimaya Gazeta.* September 26, 1991, p. 8. Reprinted in English in "I Fell Into a Demagogue's Trap: Tengiz Sigua, Former Prime Minister of Georgia, Assesses His Relations with the Republic's President." *Current Digest of the Soviet Press* 43, 39 (October 30, 1991): 12–13.

[World Bank.] "Georgia From Crisis to Recovery: A Blueprint for Reforms." Country Economic Memorandum no. 11275-GZ. Washington, DC: World Bank, 1993.

II

FORMER YUGOSLAV
REPUBLICS

6

Book title:

Slovenia

Evan Kraft, Milan Vodopivec, and Milan Cvikl

INTRODUCTION

Slovenia, the richest republic of the Socialist Federal Republic of Yugoslavia, went its own way in the 1980s, removing such onerous vestiges of communist rule as censorship, prosecution for speech crimes, and effective prohibition of the organization of independent groups. Slovenia's reform effort, among the longest and deepest in any communist nation, exposed differences with other Yugoslav republics and the League of Communists of Yugoslavia. Yet, throughout the 1980s, independence was not widely embraced as the solution to Slovenia's conflicts with the rest of Yugoslavia; widespread support for independence only materialized at the beginning of the 1990s.[1]

With the election of a noncommunist, center-right government in 1990, Slovenia began its drive to independence. Among the chief steps toward achieving independence were the December 1990 referendum on independence, which was passed with 90 percent approval; the declaration of independence of June 26, 1991, followed by ten days of hostilities between the Yugoslav army and Slovenian forces; the withdrawal of the Yugoslav army in late summer and early fall; and the effective implementation of Slovenian independence on October 8, 1991. Other notable milestones were the introduction of the national currency in October 1991 and the recognition of Slovenia by the European Community in January 1992. In contrast with other successor states of former

Yugoslavia (except Macedonia), Slovenia's independence was achieved virtually without a scar.

But what are the economic consequences of Slovenia's separation? Is Slovenia a viable country? Will Slovenes live better after separation? The purpose of this chapter is to answer these questions. We focus on issues brought about by the separation per se (and that would not have arisen had Slovenia not separated from Yugoslavia). These are distinguished as much as possible from the issues that are typically associated with the transition to a market economy. We argue that due to the fall in trade with the rest of former Yugoslavia, Slovenia will suffer in the short run, but by enhancing macroeconomic stability, avoiding subsidization of the less-developed regions of Yugoslavia, and speeding up the process of integration with Western Europe, it is likely to profit from the separation in the medium and long run.

After a brief examination of the macroeconomic and institutional background in the next section, we discuss Slovenia's economic record after separation in the third section. The fourth section focuses on the stabilization effort, while the fifth deals with restructuring experiences (privatization, bank restructuring, and labor market reform). We conclude with an assessment of Slovenia's economic prospects as an independent nation, and of the extent to which Slovenia's experience is generalizable.

MACROECONOMIC BACKGROUND

After a period of steady growth in the 1970s and stagnation during the 1980s, Slovenian GDP fell sharply at the beginning of the 1990s. The fall was the result of disinflationary policies, enterprise restructuring in response to changes in relative prices, and a collapse in trade within former Yugoslavia and between the former socialist economies.

As a part of Yugoslavia, Slovenia's economy became increasingly unstable during the 1980s. Inflation steadily increased and by 1989 the country was experiencing full-fledged hyperinflation. The federal stabilization program of 1990 was initially successful in reducing inflation, but the centrifugal forces unleashed by the first free elections at the republic level undermined the fiscal and monetary discipline needed for the program to succeed in the longer run (see Pleskovič and Sachs, 1994). The result was a new inflationary cycle in 1991, and steep declines in GDP in both 1990 and 1991 (see Table 6.1).

Since achieving independence in October 1991, Slovenia has brought inflation under control. Inflation was reduced from a monthly rate of 18 percent in the final quarter of 1991 to an annual rate of 22.9 percent in 1993 (on a December-to-December basis). Moreover, Slovenia has been running a foreign trade surplus throughout the 1990s and has in the process accumulated considerable foreign exchange reserves. These positive outcomes are the fruit of a timely and consistent stabilization program consisting of the successful introduction of a new currency (the tolar) at an exchange rate reflecting a devaluation relative to the rate for the Yugoslav dinar at the time; restrictive monetary policy; an effective incomes policy (which helped reduce the average real wage); and the running of a budget surplus in both 1991 and 1992.

But Slovenia — along with other transitional economies — has paid a high price for its achievements in macroeconomic stabilization and in restructuring according to the dictates of the transition to a market economy. From its peak in 1987 until the end of 1993, employment had been reduced by more than 17 percent; the unemployment rate had increased from a mere 1.8 percent to a worrisome 15.0 percent. In 1993, however, the fall of production was arrested, and there were signs that recovery was underway — real GDP grew at annual rates of 0.6 percent, 2.1 percent, and 2.5 percent, respectively, in the final three quarters of 1993, and 1.3 percent for the year as a whole (Bank of Slovenia, February 1994).

Although the Slovenian government has been able to implement a reasonably effective set of macroeconomic policies, it had more difficulty enacting privatization legislation and is having even more difficulty implementing it. After a two-year delay, Slovenia finally passed a privatization law in November 1992; the implementation of this law has run into considerable bottlenecks. The process of enterprise privatization, particularly the privatization of small and medium-sized enterprises, thus lags that in many other transitional economies. This undoubtedly has had a deleterious impact on economic growth, not least because of the associated disincentives for both domestic and foreign investment. Slovenia's progress on bank restructuring, which began in 1993, however, should help the privatization and restructuring process considerably.

To put Slovenia's transition to date in perspective, it is useful to compare Slovenia's macroeconomic performance to that of some other transitional economies. As shown in Table 6.2, Slovenia's record to date — at least in terms of output decline and increase in unemployment — is quite similar to what has occurred in other countries undergoing similar processes.

TABLE 6.1
Main Slovenian Economic Indicators, 1986–1993

| | Industrial Production[2] | Retail Prices[3] | Real Net Wages[2] | Unemployment Rate[5] | Balance of Payments[1] | | | M1[3] | M3[3,4] |
					Current Account Balance	Long-Term Capital[6]	Change in Official For. Reserves		
1988	-2.6	212.3	-10.6	2.2	1,364.5	35.4	n.a.	n.a.	n.a.
1989	1.1	1306.0	15.5	2.9	1,084.9	25.8	n.a.	n.a.	n.a.
1990	-10.5	549.7	-25.9	4.7	526.2	123.9	n.a.	n.a.	n.a.
1991	-12.4	117.7	-10.9	8.2	190.4	-23.8	-112.1	n.a.	n.a.
1991:9	-11.2	17.0	-20.4	9.0	-13.0	-17.6	0.0	n.a.	n.a.
1991:10	-17.0	21.5	-24.3	9.4	56.5	-11.5	-15.8	13.3	6.1
1991:11	-15.8	18.7	-27.3	9.9	0.9	0.5	-29.7	-1.6	7.1
1991:12	-18.7	15.4	-31.6	10.1	46.4	9.9	-66.8	16.5	16.7
1992	-13.2	201.3	-8.9	11.6	764.3	108.8	-603.4	100.7	132.3
1992:1	-17.6	15.2	-34.3	10.5	134.9	0.7	-12.5	-0.5	4.0
1992:2	-11.8	11.0	-30.0	10.7	112.1	-2.2	-33.9	6.2	17.1
1992:3	-11.4	11.5	-24.8	10.7	137.0	-10.7	-48.2	-0.6	8.6
1992:4	-21.0	5.1	-25.4	10.8	53.8	13.7	-40.1	17.7	8.9
1992:5	-19.6	6.5	-14.6	10.9	56.6	20.3	-64.0	-3.2	4.0
1992:6	-14.3	5.9	-9.2	11.1	58.5	-21.9	-110.5	4.9	4.5
1992:7	-8.7	2.0	-5.9	11.5	36.7	19.6	-145.7	6.1	8.1
1992:8	-19.0	1.4	-1.2	11.7	90.3	63.1	-92.1	13.0	6.8
1992:9	-13.4	2.7	3.2	12.2	177.4	-19.6	-43.2	5.0	7.4
1992:10	-9.8	3.4	10.6	12.7	62.9	36.9	-10.5	5.4	5.5
1992:11	-6.1	2.8	18.5	12.8	10.5	19.2	-8.4	2.9	4.0
1992:12	-1.0	1.1	29.6	13.4	1.1	-16.8	5.5	17.1	9.1

142

| 1993 | −2.8 | 32.3 | 16.4 | 14.5 | 200.7 | 214.3 | −54.5 | 43.7 | 72 |

Source: Bank of Slovenia (1992, 1993, 1994).

Notes:
[1]U.S.$ million.
[2]Annual growth rate for years, annualized growth rate for months.
[3]Annual growth rate for years, monthly growth rate for months.
[4]A measure that includes all demand, time, and foreign exchange deposits.
[5]Percentage of economically active population.
[6]Direct investment, portfolio investment, and other long-term capital flows, net, excluding central bank activity.

143

TABLE 6.2

**Economic Developments in Slovenia and
Other Transitional Economies (percentages)**

	Drop in GDP	Unemployment rate	
	1989–1992	January 1990	December 1992
Slovenia	24.1	4.0	12.5
Bulgaria	28.0	0.1	14.8
Czech Republic	21.2	0.1	2.5
Hungary	18.4	1.0	12.0
Poland	17.4	0.3	13.6
Romania	31.7	0.2	8.5
Slovakia	23.5	0.1	10.0

Sources: PlanEcon (1992); World Bank (1993).

STABILIZATION EXPERIENCES

Successful Price Stabilization

In contrast to the unsuccessful stabilization attempts of the federal Yugoslav authorities, Slovenia had by and large brought inflation under control by the fall of 1992.[2] Perhaps the key was the monetary policy of the Bank of Slovenia (BoS). The BoS policy, the exact opposite of the redistributive and expansionary monetary policy of the National Bank of Yugoslavia (NBY), strengthened the soundness and stability of the new currency.

Monetary policy was supported by a market-determined exchange rate policy, which resulted in a build-up of Slovenia's international reserves.[3] However, only in the summer of 1992, with the advent of a new government, was restrictive monetary policy supported by stabilization-oriented fiscal policies as well.

Table 6.1 above shows the main contours of Slovenia's attainment of macroeconomic stability. In the sections below, we outline the new macroeconomic policies and institutions, especially in the monetary sphere, that facilitated this achievement.

The Introduction of a New Currency and the Achievement of Economic Control

To assert its economic self-determination, independent Slovenia needed to gain control of fiscal and monetary policy. Fiscal control proved easier, because, like other regions in former Yugoslavia, the fiscal system and fiscal policy had been for the most part under the control of the Slovenian authorities since the constitutional reform of 1974.[4] To gain full control, Slovenia simply stopped paying taxes to the federal government and took over the customs facilities.

Slovenia began its push for monetary control in the fall of 1990 by (re)drafting the laws regulating the financial system. This legislation included the Law on the Bank of Slovenia, the Banking Law, and laws regulating bank supervision, bank liquidation, deposit insurance, international credit relations, and customs. With the exception of the Banking Law, the financial laws are similar in instrument design and institutional set-up to the old federal Yugoslav financial laws, as amended on the federal level in the late 1980s.[5] However, in order to avoid repeating Yugoslavia's experience — a central bank persistently pursuing an expansionary monetary policy — the Banking Law gave the BoS full independence in conducting such policy. This proved crucial in implementing macroeconomic stabilization policies after October 1991.

These financial laws were passed in June 1991, together with the declaration of Slovenian independence. Their implementation was temporarily suspended due to the outbreak of the war and the subsequent Brioni Accord, which froze further moves toward independence for a period of three months.

The introduction of a new currency became imperative once the NBY's monetary policy became totally subservient to Serbia's need to finance its military activity. The main impetus for implementing currency reform was thus to prevent the republic from being sucked into the inflationary spiral that characterized the dinar monetary zone.

The currency was named the tolar (abbreviated as SIT). It was decided to declare the coupons that had already been printed (in fact a full year in advance) preliminary tolar banknotes until the introduction of the real tolar banknotes, and to exchange the coupons for Yugoslav dinari (YUD) at one-to-one.

The currency exchange followed immediately. The Parliament's decision was communicated on the same night to all Slovenian commercial banks and postal savings banks. The next day, Tuesday, October 8, 1991, was declared a bank holiday in order to prepare for the currency exchange at the commercial bank level. From Wednesday, October 9, until Friday, October 11, all commercial banks in Slovenia stayed open from 7 A.M. until 9 P.M. to permit the public to exchange its dinar cash for tolars (coupons).

During these three days the BoS guaranteed an exchange rate of one tolar for one dinar. After that the tolar started to float, and appreciated immediately by 25 percent to the rate of 1 YUD for 0.8 tolar. During the exchange period, the Yugoslav dinar remained legal tender alongside the tolar, both in cash and in check form, to smooth daily transactions. To prevent a large influx of dinars from elsewhere in Yugoslavia, strict border controls were instituted and conversion was, in principle, limited to residents. The authorities wished to prevent a large tolar flow to non-residents so as to minimize destabilizing return flows and speculation.

Upon presentation of their identity cards, residents were able to exchange up to 20,000 YUD, equal to about $370. Cash in excess of 20,000 YUD but less than 50,000 YUD was exchanged by crediting the tolars to the owner's current account or savings account. Persons wanting to convert more than 50,000 YUD in cash, in principle, had to explain the origin of their cash. After the exchange process was completed, the BoS exchanged dinars with members of the public only if they had exceptionally good reasons for doing so. The public acceptance of the tolar was very good, and during three days of exchange, the BoS via the commercial banks (and the social accountancy offices in 14 Slovenia cities) took out of circulation about 8.6 billion YUD or 4,000 YUD per head, the equivalent of about $75.

Bank deposits were automatically converted into tolars. Financial contracts were left untouched by the conversion, since Slovenian law stipulates that contracts may be written in any currency. External payments with former Yugoslav regions required new arrangements, which were concluded in the ensuing month.

Fiscal Reform

In early 1991, Slovenia put its public finances on a comparable footing with those of the developed market economies. The system of direct taxation was revised and the number of taxes and contributions was drastically reduced. Slovenia introduced corporate profit and personal income taxes, while social security contributions paid by employers and employees were retained only for pension and disability insurance and health and unemployment insurance.

During 1991, the inflationary erosion of the value of collected revenues and arrears from enterprises hurt by the collapse of trade with the
rest of former Yugoslavia put revenue collection well below target.
Government expenditures were also cut significantly in real terms, and
government wages were frozen. Public expenditure was reduced to 43.2
percent of GDP in 1991, in comparison with 48.9 percent in 1990. Most
of the reduction came from reducing Slovenia's contribution to the
Yugoslav federal government budget to 0.9 percent of GDP in 1991 from
7.2 percent in 1990.

The government achieved a surplus of 2.6 percent of GDP in 1991,[6]
and 0.3 percent in 1992. However, the 1991 budget did not include
provisions for enterprise and bank restructuring, and the substantial
liability represented by frozen foreign exchange deposits was not properly taken into account. In the summer of 1992, the new government
attempted to address restructuring issues by earmarking funds for loss
makers and cutting other current expenditures. The government also
improved its cost management. These measures, along with the continuing restrictive monetary policy, brought retail price inflation in August
1992 to a monthly rate of 1.4 percent.

Restrictive Monetary Policy

The success of macroeconomic stabilization in independent Slovenia
can be largely attributed to smooth currency introduction and restrictive
monetary policy, both the result of the efforts of the BoS. The BoS's
consistently restrictive monetary policy during the first independent year
represented a genuine change from the NBY's redistributive and expansionary manner of conducting such policy.

Table 6.1 illustrates the tightness of monetary policy after independence. M1 actually shrank in nominal terms in the first full month
(November 1991) after monetary independence. M2 growth has also
generally been moderate, as has the growth of foreign liabilities.

A crucial factor enabling the pursuit of a restrictive monetary policy
was central bank independence, as established by the Law on the Bank
of Slovenia. The law mandates that the BoS alone may execute monetary
policy, free from political interference. Price stability and smoothly
functioning domestic and international payments are its only objectives.
The most important provisions of the Slovenian law that distinguish it
from that governing the NBY concern the independence of the BoS's
supreme bodies, the BoS's relationship with the government, and the role
of indirect monetary instruments.

The governor and the members of the board may not be connected with the government or any organization controlled by the BoS. The board consists of the governor, deputy governor, three vice governors, and six independent experts, all appointed by Parliament for six years. The governor and six independent experts are nominated by the president, while the governor in turn nominates the deputy governor and vice governors.

By contrast, the board of the National Bank of Yugoslavia consisted of the eight governors of the national banks of the regions (i.e., the six republics and two autonomous provinces), and the governor of the NBY. Only the governor of the NBY was elected on the federal level, while the other governors were elected by the regions' parliaments, and thus represented regional interests. Legislation passed in 1974 provided that the NBY board should vote by consensus to prevent excessive republican influence. The consensus vote was soon (in the inflationary 1980s) replaced by ordinary majority vote to accommodate the economic interests of less-developed regions and Serbia, which effectively controlled the NBY apparatus (see Cvikl, 1990).

In order to reduce direct financing of the budget deficit, the law allows the BoS to extend only short-term loans to the government for bridging cash flow problems. The stock of these loans may exceed neither 5 percent of the current budget nor 20 percent of the budget deficit.

Yugoslav legislation required a balanced federal budget, and, in principle, excluded the possibility of direct budget financing by the central bank. However, indirect budget financing through quasi-fiscal deficits was widely practiced (Rocha and Saldanha, 1992).

To enhance the effectiveness of monetary policy, the law allows the BoS to employ all commonly used monetary instruments, including a variety of open market operations that exert impact through interest rates. Although the NBY enjoyed similar provisions, it preferred direct instruments such as selective credits and credit control. The Law on the BoS totally excludes the use of selective credits, and prohibits the use of other direct credit controls after December 31, 1993. These measures underscore the authorities' commitment to the use of indirect monetary control.[7]

A Market-Determined Exchange Rate

The objectives of Slovenian exchange rate policy are to reinforce macroeconomic stabilization, to promote economic integration with the West, and to make the tolar completely convertible while pegged to the

Deutsche mark. The main vehicle for achieving this was the market-determined exchange rate for the tolar. This contrasts sharply with the administrative regulation of dinar exchange rates in the 1970s and 1980s.

The tolar is expected to derive its strength from strict macroeconomic policies and a healthy balance of payments. At the time of currency introduction, Slovenia was not a member of international organizations and was not about to receive any financial support. Since the country's level of net international reserves was low — at the end of September 1991 reserves in the banking system only amounted to $204 million, and the BoS had literally no reserves — a floating exchange rate was introduced, with some exchange restrictions imposed to protect reserves.[8]

One important exchange restriction was the freezing of foreign exchange deposits. This control was partly lifted later, as Slovenia's reserves grew. However, deposits will only be completely unfrozen after Yugoslavia's foreign exchange claims and liabilities are settled, as a component of the restructuring of bank and enterprise ownership.

Importantly, banks cover exchange risk by extending domestic credit in foreign exchange, and not by general BoS guarantee. Such a guarantee was the main source of NBY losses in the 1980s, coming to be known as the "black hole."

TRANSITION EXPERIENCES:
PRIVATIZATION AND RESTRUCTURING

While Slovenia has been a path breaker in its rapid and successful currency reform and macroeconomic stabilization, restructuring started out very slowly. In particular, ownership change was mired for years in legislative disputes. Serious progress only took place during 1994. Financial sector restructuring, on the other hand, began in 1993 and has shown some positive results. Labor market institutions are also still in flux.

Privatization Policy

Slovenia began slowly on privatization. Whereas other ex-communist states moved rapidly to privatize small enterprises, Slovenia decided not to privatize small enterprises separately.

No less than three privatization bills were considered by the Parliament of Slovenia. The two failed bills represented divergent approaches: one favored internal privatization through worker-manager buyouts, and the other external privatization through distribution of shares to citizens and pension funds, coupled with the establishment of mutual funds. The latter approach is similar to the method used in the former Czechoslovakia, Russia, and Poland.

The first bill, drafted by Economics Minister Jože Mencinger in early 1991, embodied an internal privatization approach. It was denounced by Harvard professor Jeffrey Sachs, who, somewhat strangely, was invited by the prime minister to oppose the government's proposed law (Rus, 1994). Sachs argued that the plan unfairly benefited existing managers, was open to speculation due to the impossibility of accurate evaluation in the absence of functioning capital markets, and failed to fit the circumstances of large, capital-intensive, and expensive enterprises (Pleskovič and Sachs, 1994).

Defenders of internal privatization argued that Slovenian managers are not typical of managers in communist countries. Many are highly capable, and quite familiar with management in a market milieu. Furthermore, Slovenian workers may have taken advantage of self-management structures to achieve a degree of participation in management. Insider privatization therefore makes sense in Slovenia, they argue, as a way of utilizing workers' and managers' firm-specific knowledge and of nurturing the efficiency advantages of worker participation (Štiblar, 1992).

After a bill reflecting the external approach was defeated in early 1992, a compromise bill combining the approaches was finally passed in November 1992. The bill allows for three methods: sale of the whole enterprise, employee purchase, and the transfer of shares. The last of these approaches requires that 10 percent of the book value of social capital be distributed as shares to the Slovenian Pension and Invalid Fund, 10 percent to the Compensation Fund, 20 percent to authorized investment companies, 20 percent to employees, and 40 percent to the population at large.

The method of privatization is chosen by the individual company, subject to the approval of the Agency for Privatization of the Republic of Slovenia. It is hoped that this framework will prove flexible yet simple enough to facilitate rapid privatization. However, continued wrangling over the status of enterprises "spontaneously" privatized prevented the implementation of the law through 1993. Implementation required the passage of further enabling laws and regulations, which caused considerable controversy. Between November 1992 and October 1993, only 42 companies presented privatization proposals to the Agency for Privatization, and these companies were of minimal economic significance.

Privatization Experience

Despite the legislative impasse, privatization in Slovenia, like a force of nature, cannot be completely stopped. While 96.4 percent of the total capital stock in manufacturing was socially owned in 1989, only 76.1 percent was so owned in 1992, according to Social Accounting Service data. Before 1994, the advance of privatization took place in the following ways:[9]

(1) *Employee buy outs*: These occurred via two methods, the "asset drop" and the "net worth transfer." An "asset drop" is effectuated when enterprises are transformed into a holding company, and assets, workers, and operations are transferred to a newly created subsidiary. The subsidiary is then sold to the employees. The parent emerges as a purely financial institution.

With the "net worth transfer," the social enterprise transfers its equity to a newly created enterprise in which it holds preferred shares. New common shares are issued to insiders, giving them control of the newly created but only slightly transformed firm.

While ingenious and convenient, these techniques were developed with little regulatory or legal supervision (Korže and Simonetti, 1993). They have been at the heart of continued political controversy over the ethics and fairness of various methods of privatization.

(2) *Direct sales and joint ventures*: This method has mainly been used in transactions with foreign buyers. Direct sales and joint ventures are initiated by enterprises themselves, but must be approved by the Privatization Agency. Proceeds from direct sales go to the Privatization Fund, which may reinvest part of the money in the form of a long-term loan or purchase a block of preferred shares. Joint ventures are usually new companies, with foreigners holding the majority of the shares.

Slovenia has managed greatly to increase the inflow of foreign investment in recent years. Direct foreign investment roughly tripled in value between 1989 and 1990, and grew another 40 percent in 1991 despite the war (Ministry of Finance, 1992). Although most of these investments are small, they seem a hopeful portent of things to come. Leading European companies now involved in Slovenia include Siemens, Renault, and Henkel, and three major Austrian banks, including Creditanstalt, are represented as well.

(3) *Privatization through bankruptcy*: As a result of debt-equity swaps, enterprises that emerge from bankruptcy procedures are typically owned by their former creditors, which above all are banks.

(4) *Quasi-privatization*: Through cross-ownership, socially owned enterprises have created new enterprises as subsidiaries. Even where these companies have not become majority private-owned, they have become "less social" and more subject to control by management.

(5) *Start-ups of new companies*: The number of registered commercial companies roughly tripled between 1989 and 1991. Private sector employment increased by 4 percent, and self-employment by 8.1 percent, in 1992 (Pleskovič and Sachs, 1994).[10] Thus, despite Slovenia's inability to implement large-scale privatization, a considerable amount of enterprise transformation has taken place.

Financial System Rehabilitation

Financial system rehabilitation has been recognized as a key to the transition to market economy. Functioning capital markets play a crucial role in the allocation and mobilization of resources. Moreover, banks are pivotal to the rehabilitation of enterprises, especially those in which they have large holdings.

The main weaknesses of the Slovenian banking system were inherited from the old Yugoslavia. One bank, the Ljubljanska Banka, played a dominant role. Also, Slovenian banks were owned by social sector (productive) enterprises, which had their representatives sitting on bank boards. But, at the same time, these enterprises are the bank's major debtors. The negative implications of this kind of cross-ownership were abundantly evident in the former Yugoslavia, as well as in such other countries as Chile in the early 1980s (Díaz-Alejandro, 1985).

In addition, Slovenian banks have a very high proportion of non-performing loans in their portfolios (30–40 percent). The bad debt problem was greatly exacerbated by the enormous payments problems generated by the rapid collapse of Slovenia's markets in the ex-Yugoslav republics in late 1991 and 1992. Much of the impact of this disintegration was crystallized in the financial system.

Slovenia has made a start in dealing with these problems, auditing banks in 1991 and establishing a Bank Restructuring Agency (BRA) in the fall of that year. In late 1992, the rehabilitation of Ljubljanska Banka was announced. The BRA exchanged 30-year bonds, denominated in Deutsche marks and yielding 8 percent interest, for most of Ljubljanska Banka's bad assets. These included not only loans to Slovenian enterprises, but also loans and guarantees to banks in other former republics, as well as claims on the NBY.

Similar operations were undertaken at two other banks in early 1993. Unfortunately, the exchange of bonds for bad assets is only the beginning of rehabilitation, for it leaves the banks without adequate liquidity. In addition, a certain amount of bad loans were left on the banks' books because of a lack of funds. The process of rehabilitating and privatizing Slovenian banks will last for a minimum of two to three more years, and the initial cost of DM 2.2 billion can be expected to rise.

Slovenia has taken a rather centralized approach to financial sector reform. Banks under rehabilitation actually revert to government ownership, with a management team appointed by the BoS. While under rehabilitation, banks' actions are subject to veto by the head of the BRA, and banks' liquidity position is very much in the hands of the BoS.

In the summer of 1993, a coordinating body (the Bank Rehabilitation Oversight Board) was created, including representatives of the BoS, Ministry of Industry, Privatization Agency, Committee for Credit and Monetary Policy, and the Minister of Finance as chairman of the group. The creation of the Oversight Board is meant to avoid the conflicts in policy that had been cropping up between the BRA and the Privatization Agency, with the latter advocating debt write-offs and debt-equity swaps to shore up struggling enterprises, and the former opposing such moves as contrary to the interests of the troubled banks.

Progress on bank reform in 1993 deserves a positive assessment. Ljubljanska Banka's business results in the second half of 1993 were good. It is hoped that the other two banks under rehabilitation will emerge as strong competitors to Ljubljanska Banka. Along with two or three other major banks, at least one of which is expected to be foreign, these banks will be the main ones operating in Slovenia. The BoS has announced new, higher capital requirements, which will enhance the consolidation process. Chances for a vigorous, competitive banking industry seem reasonably good.

Labor Market Legislation and Practices

As a part of the comprehensive economic transformation toward a market economy, the Slovenian labor market has undergone major changes. Above all, workers can be laid off, and thus the Rubicon of unlimited job security has been crossed. Labor mobility has also been enhanced by legislation mandating more flexible hiring practices. The rigid system of wage determination that prevailed under self-management has been replaced by collective bargaining, and active labor market policies, including training of the unemployed. Employment subsidy programs, public employment programs, and efforts to stimulate self-employment of the unemployed have been instituted.[11]

However, the last major legal improvement to the functioning of the labor market occurred in February 1991, when the required advance notification period for redundant workers was reduced from 24 to 6 months. What is more, as an independent country, Slovenia has made two moves that will hurt the economy in the longer run. In July 1991, following the fighting with the Yugoslav army in June and the pending loss of the Yugoslav market, Parliament halted new initiations of bankruptcy procedures, and the Ministry of Labor began providing employment subsidies to those enterprises unable to meet wage payments — no doubt, a bad industrial policy.

Moreover, at least through summer 1993, there was a lack of trust and coordination between the two major institutional players in collective bargaining (the government and the trade unions), resulting in the suspension of incomes policy in February 1992. By August 1992, the total wage bill had increased by 40.2 percent in real terms,[12] seriously threatening to fuel inflation. In January 1993, an extremely restrictive indexation scheme, amounting to a virtual wage freeze in the nongovernment sector (and an explicit wage freeze in the government sector) was imposed for six months. These actions, along with government intransigence toward the demands of teachers and farmers in summer 1993, contributed to an atmosphere of distrust between the authorities and the labor movement. Establishment of a more harmonious labor-management atmosphere was left for future governments.

The scope of the changes in the Slovenian labor market can be seen from the results of a study by Abraham and Vodopivec (1993), which employed two data sets: one on employment histories and another on unemployment spells that began between December 31, 1986, and April 1993. The main changes observed are the following:

(1) Both young and old workers have been disproportionately affected, with youth being frozen out of jobs and the elderly pushed into early retirement or, having lost jobs, increasingly unable to find new ones.

(2) The relative advantage enjoyed by highly educated workers has increased, reflecting the end of the wage compression that characterized self-management and the beginning of the larger wage differentials expected in a market economy.

(3) Women have been no more likely to be laid off than men and when unemployed encounter no more difficulty than men in finding jobs.

(4) Ethnic minorities have experienced growing job-to-unemployment and

job-to-out-of-the-labor-force rates, probably the result of increased discrimination.

SLOVENIA'S ECONOMIC PROSPECTS
AS AN INDEPENDENT NATION

The Status-Quo Ante: Slovenia and ex-Yugoslavia

Before evaluating Slovenia's experiences as an independent nation, it is useful to look briefly at Slovenia's relationship to the Yugoslav Federation before independence. Three factors can be singled out as having the most important influence on the fate of independent Slovenia:[13]

(1) More-developed regions (MDRs) of Yugoslavia heavily subsidized less-developed regions (LDRs), and, moreover, Slovenia was the region that was (at least in the 1980s) drained the most.
(2) Yugoslavia was continually plagued by macroeconomic instability, in part because of subsidization of less-developed regions and poorly performing enterprises.
(3) Due to the disintegrative tendencies within Yugoslavia, the production structures of its constituent regions were much less influenced by being a part of a larger entity than were the production structures of former Soviet republics.

These factors form the basis for our conclusion that Slovenia may achieve positive net benefits to leaving Yugoslavia.

The Costs of Separation

While Slovenia may well benefit in the long run from its separation from Yugoslavia, in the short run there are obvious and significant costs.[14] These include: the cost of reorienting trade; growth of autarkic tendencies; the danger of "germanization"; heightened perception of political risk in Slovenia due to the wars; and such spillovers from war-torn republics as the refugee problem.

The cost of reorienting trade has already proven significant. In 1987, 35.7 percent of Slovenia's deliveries went to the rest of Yugoslavia. The wars have at least temporarily disrupted this trade. In addition, the former Yugoslav states have erected trade barriers with each other, and most have nonconvertible currencies. Even Slovenia and Croatia now levy tariffs on each other's goods, making trade diversion a problem. Therefore, in the medium term, much of Slovenia's trade with the old Yugoslavia will have to be reoriented.

The costs of reorientation go well beyond the search costs of finding new customers. Slovenian producers had many advantages within the Yugoslav market: knowledge of the market, customers' familiarity with Slovenian goods, and superior productivity and quality relative to other Yugoslav producers. The international market is far more difficult to penetrate and profit margins are probably lower than on the old Yugoslav market.

In addition, the Yugoslav market provided a wider platform for Slovenian producers than the Slovenian market. Scale economies may be lost in the process of trade reorientation, especially if Slovenian producers are unable to redirect all of their lost sales on the Yugoslav market to third markets. Also, innovation and introduction of new products, which is generally done on the producers' home market, will be more difficult with a smaller market.

Finally, the loss of the Yugoslav market and of most of the assets that Slovenian firms possessed in other Yugoslav republics has greatly increased these firms' liquidity problems, and correspondingly the difficulties of Slovenian banks. A particularly troublesome problem here is the loss of Slovenian claims on the NBY. The rehabilitation of the banking system would not have been nearly such a big problem if Yugoslavia had not gone out of existence.

The impact of these phenomena is somewhat alleviated by the high degree of disintegration within former Yugoslavia. Yugoslav regions tended to view their balance of trade as distinct from that of the federation as a whole, and had a good deal of freedom to find their own pattern of comparative advantage. Slovenia was the most successful republic at trading with the developed market economies; by 1992, more than two-thirds of its exports were sold in Western Europe (Bank of Slovenia, February 1994).

Bole (1992) estimates that the collapse of the Yugoslav market has caused Slovenian GDP to shrink by 6 percent. This estimate, however, may not adequately take into account the longer-term impact of increased liquidity problems on both the real and financial sectors. Still, in light of the 38 percent fall of Slovenian industrial production between June 1989 and June 1992, the collapse of the Yugoslav market was far from the only factor behind the slump in output. Rather, it was one cause of problems, alongside hyperinflation, the demand shock arising from the stabilization attempt of 1990 and the stabilization of 1991–92, the collapse of the CMEA market, and the recession in Western Europe.

Slovenia's separation may also enhance other autarkic tendencies. Strategic military arguments could be made for retaining and further developing Slovenia's heavy industrial base, which includes everything from steel to computers. For such a small state, this would require a greater deviation from the country's current comparative advantage than for a larger entity such as Yugoslavia. Furthermore, such a move would reverse recent, probably healthy trends to restructure Slovenian heavy industry, eliminating outdated and ecologically damaging technology.

Irrespective of any domestic desires for autarky, the smaller size of the Slovenian market makes it a less attractive location for foreign investors. Locating production in Slovenia to supply the domestic market makes no sense for foreigners; motives such as a desire to cooperate with Slovenian partners who possess outstanding knowledge or skills, or strategic considerations such as a company's share of total production in Central and East Europe will bring foreign investment to Slovenia, not the Slovenian market.

A related, longer-term problem is fear of germanization. Given the small size of the Slovenian economy, the impact of a few significant foreign investments could be quite large. A defensive reaction, restricting the sales of Slovenian assets to foreigners, could well take hold. Such a reaction seems more likely in a small state like Slovenia than in a medium-sized entity like the old Yugoslavia. The first indications of such a reaction can be seen in the current Slovenian government's unwillingness to allow foreigners to buy land.[15]

In addition, Slovenia's proximity (both physical and political) to ex-Yugoslavia has resulted in its sharing to a certain extent the perceived political risk that foreign investors associate with Yugoslavia. The political risk is, of course, not the result of independence per se, but of the wars in ex-Yugoslavia. It took Slovenia more than a year after independence to gain admission to the IMF, and its relationship with the European Community, although good, has been far slower in developing than other Central European nations.

A further strain on the Slovenian economy is the refugee problem. While the refugee situation in Slovenia is not nearly so bad as in Croatia, an estimated 75,000 refugees (3 percent of Slovenia's population) arrived between July 1991 and October 1992.

A key question is whether these costs will continue to affect Slovenia over the medium to long term. Trade reorientation costs are essentially one-time costs incurred during the transition from one trade pattern to another. The other costs have a longer duration. Trade diversion will continue as long as trade with other ex-Yugoslav republics is disrupted, and even after that if tariff or other barriers remain in place.

Political risk, too, may linger for a considerable period of time. How long will depend on the success of Slovenian diplomacy in creating a perception that Slovenia is different from the rest of ex-Yugoslavia. The refugee problem, in turn, cannot be solved quickly, nor will the issues of autarky and germanization be immediately settled. Hence, we may conclude that the costs of separation are felt in the short run, but may continue to accumulate through the medium term (probably to the end of the decade).

Benefits of Separation

The overarching benefit of separation for Slovenia has been political: exit from the chaos of ex-Yugoslavia. Following the end of the one-week war between Slovenian forces and Yugoslav People's Army in late June–early July 1991, Slovenia has been able to separate itself from the brutality and violence of the Yugoslav wars. It has also been able to keep extreme political forces (above all extreme nationalists) from gaining significant power within Slovenia, thereby facilitating the establishment of peaceful democratic processes.

In the eyes of the Slovenian people, this political benefit justifies any short-run economic sacrifices. Nonetheless, a case can be made for the proposition that Slovenia will experience medium- and long-term economic benefits. These fall under three headings: enhanced macroeconomic stability through Slovenian sovereignty and control over monetary and fiscal policy; enhanced capital accumulation through the dismantling of the old system of redistribution; and faster access to the EC and its benefits.

Enhanced macroeconomic stability is the fruit of political sovereignty. The old Yugoslavia did not possess adequate federal mechanisms for managing the macroeconomy. The formal balance of the federal budget hid a significant but unmeasured deficit. The difficulties in achieving approval by all the federal units in Parliament for compromises on federal allocations made fiscal policy response sluggish. Disagreements over taxation policy also made it difficult to achieve a coherent federal policy in this area.[16]

Similarly, federal monetary policy was hampered by the political set-up and power balance in the NBY. With its governors chosen by republican parliaments, the central bank lacked any substantial degree of independence. Controlled by a coalition favoring redistribution and easy money, it chose to put out the fires that started at the regional level.[17] For Slovenia, which practiced greater fiscal discipline than other federal units, this meant an unwanted inflationary impulse without corresponding benefits.

It is in this context that Slovenia's assumption of fiscal and monetary independence must be understood. The introduction of the Slovenian tolar, in particular, has proved an invaluable instrument in protecting Slovenia from the hyperinflation of the dinar in late 1991 and 1992. In this sense, independent Slovenia might prove to be an optimal currency area, for it has turned out to be an area within which coherent monetary policy has been politically feasible.

Yugoslav regions — in an ethnically heterogeneous society with large differences in economic development — functioned as distributional coalitions (Olson, 1982), thereby preventing coherent fiscal and monetary policies and turning them into a vehicle of redistribution. Efficiency was subordinated to redistribution. Hence, the potential advantages of participation in a larger entity were not realized, and separation from the larger entity provided an improvement in this respect.

Another aspect of macroeconomic stability derives from Slovenia's newfound flexibility to create labor market institutions appropriate to its own circumstances. With a small economy and a fairly ethnically homogeneous work force, Slovenia is a candidate for all-encompassing corporatist bargaining between labor and management. Similar institutions have proved highly successful in such small, open European economies as Sweden and Austria. They provide a way to keep the overall rate of wage increase within the bounds necessary to ensure macroeconomic stability. They also facilitate the achievement of macroeconomic targets (e.g., on exchange rates, relative unit labor costs, and employment) (Layard, 1990).

Enhanced capital accumulation is the second benefit expected from Slovenia's separation. This benefit is contingent on ending the practice of redistribution of the old regime.

Interregional subsidization was ended immediately upon separation from Yugoslavia. But cross-subsidization is more persistent. Thanks to the economic collapse engendered by the war, Slovenia has been unable to end subsidies. Reported losses in 1991 reached 8.7 percent of GDP, and rose to a staggering 17.2 percent in 1992, according to the Social Accounting Service. Some 69 percent of losses were concentrated in industry, with three sectors — electric power, steel, and electronics — accounting for the majority. Many of the largest industrial enterprises were involved. As was mentioned above, wage subsidies have been employed to keep insolvent enterprises afloat.

The key question is whether an independent Slovenia will be in a better position to end cross-subsidization than it would have been within Yugoslavia. The passage of privatization legislation suggests that the answer may well be positive. Slovenia's political system must still find a way to carry through bankruptcy and rehabilitate the financial system. Nonetheless, Slovenia's progress so far compares favorably with what Yugoslavia achieved in 1990, when the Marković government's privatization and restructuring program became hopelessly mired in interregional conflict.

If the process of restructuring the financial and industrial sector is successful, capital accumulation should improve. The old pattern of subsidization effectively taxed relatively successful enterprises while subsidizing relatively unsuccessful ones. Estimates by Vodopivec (1989) suggest that this had a negative effect on productivity. Similarly, Kraft (1992a) has found that soft budget finance allowed enterprises to maintain their investment despite continued loss-making.

Another factor contributing to faster capital accumulation, as well as to higher living standards, will be Slovenia's ability to fashion its own tariff policies. The less-developed regions of Yugoslavia stoutly resisted lowering tariff barriers. Slovenia, with its greater competitiveness, should be able to lower tariff barriers much further than Yugoslavia as a whole.

There is a danger here as well. As a small economy, Slovenia is forced to be open. Whether it can thrive in a competitive international environment remains to be seen.[18]

A third benefit is faster access to the EC. Yugoslavia's aspirations to enter the EC were frustrated by its inability to meet EC standards on human rights and political democracy. A major impetus for Slovenian independence was the assessment that the Milošević leadership in Serbia was unwilling to resolve the Kosovo situation in a way satisfactory to the EC (as well as to the rest of the international community). Naturally, the wars in ex-Yugoslavia have only reinforced this assessment.

Slovenian independence appears to have unblocked the way to Europe. Close cooperation with both the European Free Trade Association (EFTA) and the EC have already begun, including the signing of an economic agreement building on the old EC-Yugoslavia agreement in April 1993. While the continuation of the wars and difficult relations with Italy render Slovenia's situation uncertain, Slovenia is on a much faster track to Europe than any other ex-Yugoslav republic.

What will closer association with Europe mean for Slovenia? First, it will mean a stamp of approval for foreign investment in Slovenia.

Second, it will mean guaranteed access to European markets. Third, membership would also allow Slovenes to work anywhere in the EC without special permission, and likewise would allow EC citizens to work in Slovenia. Fourth, should Slovenia accede to the EC, it will probably be eligible for funds from the EC's regional programs. These funds have provided a major source of funding to the poorer EC members (Ireland, Portugal, and especially Greece).

Of course, it is far from inevitable that Slovenia will become a full member of the EC. Such a development is hard to foresee within the current decade. However, closer association seems highly realistic, with ties growing stronger rather rapidly.

CONCLUSIONS

Nearly three years after the declaration of Slovenian independence, things are looking up: inflation is under control, the economy is growing again, and real wages are nearly back to pre-independence levels. Unemployment remains a serious problem, however. Furthermore, given the uncertainty surrounding the future of the region, and the nature of internal Slovenian politics, any conclusions drawn at this early stage must be tentative.

First, despite the obvious costs Slovenia has incurred in the short run, prospects of medium- and long-run economic benefits seem fairly good. Above all, the ability to pursue macroeconomic stability, the fruit of political independence and a separate currency, appears to be yielding tangible benefits. Membership, or at last a closer relationship with the EC, appears likely, and will prove highly advantageous. The ending of the old interregional redistributive practices, if combined with a halt in cross-subsidization and the fashioning of functional new institutions which are appropriate for Slovenia, especially in the labor market, holds great promise.

Second, Slovenia's case does not prove that any separation from a larger entity would be welfare increasing. In fact, Slovenia's separation from Yugoslavia might not have been as beneficial as it has been already had Yugoslav politics turned out differently. Had forces amenable to rational debate and compromise prevailed in Yugoslavia, Slovenian secession might actually have been welfare decreasing.

Slovenia's experience suggests that secession from a larger entity that is racked by political instability may yield positive net economic benefits. If local political autonomy provides an opportunity to introduce a new currency and achieve macroeconomic stability, separation can become economically attractive. However, this can only take place if the local political constellation is not controlled by distributive coalitions bent on preserving the old redistributive system, and is not hampered by major political divisions that paralyze decision making. In short, secession can be beneficial if the new state is more homogeneous in its composition and coherent in its functioning than the old state.

Not all of the costs Slovenia has faced would be felt by other newly independent states. In the Czech-Slovak breakup, for example, political risk and refugee cost (or, more properly, costs due to migration) are much smaller than in the Slovenian case. On the other hand, the Czech Republic may well face a similar situation to Slovenia's: short-term costs but potential long-term gains.

Slovenia's circumstances are fortunate. It is ethnically homogeneous, culturally and historically compatible with the West, and enjoys proximity to (and some protection from) friendly Western neighbors. Furthermore, even though political divisions have been sharp, it has shown a political will to fight counterproductive redistribution.

There may not be a Slovenian model for anyone to copy. But there is a growing body of useful experience that Slovenia has to offer other new postcommunist nations.

NOTES

The authors would like to acknowledge helpful comments from Cheryl Gray and Nemat Shafik. Any remaining errors are the authors' sole responsibility. The views presented here are those of the authors and do not imply any policy or judgment on the part of the World Bank.

  1. For background on the Slovenian experience, see Benderly and Kraft (1994) and Huttenbach and Vodopivec (1993).

  2. We do not mean to argue that Slovenia achieved complete stabilization at that point. Inflation in January 1993 rose to 3.7 percent, following substantial wage increases; but by April it was down to 1 percent. Unemployment continued to grow, exceeding 15 percent by early 1994. Nonetheless, Slovenia's accomplishments in dealing with inflation compare well with the hyperinflation or near-hyperinflation prevailing in the rest of ex-Yugoslavia through the end of 1993.

  3. Reserves were also built up in the process of housing privatization, which began following the passage of the Housing Law in November 1991 (Gray and Štiblar, 1992).

  4. This puts Slovenia at a great advantage compared to the states of the former Soviet Union. Even the former Czechoslovakia had to revamp the entire budget process just before the separation of its two component republics.

  5. Indeed, the organizational structure of the central banking system of the former Yugoslavia provided the basic institutional set-up for the currency reform. In

Yugoslavia the regional national banks executed commonly agreed upon monetary policy on the territories of the respective regions. This institutional heritage gave Slovenia and other former Yugoslav republics a big advantage over the ex-Soviet republics.

6.   This figure is the so-called "out-turn." On a cash basis, the budget was in deficit in 1991 (2.6 percent of GDP). Even this figure is not alarming by international standards, and is indeed quite modest compared to the other Central European economies in transition.

7.   The effectiveness of indirect monetary instruments will be impaired as long as loss-making enterprises and banks are not restructured. Important preconditions also include the development of financial and capital markets.

8.   An excellent discussion of the motivation for the choice of a floating exchange rate is found in Mencinger (1993).

9.   this discussion draws on Vodopivec and Korže (1993).

10.   See also Kraft (1993) for information on the growth of the private sector in prewar Slovenia and ex-Yugoslavia.

11.   For a discussion of recent trends, legislation, and major issues concerning the labor market, see Vodopivec and Hribar-Milič (1992).

12.   The source of this figure is unpublished data from the Ministry of Planning.

13.   For a more complete account of Slovenia's relationship to ex-Yugoslavia, see Cvikl, Kraft, and Vodopivec (1993).

14.   Even before the civil war, these costs were so apparent that the leading Slovene economist, Aleksander Bajt, warned that the drive for independence could not be justified on economic grounds (Bajt, 1991). However, Bajt's argument makes sense only if the alternative is an integrated, peaceful Yugoslavia. Lacking such an alternative, independence was simply a necessity.

15.   It should be noted, however, that several other East European countries have forbidden foreign land ownership as well.

16.   An old, but nonetheless relevant diagnosis of Yugoslavia's institutional inability to conduct fiscal policy is found in Horvat, Hadžiomerac, and Gluščevič (1972–1973).

17.   The same forces also undermined the ability of the federal government to conduct consistent policies in other areas, for example in the administration of price controls.

18.   Boris Majcen (1992) argues that, since 1989, Yugoslav and Slovenian legislation may have lowered tariffs too fast. He points out that the old system of quantitative restriction, export licenses, and special measures has not been replaced by an equivalent tariff, and provides evidence that Slovenia's effective rate of protection may be below the EC average.

REFERENCES

Abraham, Katherine, and Milan Vodopivec. "Slovenia: A Study of Labor Market Transitions." Mimeograph, World Bank, October 1993.

Bajt, Aleksander. "Visoka cena samostalnosti." *Danas*, February 19, 1991.

[Bank of Slovenia.] *Monthly Bulletin*. Ljubljana: Bank of Slovenia, various 1992, 1993, and 1994 issues.

Benderly, Jill, and Evan Kraft (eds.). *Independent Slovenia: Origins, Movements, Prospects.* New York: St. Martin's Press, 1994.

Bole, Velimir. "Slovensko gospodarstvo v splošnem 'neravnotežju'." *Gospodarska gibanja* 230 (August 1992): 23–36.

Cvikl, Milan. "Denarna politika osemdesetih let v Jugoslaviji." Unpublished M.Sc. thesis, University of Ljubljana, July 1990.

Cvikl, Milan, Evan Kraft, and Milan Vodopivec. "Costs and Benefits of Independence: Slovenia." *Communist Economies and Economic Transformation* 5, 3 (September 1993): 295–315.

Díaz-Alejandro, Carlos F. "Goodbye Financial Repression, Hello Financial Crash." *Journal of Development Economics* 19, 1–2 (September–October 1985): 1–24.

Gray, Cheryl, and Franjo Štiblar. "The Evolving Legal Framework for Private Sector Activity in Slovenia." World Bank Policy Research Working Papers, WPS 893, April 1992.

Horvat, Branko, Hasan Hadžiomerac, and Boris Gluščevič. "The Economic Functions of the Federation." *East European Economics* 2 (1972–73): 3–46.

Huttenbach, Henry R., and Peter Vodopivec (eds.). "Voices from the Slovene Nation." Special issue of *Nationalities Papers*, Spring 1993.

Korže, Uroš, and Marko Simonetti. "Privatization in Slovenia — 1992." In Andreja Bohm and Marko Simonetti (eds.), *Privatization in Central and Eastern Europe 1992*. Ljubljana: Central and Eastern European Privatization Network, 1993.

Kraft, Evan. "Soft-budget Subsidies and Investment Finance in Yugoslavia: A Model with Estimates for 1986–7." Mimeograph, Salisbury State University 1992.

Kraft, Evan. "The Growth of Small Enterprise and the Private Sector in Yugoslavia." In Perry L. Patterson (ed.), *Capitalist Goals, Socialist Past: The Rise of the Private Sector in Command Economies*. Boulder, Colo.: Westview Press, 1993.

Layard, Richard. "Wage Bargaining, Incomes Policy and Inflation: Possible Lessons for Eastern Europe." World Bank Seminar on Managing Inflation in Socialist Economies, Vienna, March 1990 (mimeo).

Majcen, Boris. "Protection of the Slovene Economy and Slovenia's Approach to the European Community." *Development and International Cooperation* 7, 14–15 (June–December 1992): 87–108.

Mencinger Jože. "Rojstvo in otroštvo tolarja." *Slovenska ekonomska revija* 44, 1–2 (1993): 24–47.

[Ministry of Finance.] "Sponsorship Statement." Ministry of Finance, Republic of Slovenia, reprinted in *Euromoney*, September 1992, pp. 190–193.

Olson, Mancur. *The Rise and Decline of Nations: Economic Growth, Stagflation, and Social Rigidities*. New Haven, Conn.: Yale University Press, 1982.

[PlanEcon.] *Plan Econ Report*, Vol. 8, various 1992 issues.

Pleskovič, Boris, and Jeffrey D. Sachs. "Political Independence and Economic Reform in Slovenia." In Olivier J. Blanchard, Kenneth A. Froot, and Jeffrey D. Sachs (eds.), *Transition in Eastern Europe*. Chicago: University of Chicago Press, 1994.

Rocha, Roberto R., and Fernando Saldanha. "Fiscal and Quasi-Fiscal Deficits, Nominal and Real." World Bank, Working Series no. 919, 1992.

Rus, Andrej. "Quasi-Privatization: From Class Struggle to a Scuffle of Small Particularisms." In Jill Benderly and Evan Kraft (eds.), *Independent Slovenia: Origins, Movements, Prospects*. New York: St. Martin's Press, 1994.

Štiblar, Franjo. "Privatization in Slovenia." *Development and International Co-operation* 8, 14–15 (June–December 1992): 185–196.

Vodopivec, Milan. "Productivity Effects of Redistribution in Yugoslavia." Unpublished Ph.D. dissertation, University of Maryland, 1989.

Vodopivec, Milan, and Uroš Korže. "The Incidence and Effects of Spontaneous Privatization in Slovenia." World Bank, 1993 (mimeo).

Vodopivec, Milan, and Samo Hribar-Milič. "The Slovenian Labor Market in Transition." 1992 (mimeo).

[World Bank.] *Trends in Developing Countries: Extracts.* Washington, D.C.: World Bank, 1993.

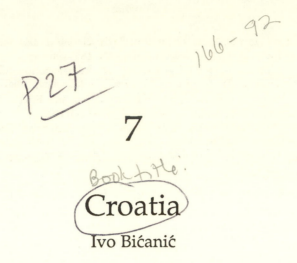

7

Croatia

Ivo Bićanić

INTRODUCTION

The great historical rifts that have accompanied the global abandoning of the socialist "experiment" have imposed three very expensive social projects on Croatia. These are respectively the establishment of a nation-state, the defense of its independence, and the attempt to sketch the outlines of its postsocialist economic development. These three processes are complex and influence all aspects of society, its economy, and politics. However, only one aspect, the economic one, is addressed in this chapter.

All three processes necessitate deep-rooted changes in the economy and have, by definition, major destabilizing effects. Creating a new national economic space by drawing new national boarders and by introducing a new institutional and legal environment inevitably disrupts the flow of goods and services and changes the terms of trade. War reallocates resources and redirects production priorities, which, along with the financial burden that it inflicts and the direct and indirect losses it imposes, have further major disruptive effects. Finally, the transition to a full-fledged market economy — which necessitates a redistribution of economic power, restructuring, and the deriving of new criteria for economic decision making — seeks to replace old social relations with new ones. The first three sections of this chapter deal with each of these aspects in turn.

The Croatian economy steadily deteriorated from the early 1980s through 1994. By the beginning of the 1990s, when the implementation of the three aforementioned projects began, this deterioration had gained momentum. While the individual contributions to economic destabilization of each of these three processes cannot yet be measured, their cumulative (and probably synergistic) effects can be. This course of events has understandably led to attempts at macroeconomic stabilization, of which three have been made to date. The next two sections of the chapter deal with economic policy and its effects.

The final section of the chapter offers some conclusions regarding the three projects on which Croatia has embarked. These can be only tentative since all three are ongoing.

THE PATH TO CROATIAN
ECONOMIC INDEPENDENCE

Croatia's economic independence was established during the early 1980s. This turn of events is the result of a long historical process which gained momentum during the 1980s. Its acceleration started with the so-called "Crisis of the 1980s." During this decade-long crisis, all the underpinnings of the Yugoslav economy were brought into question. The 1990s opened with a brief period during which the economy of this multinational federal state was segmented. This segmented phase did not last long — the Yugoslav economy had irreversibly decomposed by the beginning of 1992.

Yugoslavia's Crisis of the 1980s began with the world debt crisis and over time evolved into the longest, harshest, and deepest economic crisis that the Yugoslav economy had experienced in its 73-year history (Bićanić, 1986; Bićanić and Škreb, 1992). The accelerating economic decline brought the long-run failures of the Yugoslav economy into the limelight[1] and led to discussions (often fierce ones) among economists concerning the economic underpinnings of Yugoslavia. Self-management, arguably the best known feature of the economy, lost the aura of being less crisis-prone than other forms of socialist management, while the "associated labor paradigm" was increasingly seen as a significant contributor to the crisis, if not its chief cause.[2] The enormous sacrifices demanded by the frequent attempts to promote economic growth, which began in the interwar period — at times Yugoslavia invested almost 40 percent of its social product (Sirotković and Stipetić, 1990) — failed to establish modern economic growth or to change Yugoslavia's relative place on Europe's development gradient.[3]

In addition, internal differentials in economic development — that is, those between republics and autonomous provinces — widened and Yugoslavia itself increasingly came to be perceived as a "negative sum game." All republics argued that they were experiencing a net outflow of funds and an unfavorable redistribution of income and wealth.[4] Especially important was the discussion among economists on the "unity of the economy," many arguing that the level of economic integration among the regions was falling. Finally, all crisis-management policies, the first of which dates back to 1961, had failed,[5] as they eventually degenerated into soft policies and back-tracking once the austerity measures started impinging and social tension rising.

As a result of the deepening economic crisis and the growing realization of the need for change, Yugoslavia's transition began in the mid-1980s. As the crisis continued, the real world economy demanded additional changes, and society as well as many politicians and economists recognized the need for deep-rooted changes in the economic system. The initial steps in the transition were reflected in a number of major legislative changes promulgated during the 1980s. These changes gathered momentum as they accelerated over time and each step became more radical if ultimately one step behind events.[6]

By the end of the transition of the 1980s, Yugoslavia had achieved three major breakthroughs: one concerning ownership, the second with regard to markets, and the third related to entrepreneurship. Regarding forms of ownership, by the end of the decade a level playing field was introduced that eliminated almost all the privileges of social ownership and introduced a very limited privatization plan (Uvalić, 1991). Equally importantly, legislative barriers to capital and labor markets were eliminated (markets for commodities and services had existed since the 1960s), so that these markets, which had existed informally and imperfectly (thus inefficiently), could be organized in a transparent and competitive manner. Finally, the scope for private entrepreneurship widened, as virtually all restraints were eliminated and market entry for private entrepreneurs was made easier. All of these changes were effected in the established postwar way: first, after consensus building at the federal level, and then with minor variations, at the republican one. As a result, during this initial transition phase Yugoslavia remained institutionally a single economic space.

The Yugoslav economy's brief period of segmentation started in 1990, after the first postwar multiparty elections — the Croatian elections were in May 1990 — which led to quite different results in individual republics.[7] During late 1990 and early 1991, institutional barriers to interrepublican trade were erected in the form of internal tariffs, embargoes, bans,[8] discriminatory taxes (charging out-of-republic enterprises special tax rates),[9] and the breaking up of enterprises with plants in more than one region, usually as regional plants unilaterally re-registered as independent enterprises.[10] The federal monetary system collapsed, as federal control over the quantity of money broke down,[11] while the fiscal system fell apart as republics stopped contributing taxes and customs to the federal budget.[12] Legislation was passed in different sequences in the various republics, creating divergent institutional frameworks, especially as regards privatization and social ownership.[13] Simultaneously, negotiations for "recontracting" the country were taking place.[14]

The period of segmentation did not last long and ended in December 1991. In Croatia's case three sets of events are important. First, the recontracting negotiations led to a stalemate and were discontinued by mid-1991 with no results and not even an official statement. Second, institutional segmentation increased. Third, the Croatian authorities organized a referendum in which 94 percent of the votes cast were in favor of independence, although leaving open the possibility of recontracting a new state. Acting along these lines, the Croatian Parliament passed a Declaration of Independence in June 1991 (see the official state legal digest, *Narodne novine*, no. 31, 1991, or the English translation in *Yugoslav Survey*, 1991b, pp. 51–53), but at the insistence of the EC, a "time-out" postponed its application (together with Slovenia) until the end of the year. The new Croatian constitution was passed in December 1991.

Fourth, the "wars of Yugoslav succession" escalated during 1991. The first of them, that is, the Slovenian episode, lasted for ten days in July. The second conflict, the one in Croatia, which started on August 20, 1990 (when the barricades were put up in Knin, "capital" of Krajina), developed into a full-fledged conflict during the summer of 1991. Since the UN/EC-brokered ceasefire of January 3, 1992, and the UN Vance-Owens peace plan, it has been rumbling on as a continuous but low-intensity conflict. The third episode, in Bosnia-Herzegovina, started in the spring of 1992.

Yugoslavia's final and irreversible decomposition had occurred by early 1993 with the formal international recognition of certain of Yugoslavia's successor states. Croatia and Slovenia won international recognition on January 15, 1992, when Germany recognized them, with the remaining EC countries and numerous others following suit. Croatia became a member of the UN on May 22, 1992, and a member of the

IMF on December 14, 1992 (together with Slovenia and Macedonia as successor states to Yugoslavia).

ESTABLISHING A NEW ECONOMIC SPACE

The four immediate economic concerns of any new state are establishing monetary, fiscal, payments, and international trade systems. With the exception of the fourth, Croatia encountered no major problems, due to Yugoslavia's federal structure.

The establishment of a national currency went quickly and smoothly. The National Bank of Croatia, established in 1945, could easily take over the duties of a central bank and monetary authority.[15] After its expulsion (together with Slovenia) from the federal monetary system in late 1991, the National Bank of Croatia (NBC) could immediately begin its new role of a central bank. Legislation regulating central banking was passed in three stages. First, Yugoslav monetary legislation was applied in such a way as to turn the NBC into a central bank (*Narodne novine*, no. 71, 1991); second, the Law on the Central Bank was passed; and, finally, legislation on foreign currency and on the banking system was enacted, and amendments were passed to the Law on the Central Bank.

The exchange of Yugoslav dinari for Croatian dinari took place over a two-day period that began on December 23, 1991, at a ratio of 1:1,[16] with savings being converted automatically. It was envisaged that the Croatian dinar would be a temporary currency until macroeconomic stabilization was achieved, at which time Croatian dinari would be replaced by the permanent currency, the kuna.[17] The kuna was indeed introduced on May 30, 1994.

The fiscal system was also changed without great difficulty. Yugoslav republics had a wide range of fiscal autonomy[18] — all customs duties and part of the turnover tax being the federal government's only direct revenue sources — which included drawing up an autonomous republic budget, determining some turnover tax rates, and collecting all turnover and income tax proceeds. Nationalizing this fiscal system proved easy, although transforming it into one consistent with an ordinary market economy is another issue.

The payments system could also easily be transformed from part of a federal structure into a national one. The Yugoslav payments system was organized into territorial units that coincided with the republics. As a result, the Croatian branch of the Social Accounting Service could easily become an independent Croatian payments system.

Croatia however, did not inherit an international trade system, since in this instance matters had been strictly under the auspices of the federal government (Stakić, 1987). Establishing a Croatian foreign trade system involved solving two sets of issues. The easier one concerned "old" trade partners. The international trade system of the former Yugoslavia (i.e., its tariff structure, export subsidies, and foreign currency regulations) was initially transferred unchanged.

Concerning Yugoslavia's successor states, matters were more complex since what was previously internal trade had now become international. The customs infrastructure was expanded to include the new borders (toward Slovenia, Serbia, Montenegro, and Bosnia-Herzegovina), but the most important issue was the payments regime with these neighboring republics, which now belonged to foreign states. This problem was solved through the creation of bilateral payments regimes with Slovenia, Macedonia, and Bosnia-Herzegovina;[19] the war has stopped all economic relations with Serbia and Montenegro. The arrangements involved special bilateral accounts and no customs payments.[20] The more difficult question of policing the borders remains. Large sections of the frontier are under the control of Serbian rebel forces, while the borders with Slovenia and Bosnia-Herzegovina are inefficiently administered and policed, especially with respect to the latter. Thus trade with Slovenia, and to a greater extent Bosnia-Herzegovina, has included many illegal deals. Fictitious trade arrangements have been set up by which either payments of tariffs is avoided or export subsidies are received for goods that are not exported.[21]

The other key economic institutions, such as a statistical office, economics ministry, social welfare system, and unemployment agency, were already organized along republic lines and thus easily transformed into sovereign institutions.

THE DIRECT COSTS OF CROATIAN INDEPENDENCE

Croatia's statehood was not achieved peacefully. In August 1990, following the results of the May 1990 multiparty elections, a fraction of Croatia's Serbian minority rebelled. With the Yugoslav National Army providing equipment and logistical support, rebel Serbian paramilitary units on August 20, 1990 — during the peak of the tourist season — blocked road and rail links leading to Croatia's main tourist area. The immediate results were blocked transport (road and rail) and energy links, cutting Croatia first into two pieces (as Dalmatia was isolated), and as the war progressed, into three pieces (as Slavonia was semi-isolated). These amputations remain, albeit in a somewhat less severe form; the increased transport cost and the uncertainty of resorting to roundabout routes continue to take their toll. The conflict is still unresolved in spite of the EC/UN-brokered ceasefire of January 3, 1992, the establishment of four UN-protected regions with UN peacekeeping forces, and EC monitors, and the Vance-Owens peace plan. Over 50 percent of Croatia's population currently lives within artillery range of Serbian rebel positions and over 80 percent within range of their missiles.

Croatia's losses in terms of human life and forced resource reallocation have been considerable. In addition to significant direct losses, there are have been sizable indirect costs of both a demographic and an economic nature. The latter include a delay in the country's economic transition, the creation of a nontransparent economic system, and the rise of an unofficial economy.

Because the war continues, the direct costs continue to rise and in many cases, especially in rebel-administered areas, have yet to be calculated. The Croatian authorities claim that up through early November 1993, 6,970 people were killed and 26,276 wounded, of whom over 7,000 were civilians; the ranks of the unaccounted-for contain some 12,000 souls.[22] By July 1993, the number of displaced persons had fallen from its peak of over 800,000 people to 249,000. In addition, Serbia has registered 160,000 refugees from Croatia (UNHCR, 1993).

On the Croatian side, 590 villages and towns were attacked during the war (35 completely leveled), around 210,000 housing units (12 percent) were destroyed or heavily damaged, there was extensive damage to social infrastructure, and many cultural monuments were damaged or destroyed (SIMAF, no. 3, 1993). In the rebel-administered area, which is inhabited by 25 percent of the population, extensive ethnic cleansing has changed the demographic picture. Almost the entire Croatian population has been forced out and Serbian inhabitants from other parts of Croatia and Bosnia-Herzegovina have moved into the area (Bićanić and Dominis, 1993a). The region in question encompasses around 33 percent of Croatian territory, and includes a quarter of the agricultural land (including Baranja, which has some of the most fertile soil and produces 35 percent of agricultural output) and 38 percent of the forests (SIMAF, no. 3, 1993).

The Croatian authorities have estimated that direct damage during the period of the most intense fighting (through January 1992) amounted to some $20 billion (SIMAF, no. 3, 1993), about 2.5 times the present social product. The indirect costs have not been estimated, but there is no doubt that the declines in tourism[23] and transport[24] were directly related to the war, as were the extensive electric energy cuts that occurred in some areas.[25] The means of financing the war are still impossible to ascertain, since weapons were bought during a UN arms embargo — leading one to presume the existence of a secret, parallel budget — and military expenditures appear in more than one budgetary category (certain items are included under salaries and other expenses). The 34 percent of the 1993 budget officially earmarked for military expenditures (*Privredni vjesnik*, April 19, 1993, p. 12) should thus be taken as a very conservative estimate.

Another economic consequence of the war is the regional realignment that it has engendered. Thus, Dalmatia, once among the most affluent regions, is now among the poorest, with a crippled economy, high unemployment, and many displaced persons and refugees (temporarily housed in its hotels).

DEFINING A TRANSITION PATH

Croatia's independence provided it with two important transition-related opportunities. The first is the opportunity to define a transition path best suited to a new, smaller economic space. The second results from the need for new national legislation, which can make it easier to pass transition-related laws. Of course, both opportunities may be unused, partially used, or even misused. In this respect Croatia's record is mixed.

As of the end of 1993, an evaluation of the Croatian transition record can be reduced to the following seven points. The three points on the "credit" side are as follows:

- extensive legislative change has introduced a general framework and most of the basic legislation required for a mixed market economy;
- privatization has been well under way since 1991 and the relevant legislation has been modified to enable a more efficient realization of the chosen methods of privatization; and
- some of the most important institutional components of a market economy are operating.

The three points on the "debit" side include:

- large enterprises and banks, the most difficult units to be privatized, remained untouched and the issues pertaining to them unresolved;

- economic restructuring had not advanced very far, so that many of the related social costs have not yet appeared; and
- some the most important institutions of a market economy were not yet functioning in an orderly way.

The final feature is the generally decelerating effect the war has had on the transition.

The economic section of the new constitution passed in December 1991 represents a clean break with socialism. It envisages a completely different economic system from the inherited one. It thus abolishes all that remained of self-management and worker participation in the economy and introduces a market economy with mixed forms of ownership (state, private, and cooperative). Croatia was the only one of Yugoslavia's successor states to choose such a seemingly abrupt and radical departure.

As was already mentioned, initially economic legislation from the Yugoslav legal system was transplanted and marginally adapted to the needs of the new economy and the legal requirements of the economic transition were ignored. Over time these laws have been replaced by newer ones providing the legal underpinnings for this transition. This concerns primarily the monetary and payments systems and to a lesser extent the fiscal system, which was changed least.

The inherited monetary system, after being adapted so as to enable the NBC to act as a central bank, has been transformed. The NBC, whose Governor is appointed by Parliament, independently conducts monetary policy by regulating business banks and by conducting open-market operations. A banking law regulates the private banking system and determines the conditions for market entry. The payments system has been completely changed — the Social Accounting Service has been abolished — and simplified, so that it now resembles those in other market economies. Financial control has been transferred to the newly established financial police, which is under the Ministry of Finance. New, liberal legislation on foreign exchange transactions has been passed, which allows for a market-determined exchange rate. The legislation required for a stock exchange has also been passed.

The glaring omission in the transitional institutional framework is a labor law. The government proposal for such a law has been discussed by Parliament for over a year and both procedural and political pressure has been brought to bear for its passage. The proposal, especially the sections significantly reducing job security, has met with strong objections from all four trade unions and as of early 1994 remained unpassed.

As elsewhere, the central issue of the transition has become changing property rights, that is, privatization (Bićanić, 1993a; 1993b). Privatization in Croatia can be broken up into three closely related but separate processes: the privatization of business assets, the privatization of housing, and the restitution of property. While the first two got off to an early start and have largely been proceeding along the initially envisaged track, the legislative framework for restitution has yet to be defined.

The privatization of Croatia's business assets formally began while Croatia was still part of Yugoslavia. Due to foot-dragging and the force of circumstances, little was accomplished.[26] Actual privatization in Croatia began in April 1991, when Parliament passed major legislation on this topic (*Narodne novine*, no. 19, April 23, 1991). Since then, the institutional framework has been changed three times and the legislation has been amended on four occasions. None of these changes has significantly altered the original legislation's underlying principles. The first changes took place in July 1992 and redefined the discounts offered past and present workers (*Narodne novine*, no. 45, July 20, 1992). The amendments of December 1992 sought to close a loophole that had arisen because prices were set in Deutsche marks and converted to dinari at exchange rates that had become unrealistic under the influence of inflation and currency depreciation (*Narodne novine*, no. 83, December 2, 1992). The modifications passed in February 1993 changed the auction system, opening it further to foreign capital in an attempt to attract the capital of expatriates (*Narodne novine*, no. 19, February 24, 1993). Further amendments in October 1993 widened the secondary market in shares.

The first change in the institutional structure involved renaming the inherited one, which consisted of a privatization fund and a privatization agency. When the first Croatian legislation on privatization was passed in April 1990, it merely redistributed the powers of these bodies, retaining the inherited structure (*Narodne novine*, no. 19, April 23, 1990). The most important institutional change was made in January 1993, when the fund and agency were merged into the Croatian Privatization Fund, which appraises, approves, manages, and reviews the privatization process; it also owns enterprises prior to privatization (*Narodne novine*, no. 84, December 4, 1992). The framework for privatization includes two additional important laws. The first was inherited from Yugoslavia and allows for the establishment of state-owned firms ("public" firms). The second putatively seeks to protect the "national interest," by enabling state ownership in all sectors (*Narodne novine*, no. 43, October 24, 1990).

The basic law governing privatization was discussed and passed by parliament in April 1991 amid less discussion and controversy than such an issue warrants. This is less the result of undeveloped democratic procedures than of the fact at the time issues related to Croatian sovereignty were in the limelight; the rapidly widening war understandably forced military questions to the top of the agenda. The discussion that took place was largely along the same lines as elsewhere and related to speed, revenue, and role of the state.[27]

The final legislation envisaged a state-dominated, revenue-oriented, "four-track" form of privatization. The privatization agencies — both the central office which deals with large firms and the regional offices which perform the same functions for smaller ones — approve and review privatization plans and organize the sale of shares; in certain instances they draw up privatization plans themselves. All revenue from privatization belongs to the state budget. The changes have not altered this general approach, but sought to close a number of legislative loopholes, protect small investors, attract foreign capital (especially that of expatriates), and change the selling procedure.

Four types of enterprises will emerge from the privatization process currently taking place in Croatia. The first and dominant type comprises firms whose "autonomous" privatization has been approved. These firms have drawn up their own privatization plans and submitted them to the authorities by a given deadline (one year of the law's passage). The authorities appraise them and either return them if they comply only partially with the law, refuse them, or approve them. Following approval, privatization proceeds according to the approved plan. The second form of enterprise consists of those subject to privatization but which have not submitted privatization plans to the authorities. They automatically become the property of the privatization authorities, so that the process is managed by those authorities and is at their discretion.

The third category of enterprise comprises those explicitly to be included within the state sector. Legislation inherited from the Marković era in Yugoslavia, which states that all enterprises of "national interest" will remain in state hands, has provided the base for similar legislation in the independent Croatia. This conception encompasses not only railways, electricity generation and distribution, water provision, public utilities, and forests, but also the INA oil company — the largest enterprise in former Yugoslavia — and the largest foreign trade enterprise. As a result, the state will come to dominate a substantial portion of the economy. This tendency reflects both the vicissitudes of the ongoing war, including the need to purchase arms in the face of a UN arms embargo, and a desire on the part of the ruling elite to exert control over economic developments. In any case, demands have been made that some state enterprises, such as INA and the aforementioned foreign trade company, be wholly or partially privatized.

The fourth type of firm are those whose "fuzzy" inherited social ownership was resolved by placing them in state ownership. Some sort of privatization is now envisaged for these firms.

The Croatian privatization plan does not envisage the free distribution of shares (even though such proposals are made from time to time by the trade unions and opposition parties). However, the sale of shares with large discounts — or through the provision of loans on favorable terms to present and past employees — is permitted up to the value of 20,000 DM per buyer,[28] with additional purchases possible at fixed, nonmarket prices.

The system is thus geared for managerial buyouts and surrogate buying. Abuses of the process have been frequent. Attention has been regularly drawn to them in Parliament, mostly by the opposition parties although also to a lesser extent by the ruling party. Opinion polls register widespread public skepticism regarding the equity of the whole process,[29] while the press increasingly contains articles about abuses and corruption.[30] Even the government has described privatization as one of the major generators of economic crime (*Večernji list*, February 20, 1993, p. 3; *Slobodna Dalmacija*, September 24, 1993, p. 3), while the Bishops' Synod stated that "ethics have faced great challenges . . . especially in privatization" (*Novi vjesnik*, April 25, 1993, p. 4).

The main abuses occur in the writing of the privatization programs and the undervaluation of firm assets; the authorities' acceptance of these programs, their insider knowledge, and the fact that they occasionally turn a blind eye to corruption; the means by which managers raise cash for buying shares, including favorable "managerial loans," acceptance of dubious collateral, and cashed insurance premiums; and the purchase of shares at low prices using surrogate buyers, thereby avoiding markets and auctions and the transparency that they entail.

Of the 3,700 firms eligible for privatization by the deadline of June 30, 1992, 2,860 submitted plans, and by the end of October 1993, 2,082 applications were processed. In 1,805 firms privatization has been completed (i.e., shareholders' meetings have taken place, the official criteria for completed privatization), among which 868 have been completely privatized, in 698 the privatization fund has less than 50 percent ownership, and in 239 the fund has majority ownership

(*Privredni vjesnik*, December 6, 1993, p. 3). The ownership structure of a sample of enterprises is given in Table 7.1.

TABLE 7.1

Results of 1,805 Completed Privatizations in Croatia

	Fund[1] Has No Share of Firm's Assets	Fund[1] Has Less Than 50% of Firm's Assets	Fund[1] Has More Than 50% of Firm's Assets	Total
Number of Firms	868	698	239	1,805
Average Value of Assets[2]	1.54	9.62	28.05	8.17
Average Number of Buyers	76.32	310.87	280.35	194.03
Share of Assets Sold[3]	92.02	58.09	14.69	41.46
Share of All Funds[3,4]	0.0	31.67	82.78	52.01
Share of Privatization Fund[1,3]	0.0	21.11	55.19	34.67

Source: *Privredni vjesnik*, December 6, 1993, p. 3.

Notes:

[1]Refers to the Croatian Privatization Fund.

[2]Millions of DM.

[3]Percent.

[4]The category "All Funds" includes such entities as the state-dominated Pension Fund and Veterans Fund, along with the Privatization Fund.

A completed privatization is one in which the shareholders' meeting has passed the firm's statutes and elected a chief executive officer and members of the board of directors.

The table clearly shows that the importance of state-controlled buyers — pension funds and the privatization fund — increases with the value of the firm. In an interview the director of the Croatian Privatization Fund estimated the value of assets privatized at 20 billion DM, of which 6 billion DM would end up in the fund's ownership, 2 billion DM would be owned by the pension funds, 3 billion DM would be set aside for future restitution, and 9 billion DM would wind up in other forms of private ownership (*Slobodna Dalmacija*, October 31, 1993, p. 2). In addition, it is expected that there will be 220,000 "small shareholders." Most of these shareholders bought their shares on installment credit; due to the falling living standard (through the end of 1993), it was expected that many would either stop making the payments or sell their shares on the secondary market, thus dropping out of the privatization process. By the fall of 1993, not a single large Croatian firm had been completely privatized, and many were still waiting for the approval of the authorities.

Privatization of housing — mostly urban apartments — started very early, with the proceeds largely going to the state.[31] Extensive discount schemes (up to 70 percent of estimated value, which itself was below the market value) were devised for tenants, the largest ones for up-front purchases in foreign currency and the smallest for dinar payments in installments. An attempt was made to accelerate this type of privatization by introducing a deadline for applications. This deadline was pushed forward three times due to an insufficient number of applications, with authorities complaining all the while of a fall-off in interest.[32]

The restitution law has not yet been passed by Parliament. However, each piece of legislation described above requires that a certain sum be put aside in every privatization plan for covering the expenses of restitution.

THE COST TO DATE OF CROATIA'S THREE SOCIAL PROJECTS

All three social and economic projects that Croatia has undertaken since 1990 have had major destabilizing effects on its economic performance (both micro and macro).

The decline of Croatia's gross social product (GSP)[33] had leveled off by mid-1993, at which point it stood at about half of its pre-independence[34] value. In August 1993 GSP was 48 percent of the 1990 monthly average; GSP in 1993 has been estimated at U.S. $8 billion. At the end of 1993, aggregate supply was less than half, real household income less than a third, and investment less than a quarter of their respective levels in 1990. Unemployment remains high but stable at around 18 percent — an underestimate since many are in the army who would otherwise be unemployed — but as of the end of 1993 employment was falling in the nonprivatized sector, which continued to account for 85 percent of employment (SIMAF, nos. 5–7, 1993). For basic macroeconomic data on Croatia from 1990 onward, see Table 7.2.

At the end of 1993, the government budget was in deficit to the tune of 12 percent of social product (Anušić, 1993), largely due to losses incurred by state-owned enterprises in the spheres of health, energy, and transport. However, the budget deficit of the central government proper disappeared in late 1993, not so much due to expenditure reductions as to the effects of inflation on revenue.

TABLE 7.2
Basic Macroeconomic Indicators for Croatia

	1990	1991	1992	1993
Industrial production[1]	87.5	55.3	63.1	55.6
Retail prices[2]	235.6	349.8	1,038.2	1,249.7
Employment[3]	1,507	1,187	1,098	1,043.0[4]
Average monthly unemployment	160.6	253.7	266.6	250.8
Average real wage[2]	10.0	–21.3	–33.1	18.1
Commodity imports, excluding				
ex-Yugoslavia[5]	5,188	3,441	3,429	3,893
Commodity imports, ex-Yugoslavia[5]	n.a.	n.a.	1,034	774
Commodity exports, excluding				
ex-Yugoslavia[5]	4,020	2,976	3,127	2,938
Commodity exports, ex-Yugoslavia[5]	n.a.	n.a.	1,472	963
Foreign exchange reserves[5,6]	n.a.	200.9	669.1	1,325.3

Sources: RHDZS (1993, 1994); SIMAF (1993); *Privredna kretanja i ekonomska politika*, various 1993 issues; *Privredni vjesnik*, various 1993 issues.

Notes:
   [1]Index for December of relevant year, with 1990 average set equal to 100.
   [2]Rate of change, December to December, unless otherwise noted.
   [3]Millions, December of given year, unless noted otherwise.
   [4]As of end of October 1993.
   [5]U.S.$ millions, converted at prevailing exchange rates.
   [6]Total reserves at NBC and commercial banks at end of year.

Inflation, arguably the most reliable indicator of macroeconomic instability, has shown a rising trend from 1990 through early autumn 1993, when it reached the nearly hyperinflationary level of almost 40 percent monthly (*Privredni vjesnik*, November 22, 1993, p. 7). The rising average inflation rate masked large monthly oscillations. The volatile inflation rates inherited from Yugoslavia were about 18 percent monthly.[35] During the most intense part of the war — the second half of 1991 — monthly inflation levels remained below 10 percent, there were no shortages in the shops, and goods were not rationed.

In late 1991 monthly inflation surpassed the 20 percent mark, but fell in early 1992 to around 15 percent. In late 1992 monthly rates reached 30 percent, only to fall again in early 1993 to around 25 percent. The final acceleration occurred in the late autumn of 1993; monthly inflation had reached 39 percent (over 2,300 percent yearly) by November 1993 (NBC/MSI, no. 6, 1993). Continued expansionary monetary policy, rising money wages, a persistent deficit, and administratively changed energy prices were among the causes of this last increase.

Croatia's international trade situation has changed completely since independence. New borders (in both the former Yugoslavia and the former Soviet Union, a major trading partner) and postsocialist development in other economies have altered its competitive position, leading to a loss of markets. At the same time, a fall in domestic production has led to an overall decline in trade volumes. Prior to economic independence Croatia had a lively trade with the rest of Yugoslavia. In 1987, the last year for which statistics were complied (Grubišić, 1990), Croatia traded 19.1 percent of its social product with the rest of the former Yugoslavia. Its main Yugoslav trading partner was Slovenia, to which it sold 6.1 percent of its social product, followed by Serbia without its autonomous provinces and Bosnia-Herzegovina, which bought 4.6 and 4.3 percent of its production, respectively.

In 1987 — indeed, consistently since 1972, when the authorities began to collect the relevant data — Croatia had an overall surplus in its sales to the rest of Yugoslavia and deficits only with Slovenia and Vojvodina. This trade has since collapsed, partly as a result of the wars, at least with respect to Serbia and Bosnia-Herzegovina, and partly because of changed competitive conditions. What was previously internal trade has became international, forcing domestic producers to compete on an equal footing with those from outside the former Yugoslavia.

In spite of the signing of payments agreements with three successor states, only trade with Slovenia has picked up. In the first five months of 1993, Croatia's trade with Yugoslavia's successor states was only 27.3 percent and 16.7 percent of its exports and imports, respectively, with Slovenia emerging as the only important ex-Yugoslav partner. At present, Slovenia's shares of Croatian imports and exports to the rest of former Yugoslavia are 68.8 and 79.9 percent, respectively. Slovenia's shares in aggregate Croatian exports and imports were 18.8 and 16.7 percent, respectively (NBC/B, nos. 1–5, 1993).

After the establishment of its new borders, Croatia's main trading partners in the first half of 1993 were Germany, Italy, and Slovenia, whose respective export shares were 21.4, 22.0, and 18.5 percent, and whose import shares were 20.8, 18.1, and 14.8 percent, respectively (*Privredni vjesnik*, September 20, 1993, p. 7). In comparison with the whole of 1992, Slovenia's position fell from first to third place.[36]

Overall, a foreign trade surplus in 1992 turned into a $512 million deficit in 1993 (SIMAF, nos. 5–7, 1993). In addition, the government alleged that Croatia's exports were subject to a tacit embargo on the part of the EC. One area in which the government claimed to have had some success was in accumulating $1.2 billion of foreign reserves by August 1993. Some 38 percent of these reserves were held by the National Bank of Croatia, with the remainder belonging to the commercial banks.

Croatia's three social projects have led to a large decline in the welfare of its population. The effects of the war are still felt; not only do war losses continue to increase, but the majority of the population still lives within artillery range (i.e., 30 kilometers) of rebel Serbian forces. Through the end of 1993, average monthly real wages fell,[37] to around 200 DM,[38] some 40 percent of the statistical minimum consumption level for a family of four.[39] Household incomes and expenditures fell to 33.5 and 40.9 percent, respectively, of their benchmark levels, while households' average expenditures began to exceed their incomes in May 1992; in July 1993 incomes covered 81.3 percent of expenditures (SIMAF, nos. 5–7, 1993). This deficit was largely covered by increased family debt (unpaid bills), unofficial economic activities, and remittances from abroad, while living standards were maintained to an increasing extent by produce obtained from relatives in the villages.

Movements in aggregates and averages mask major changes in economic inequality caused by the often arbitrary effects of war and transition. The ranking of regions with respect to their prosperity has been redrawn — the economy of Dalmatia has effectively collapsed under the weight of transport isolation, the virtual disappearance of tourism, and the need to house a large number of refugees. The regions administered by Serbian rebels, which coincide with the UN Protected Zones, were always poor — with the exception of Western Srijem and Baranja — but even they have fallen in relative position. In addition to the changed regional ranking the dispersion has widened.

Similarly to regions, economic sectors have experienced major changes, the largest of which are the collapses in tourism and rail transport. Economic inequality in the narrow sense has increased significantly. The ratio of the highest to the lowest wages and salaries has risen from the inherited 10:1 to 67:1 (*Privredni vjesnik*, August 20, 1993, p. 10). At the same time, most income earners find themselves concentrated in the lower income categories, which now include most of the educated middle class, whose salaries are increasingly dependent on public spending.[40] Finally, inequality of wealth has increased as a result of privatization (Bićanić, 1993b).

ATTEMPTING MACROECONOMIC STABILIZATION

Since 1990 three macroeconomic stabilization programs have been designed to deal with a deteriorating Croatian economy.[41] The first one was announced in mid-1992, the second in early 1993, and the third in the early autumn of 1993.

The first economic stabilization plan was constructed in the summer of 1992 — at a time when the war was escalating daily — by the popular, multiparty National Unity Government and its respected prime minister, Dr. Franjo Gregurić. Its aims were to reduce public spending and inflation without resort to price controls (with the exception of milk, bread, oil, electricity, and a few other items), increase the autonomy of the central bank, define a framework for financial rehabilitation, and stimulate growth. Marijan Živković, the assistant minister for economic development and one of the plan's architects, noted at the time that its underlying assumption was a cessation of the war in Croatia and a consequent substantial demobilization (*Privredni vjesnik*, July 13, 1993, p. 1). He also observed that given the war and the state of the economy, a fully fledged IMF-type stabilization would not be not possible.

The plan had very limited success, due both to the war and to criticism by influential local economists regarding its restrictive features.[42] Inflation remained more or less unchanged and major problems did not appear in the realm of foreign trade. However, public spending and the public debt rose, while the central bank's independence was actually diminished,[43] and bank rehabilitation did not get very far.

The drafting of the second stabilization program began in the fall of 1992. This took place under the auspices of the single-party government of Hrvoje Sarinić, who received the premiership on the heels of the decisive victory of the ruling Croatian Democratic Union (CDU) in the August 1992 elections (Bićanić and Dominis, 1992). It coincided with an intense attempt to court the international financial institutions, including the hosting of many IMF and World Bank missions. The program finally came before Parliament at the end of 1992,[44] by which time the economy had worsened considerably.

The second plan aimed at introducing a balanced budget, financial discipline, and a strict monetary policy, and explicitly supported tourism. Although it got through Parliament and won IMF approval, it was never implemented. The February 1993 elections (in which the CDU did worse than previously but remained in control at the national level and in the majority of regions; see Bićanić and Dominis, 1993b), a continued economic downslide, and the widespread view that other economic topics were more important politically (especially the privatization process and its abuses) led to a government crisis. As a result, macroeconomic stabilization was pushed down the agenda.

In addition, the conservative critique continued, arguing for expansionist policies and public works and criticizing the fact that the IMF had inspired the plan. A government reshuffle resulted in the appointment of a new deputy prime minister in charge of the economy. Although he appreciated the importance of macroeconomic stabilization, he also had considerable sympathy for using public works as a means of economic recovery. The ad hoc policy measures of early 1993 were not in the spirit of the program, which in any case attracted merely rhetorical support. The only possible real effect of the second stabilization effort was in promoting Croatia's membership in the IMF and World Bank.[45]

The long-running government crisis was finally resolved when a new government took office on April 2, 1993. This government immediately announced that it would postpone drawing up a macroeconomic stabilization program until the fall of 1993. The reason given for the delay was that the preconditions for a successful program had first to be established.[46] This implied the need for further reform of banking and foreign currency regulations, an increase in relative price of energy, greater control over the quantity of money, a reduction in the extent of tax and customs duty evasion,[47] and an increase in the foreign currency reserves.

The third macroeconomic stabilization program[48] was unveiled in early October 1993.[49] Its main task is to reduce in one blow inflationary expectations, which the government blames for two-thirds of inflation, and bring monthly inflation down to 10–12 percent. By March 1994 the inflation rate was to have fallen to 5 percent, a goal that was more than realized, as inflation for the whole year was less than 10 percent.

The plan includes three packages of policy decisions and decrees. The first concerns monetary policy: the dinar will be devalued and the exchange rate supported by open-market operations, partial internal convertibility, restrictive monetary policy, and a discount rate in line with targeted rather than actual inflation. Fiscal policy measures make up the second package of measures. These include an across-the-board reduction in turnover tax rates, elimination of tax and customs duty exemptions, and an attempt to increase financial discipline. The third package involves incomes policy, and entails such steps as the suspension of all wage negotiations and collective bargaining, along with the placing of limitations on the wage bills of nonprivatized firms.

This stabilization program was not backed by a wide-ranging social consensus. The opposition parties and trade unions, while understanding the need to reduce inflation, viewed the social costs of the program as unacceptably high. Moreover, influential factions of the ruling party had other priorities, especially war and economic renascence.

The quantitative targets for October, November, December, and January were partially fulfilled. Instead of depreciating, the value of the Croatian dinar significantly appreciated in real terms, leading to major difficulties for an economy with a more-than-decade-long tradition of indexing transactions to the DM. Following an October rise in retail prices of 38 percent, the succeeding months saw price changes of 1.4, –0.5, and –0.2 percent, respectively (RHDZS, no. 2, 1994, pp. 52–53). A shortage of dinari emerged and interest rates fell.

In spite of frequent visits by high-level IMF missions, in its first five months the stabilization plan did not receive any international financial support. The plan's success in the short term will depend on whether its fiscal achievements — a balanced budget and a fall in government spending as a share of GDP — can be maintained. The still unresolved military conflict and social tensions will reduce the probability of doing so. The long-term success of the plan will depend on the incentives that it provides to workers and entrepreneurs and on whether an environment conducive to economic growth and restructuring is created. The changes in tax legislation to date have failed to provide the appropriate incentives, while the latter two issues have yet to be addressed.

In addition to the stabilization program, two further areas of economic policy making deserve mention: an ambitious public works program and a social policy. The construction of a large number of major infra-structural works was inaugurated in 1993 with ceremonies befitting their alleged national and historic importance.[50] Croatia thus arguably became the largest per capita and per square kilometer building site for highways and tunnels in the world. In fact, at least until recently high-ranking government politicians were continuing to add to the list of construction projects for highways and tunnels.[51] The social policy implemented after mid-1993, due to its limited scope and even more limited resources, left the main burden of unemployment and low wages to the family.[52]

CONCLUSION

A balance sheet cannot yet be drawn up for any of the three dominant economic processes in which Croatia has been engaged since 1990. This is partly the result of inadequate data, a lack of historical perspective, and unsolved methodological questions (primarily connected to distinguishing the costs of the transition from those of independence). The main problem, however, is the fact that all three processes are still under way. Moreover, each of them has a completely different intertemporal distribution of costs and benefits. In all three cases, there are large upfront costs and immediate destabilizing effects, with the benefits coming only later.

In spite of these disclaimers two conclusions can be drawn. The first is that establishing a new economic space was achieved quickly and the costs were not prohibitive, largely due to the inherited federal features of Yugoslavia and an adequate supply of human capital. The second conclusion concerns the opportunities that independence offers for the shaping of transition policy. Freeing oneself from the "convoy effect" — by which the slowest moving party slows down all the others — and concentrating on the problems of a smaller economy may enable those in power to focus on the most relevant issues and to find solutions suited to Croatian conditions. The divergence of the transition paths of former Yugoslav republics is a clear illustration of this point. Moreover, economic independence has simplified decision making by eliminating the need for extensive negotiations and compromises with the other regions of the former Yugoslavia. Of course, the extraordinary costs of the war must be subtracted from these present and future benefits. These costs could not have been anticipated, for it was impossible to imagine beforehand the brutality of the Wars of Yugoslav Succession.

NOTES

1.   Of course, there had always been criticism of various aspects of the Yugoslav economy, but during the 1980s not only did its level and popular following increase, but there was much more receptiveness to it among politicians.

2.   During the 1980s three efforts were made by the ruling elite to reform and resuscitate self-management and socialism. The first one was in 1983 on the basis of the report of the Kraigher Commission, on which see Lazović (1983). The second was in 1986 in the aftermath of the recommendations of the Vrhova Commission, on which see Pašić (1986). The third and last effort was in 1989 when Prime Minister Ante Marković offered his so-called "new socialism"; see Marković (1989). Interestingly, the first proposal received the official support of all political structures (party, state, and other organizations on all levels), the second got partial and much more low-key support (mostly within the party), while the third was a "white knight" effort (backed only by a small part of the ruling elite).

3.   Yugoslavia's relative position in comparison to the Western economies remained unchanged, even though relative to certain East-Central European ones (notably, Czechoslovakia) it performed well; see Bićanić and Škreb (1994).

4. The literature is extensive and dates from the late 1960s. The results were based either on a comparison of actual prices (many administratively determined) and calculated equilibrium prices, or on an analysis of biased administrative decisions.

5. During the 1980s there were four attempts at macroeconomic stabilization. The first began in 1982 under the premiership of Milka Planinc and attempted to establish external liquidity, to make cuts in domestic consumption, and to effect staggered relative price changes. The second started in 1987 under the premiership of Branko Mikulić and was based on inflationary expectations and "programmed inflation," whereby prices were adjusted to planned and not real levels of inflation. The third was designed by the same premier and implemented in 1989 by selecting four macroeconomic variables as anchors. The fourth and final federal attempt at stabilization started in 1990 and was implemented during the Marković premiership; it concentrated on influencing inflationary expectations and achieving internal convertibility.

6. This point is best illustrated by the Enterprise Law. The law regulated self-management and nonsocialized ownership; after passage in 1988 it was significantly amended three times in the ensuing year. Each set of changes further eroded the privileges of social ownership, leading to an increasingly level playing field regarding forms of ownership. A similar fate was shared by the Foreign Trade Law, as well as by proposed changes of the constitution. See Bićanić and Škreb (1992).

7. In two republics the renamed communist party retained complete control, in a further two there was power sharing with ex-communists elected as presidents and parliaments and governments led by noncommunists, while in another two the renamed communist party lost all control. Croatia was in the third group. Federal elections did not take place, so that at that level only some of the republic delegations to the Chamber of Nationalities changed composition based on the results of the republic elections.

8. In October 1990 Serbia introduced special taxes on Slovenian and Croatian goods and blocked all payments (bank, giro, and other) to those republics.

9. Serbia was the first to introduce property taxes and rents that were higher for assets owned by out-of-republic enterprises. Croatia introduced discriminatory property taxes in 1991.

10. These hostile, "Balkan-style" takeovers began in the summer of 1990. For example, branches of Croatian and Slovenian enterprises in Serbia declared themselves independent from their parent companies and in certain instances merged with similar Serbian companies. No legal action was possible — indeed local courts sanctioned such takeovers. Enterprises in other republics followed the Serbian example. In mid-1991, the Croatian Chamber of Commerce estimated the value of property thus lost in Serbia at around 3 billion DM (*Novi vjesnik*, August 12, 1993, p. 2). These takeovers inspired an interesting form of defensive collusion among enterprises with units in more than one republic, which swapped plants, offices, and wholesale and retail outlets among themselves, so that they all ended up as single-republic enterprises. Note that citations such as the one above to *Novi vjesnik* generally refer to articles in Croatian newspapers.

11. First, Serbia without regard for proper procedure took out large loans of primary money from the National Bank of Yugoslavia (NBY) during the fourth quarter of 1991. Second, in late July 1992 the NBY expelled Croatia and Slovenia from the Yugoslav monetary system.

12. In September 1990 Serbia stopped transferring part of its fiscal revenue to the federal authorities. By the end of that year, Slovenia and Croatia retaliated and did the

same. Slovenia also stopped transferring customs duties to the federal budget, a practice later followed by Croatia.

13.   Instead of following the previous practice of first hammering out a federal consensus about change and then changing the legislation from the federal level on downward, individual republics now chose to amend their legislation independently. Serbia was the first to break with the usual sequencing when it passed its new constitution in 1988, although this change did not affect the economy. With respect to the economy the legislation on privatization passed during 1990 and 1991 in Croatia and Slovenia was more important. Finally, Croatia and Slovenia independently passed their new constitutions in December 1992.

14.   These negotiations were initiated by the federal presidency. Three options were tabled: a confederation of republics (implying looser relations than the then-existing ones); an "asymmetric" federation (a "two-track" Yugoslavia); and a tighter federation (reducing the autonomy of the republics). Croatia, together with Slovenia, argued in favor of a loose confederation, which in the economy meant a customs union, joint mutual market, and coordinated monetary policy. Interestingly, economics did not figure prominently in these options, with the exception of the third one, which required centralization due to its claim that only centralized economic policy can provide efficient crisis management. All other options accepted the notion of a single economic space — that is, a common currency and tariff system, and internal free trade. English translations of the relevant documents were published in *Yugoslav Survey* (1990; 1991a; 1991b).

15.   The scope of the republic national banks within the federal central banking system is described in Gajić (1989).

16.   The time of year at which the exchange took place was chosen because the Christmas shopping spree would reduce the cash balances held by households, making the operation easier: the conversion of bank balances is a mere accounting formality, while that of cash is a more involved process. Indeed, while special provisions were made for those who could not change their cash holdings during the specified period (soldiers, displaced persons, and so on), queues and inflation soon reduced any interest on their part.

17.   The first name chosen for the permanent currency was the kruna or crown, but in the autumn of 1993, this name was replaced by the kuna (*kuna* is the Croatian word for mink). The change was very controversial and did not receive the support of the opposition parties or of large sections of the public, since the new name coincides with that of the currency used in Croatia during the Second World War.

18.   For a description of fiscal federalism in Yugoslavia, see Raičević and Popović (1990).

19.   For the November 1991 agreement with Slovenia, see *Narodne novine*, no. 57, 1991; for the February 1992 agreement with Macedonia, see *Narodne novine*, no. 6, 1992; and for the agreement with Bosnia-Herzegovina of later that same month, see *Narodne novine*, no. 8, 1992.

20.   During late 1991 Croatia imposed a special war tax on all non-Croatian goods, including imports from other former Yugoslav republics, a move that caused great dissatisfaction in Slovenia.

21.   By the autumn of 1993 the government had come to see this as one of the main and most lucrative forms of economic crime.

22.   These official statistics are as of November 8, 1993, and were communicated to the author by Dr. Miloš Judaš, a government representative.

23.   In 1992, the registered number of nights spent by tourists fell to 16 percent of the 1988 level (RHDZS, no. 7, 1993, p. 33), although tourism began to recover in 1994.

24.   The tonnage of goods in rail transport fell by 40 percent, while sea transport levels remained almost unchanged (RHDZS, no. 7, 1993, p. 53).

25.   From march until the end of September 1993, electricity reductions for industry and households in Dalmatia averaged ten hours daily and were as long as twelve hours in certain instances. These power cuts were no longer necessary after the autumn rains arrived.

26.   During this time enterprises reorganized themselves as shell (or daughter) companies around a nonprivatized core (or parent) company. The few genuine privatizations that took place were worker buyouts of small enterprises. See Uvalić (1991).

27.   These discussions were dominated by the deputy prime minister, who favored slow privatization and a dominant role of the state, and by the minister for privatization, who argued in favor of rapid privatization and a voucher scheme. The latter resigned on grounds of principle when the legislation was passed; the former did so a little later under unclear circumstances and in the face of a great deal of unproved gossip.

28.   There are special provisions for those employed in state-owned firms or in the administration who would otherwise be excluded.

29.   In an opinion poll conducted in early 1992, 43.6 percent of the respondents were dissatisfied with the course and method of privatization and only 18.9 percent were satisfied, as reported in *Večernji list*, February 27, 1993, p. 5.

30.   The first case noted in the press occurred in October 1992 and concerned the use of "managerial loans" by a firm in Split.

31.   Privatization legislation was geared to the fact that the state owned most nonprivate housing. Enterprises were induced to cede the ownership of apartments to the state, thereby decreasing their value and easing their privatization. The state was able to gain from this procedure in one of two ways; either it obtained cash — up front or in installments — which went directly to the budget, or it decreased the public debt by reducing its obligation to repay citizens' frozen foreign currency savings.

32.   By the end of June 33,000 apartments had been sold, which represents just under half of those owned by the state (*Vjesnik*, August 26, 1993, p. 17).

33.   The statistical office has yet to calculate data on gross national or domestic product.

34.   The benchmark for measuring Croatia's economic performance is monthly average values for 1990, that year being the last before independence.

35.   Inflation was a major problem in Yugoslavia since the first price reforms of the early 1960s. However, during the 1980s it rose to such levels that it was best described on a monthly basis. By the end of the 1980s monthly inflation rates were nearly hyperinflationary (over 40 percent), although they did plummet in early 1990 under the Marković program, before rising again to around 20 percent.

36.   The shares of Germany, Italy, and Slovenia in Croatia's exports in 1992 were 16.8, 19.8, and 24.0 percent, respectively, while their proportions of Croatia's imports that year were 17.2, 17.1, and 19.6 percent, respectively (*Privredni vjesnik*, September 20, 1993, p. 7).

37.   There was a brief increase in real wages in mid-1993 due to the introduction

of new collective bargaining procedures and, more importantly, to the policies of the new government appointed in April 1993.

38.   Due to high and variable rates of inflation, the nature of the monthly wage calculations, and the daily devaluation of the Croatian dinar, the value oscillates around this benchmark figure. The average wage in Zagreb in June 1993 was 204 DM (*Večernji list*, August 31, 1993, p. 9).

39.   This figure has been officially estimated at 450 DM (*Privredni vjesnik*, August 15, 1993, p. 13), while the trade unions have suggested a figure of 491 DM (*Večernji list*, September 2, 1993, p. 2).

40.   The state budget now directly finances health, primary and secondary education, the universities, public sector research, and, of course, the salaries of civil servants.

41.   This section draws heavily upon Bićanić (1994).

42.   The critics, who are misleadingly referred to in Croatia as "conservatives," support a package of measures that they refer to as "national rejuvenation and national priorities." Their position combines a nationalistic focus on war-related issues with a belief in what they see as Keynesian-type measures to stimulate the economy. They (correctly) pointed out that the architects of this first stabilization effort were among the authors of the many failed Yugoslav stabilization programs, pointed to its IMF inspiration, and suspected an IMF conspiracy. As an alternative they proposed programs based not on monetary restrictions but on stimulating aggregate demand, primarily through measures of a public works nature.

43.   During a row over a virtually free loan to the government, the NBC governor, Dr. Ante Čičin-Šain — who was not a member of the ruling party — unsuccessfully stood up for the bank's independence. He subsequently became Croatia's ambassador to the EC and was replaced by Pero Jurković, a member of the ruling party with no independent power base. Jurković has managed to avoid public conflict with the government while working with three prime ministers in succession.

44.   See "Osnove" (1993); a more detailed version of this program received only a limited circulation.

45.   Croatia, along with Slovenia and Macedonia, succeeded to the former membership of the Socialist Federal Republic of Yugoslavia on December 15, 1992.

46.   A point frequently made by the then deputy prime minister in charge of economics, Dr. Borislav Škegro; see for example *Slobodna Dalmacija*, June 3, 1993, p. 3.

47.   The NBC admitted to controlling only 40 percent of the quantity of money, while the government acknowledges that only half of taxes were collected; see Bićanić (1993a, p. 38). Considerable "quasi-export" activity takes place in order to collect export subsidies, as do imaginative schemes designed to avoid import levies. These activities are mostly connected to trade with war-torn Bosnia-Herzegovina, where there is no real border control on either side, and along the "soft" frontier with Slovenia.

48.   Written over a six-month period by Croatian and foreign economists, the program is claimed by its authors to have earned IMF support, as stated by the prime minister on numerous occasions (see, e.g., *Vjesnik*, October 13, 1993, p. 10).

49.   The promulgation of the program was announced in a three-step procedure. The main elements were unveiled following an emergency meeting of the government on Sunday, October 2, 1993. Earlier that day, the National Security Council and ruling party presidency discussed and gave their support to the program. However, the leaders

of the trade unions supported it only grudgingly. Relevant decisions on monetary policy were taken at two meetings of the NBC's council, one before and one after the program went into effect.

50. The various projects include the continuation of the highway from Zagreb to the Slovenian border and thence Graz, the building of a highway from Zagreb to the Hungarian border, and the opening of a new section of the road from Zagreb to Rijeka, all inaugurated in the late spring of 1993. In addition, work on two major tunnels was started in the late summer of 1993. One is 12 kilometers long and runs through Velebit; when finished in five years, it will link Dalmatia with the rest of Croatia by bypassing areas currently administered by Serbian rebels and the UN. The other is a 14-kilometer-long railway tunnel through Učka, which will link Istria with the rest of Croatia, bypass Slovenia, and take five-and-a-half years to build (see *Večernji list*, September 25, 1993, p. 17).

51. Since the late summer of 1993, President Franjo Tudman has opened the construction sites for the two long tunnels described above and talked about the need for a Croatian economic renascence. Meanwhile, the president of the chamber of commerce has continued to offer his strong backing for building tunnels and highways (*Vjesnik*, October 3, 1993, p. 3) and to promise a "Croatian New Deal" (*Vjesnik*, August 10, 1993, p. 7).

52. For a more detailed discussion of social policy and the deterioration in living conditions through 1993, see Bićanić (1993c).

REFERENCES

Anušić, Zoran. "Budžetski deficit i inflacija: Hrvatska u 1991. i 1992. godini." *Privredna kretanja i ekonomska politika*, no. 21 (May 1993): 23–36.

Bićanić, Ivo. "Some General Comparisons of the Impact of the Two World Crises of the Twentieth Century on the Yugoslav Economy." In Iván T. Berend and Knut Borchardt (eds.), *The Impact of the Depression of the 1930's and Its Relevance for the Contemporary World*, pp. 248–275. Budapest: Academy Research Center for Eastern Europe, 1986.

Bićanić, Ivo. "The Croatian Economy: Achievements and Prospects." *RFE/RL Research Report* 2, 26 (June 25, 1993a): 33–38.

Bićanić, Ivo. "Privatization in Croatia." *East European Politics and Society* 7, 3 (Fall 1993b): 422–439.

Bićanić, Ivo. "Croatians Struggle to Make Ends Meet." *RFE/RL Research Report* 2, 45 (November 12, 1993c): 29–34.

Bićanić, Ivo. "Croatia's Economic Stabilization Program: Third Time Unlucky?" *RFE/RL Research Report* 3, 3 (January 21, 1994): 36–42.

Bićanić, Ivo, and Iva Dominis. "Tudjman Remains Dominant after Croatian Elections." *RFE/RL Research Report* 1, 37 (September 18, 1992): 20–26.

Bićanić, Ivo, and Iva Dominis. "Refugees and Displaced Persons in the Former Yugoslavia." *RFE/RL Research Report* 2, 3 (January 15, 1993a): 1–4.

Bićanić, Ivo, and Iva Dominis. "The Multiparty Elections in Croatia: Round Two." *RFE/RL Research Report* 2, 16 (May 7, 1993b): 17–21.

Bićanić, Ivo, and Marko Škreb. "The Independence of Croatia: Economic Causes and Consequences." Paper presented at the conference on the Assets and Liabilities of Independence, held in Trento, December 10–11, 1992 (mimeo).

Bićanić, Ivo, and Marko Škreb. "The Yugoslav Economy from Amalgamation to Decomposition: Failed Efforts at Moulding a New Economic Space, 1919–91." In David Good (ed.), *Economic Transformations in Central and Eastern Europe: Lessons and Legacies from the Past*, pp. 147–62. New York: Routledge, 1994.

Gajić, Dragutin. "The National Bank of Yugoslavia." *Yugoslav Survey* 30, 3 (1989): 71–93.

Grubišić, Mirko. "Medurepublički promet robe i usluga od 1968 do 1987." *Analize i prikazi*, no. 73. Zagreb: Zavod za statistiku Republike Hrvatske, 1990.

Lazović, Budimir (ed.). "Long-Term Programme of Economic Stabilization." *Yugoslav Survey* 24, 4 (1983): 3–26.

Marković, Ante. "Statement by Ante Marković in the Assembly of the SFRY on the Occasion of His Election to the Office of President of the Federal Executive Council." *Yugoslav Survey* 30, 1 (1989): 39–60.

[NBC/B.] *Bulletin*. Zagreb: National Bank of Croatia, various 1993 issues.

[NBC/MSI.] *Main Statistical Indicators*. Zagreb: National Bank of Croatia, various 1993 issues.

["Osnove."] "Osnove stabilizacijskog programa." Zagreb, December 22, 1993 (mimeo).

Pašić, Najdan (ed.). *Kritička analiza funkcioniranja političkog sistema socijalističkog samoupravljanja*. Belgrade: Center za radničko samoupravljanje, 1986.

Raičević, Božidar, and Dejan Popović. "Fiscal System and Fiscal Policy." *Yugoslav Survey* 31, 3 (1990): 27–52.

[RHDZS.] *Mjesečno statističko izvješće*. Zagreb: Republika Hrvatska Državni zavod za statistiku, various 1993 and 1994 issues.

[SIMAF.] *Croatian Economic Trends*. Zagreb: State Institution for Macroeconomic Analysis and Forecasting, various 1993 issues.

Sirotković, Jakov, and Vladimir Stipetić (eds.). *Ekonomika Jugoslavije*. 12th edition. Zagreb: Informator, 1990.

Stakić, Budimir. "The Foreign Trade System." *Yugoslav Survey* 28, 2 (1987): 43–58.

[UNHCR.] "Information Notes on Former Yugoslavia." no. 8. Office of the Special Envoy for Former Yugoslavia, UN High Commission for Refugees, 1993.

Uvalić, Milica. "How Different is Yugoslavia?" *European Economy*, special edition no. 2, 1991, pp. 199–214.

[*Yugoslav Survey*.] Documents on the Future Organization of Relations in Yugoslavia." *Yugoslav Survey* 31, 4 (1990): 3–60.

[*Yugoslav Survey*.] "Documents on the Future Regulation of Relations in Yugoslavia." *Yugoslav Survey* 32, 1 (1991a): 3–26.

[*Yugoslav Survey*.] "Documents on the Yugoslav Crisis." *Yugoslav Survey* 32, 3 (1991b): 15–96.

8

Macedonia

Michael L. Wyzan

INTRODUCTION

This chapter addresses the first steps toward economic independence of
Macedonia, a new nation that has been beset by enormous external
shocks and internal ethnic cleavages but that has shown an encouraging
— if up to this point less than entirely satisfactory — degree of policy
competence in dealing with its economic, foreign policy, and ethnic
problems.

From the point of view of Macedonia's external environment, everything that can go wrong has done so. Trade, transport, and communications have traditionally been oriented on a north-south axis; for
topographical and geopolitical reasons, little such activity has been
conducted with Bulgaria to the east or Albania to the west. The UN
sanctions against the rump Yugoslavia — especially Security Council
Resolution 820 of late April 1993 prohibiting goods transit through
Macedonia's northern neighbor — as well as two blockades of the
southern border by Greece, have been enormously costly.[1]

Greek objections greatly delayed Macedonia's admittance to the
leading international institutions and the establishment of diplomatic
relations with the larger Western countries. Macedonia was finally
allowed to enter the UN, the International Monetary Fund (IMF), and the
European Bank for Reconstruction and Development in April 1993 as
the Former Yugoslav Republic of Macedonia, a year-and-a-half after its
declaration of independence. Entry into the World Bank did not come

until early February 1994, when a group of Western countries donated funding for settling the country's $107 million arrears to that organization. In mid-December 1993, several European Community (EC) members extended diplomatic recognition to Macedonia, including France, Germany, Great Britain, and the Netherlands. This move infuriated Greece, which on February 16, 1994, barred Macedonia from using the port of Thessaloniki, closed its border with the country to all goods but those of a humanitarian nature, and closed its consulate in Skopje.[2]

Internally, Macedonia is among the world's most ethnically divided countries, with a restive ethnic Albanian minority of between 20 and 30 percent of its population.[3] Ethnic polarization sometimes manifests itself in strange ways: the Albanian political parties called for the resignation of the governor of the National Bank of the Republic of Macedonia (NBRM) to protest the monuments depicted on the banknotes and coins issued in May 1993. Ethnic Albanians have not been employed in the social sector to an extent commensurate with their numbers. Those who have found such employment are generally teachers or blue-collar workers, with senior management positions exceedingly rare (Poulton, 1993, p. 26)l Albanians make up only about 15 percent of registered job seekers (Čangova, 1993).

Nonetheless, the first two postcommunist governments scored a number of economic successes. The first, under Independent Prime Minister Nikola Kljusev, who took office in March 1991, after multiparty elections in November and December 1990, oversaw the introduction of a new currency — the denar — and an anti-inflation program in late April 1992. The second government, that of Prime Minister Branko Crvenkovski, leader of the Social Democratic Alliance, was formed in September 1992. It was a coalition in which academic economists hold most economic ministries and there are five ethnically Albanian ministers. Crvenkovski formed another government in December 1994, following elections in October 1994.

The first Crvenkovski government made a number of adjustments to the anti-inflation package in October 1992, with limited success. It subsequently introduced a new set of measures in December 1993, in this instance — for the first time — with financial, moral, and technical support from the international financial community.

Although the anti-inflation programs have had serious flaws, mostly due to their failure to provide a comprehensive approach to the problem, much has been achieved. Since monetary independence, Macedonia, traditionally the poorest Yugoslav republic, through late 1993 had enjoyed a more stable and prosperous economy than any other former Yugoslav economy other than Slovenia. Macedonia's monthly average rate of retail price inflation during June 1992–December 1993 was 12.0 percent (see Table 8.1), compared with 5.9 percent in Slovenia and 23.7 percent in Croatia since their respective realizations of monetary independence.[4] The monthly wage in Macedonia has been on the order of $150–200, well below Slovenia's, but greatly in excess of that in the rump Yugoslavia and somewhat above Croatia's, at least until the late fall of 1993.

The pace of structural change was glacial until May 1993, when laws on foreign investment, privatization, foreign trade, the foreign exchange market (creating a unified, foreign exchange market with a flexible exchange rate), and foreign credit relations were passed. December 1993 saw the passage of important legislation governing the budget process and taxation.

The organization of the remainder of this chapter is as follows. The next section describes Macedonia's starting conditions at independence, including its level of development and external economic relations. The third section looks at the vicissitudes of macroeconomic stabilization policy from independence through the end of 1993. The fourth examines legal and structural issues, with the focus on foreign economic relations, privatization of industrial enterprises, and tax and budget policy. The final section of the chapter evaluates Macedonia's first steps toward economic independence in the light of the discussion in the introductory chapter of this volume.

THE YUGOSLAV LEGACY

Level of Development

Macedonia trailed far behind Slovenia and somewhat behind the Yugoslav average with respect to most important socioeconomic matters; for many key variables, the gap increased over time. However, rapid industrialization fed by formal and informal resource transfers succeeded in turning Macedonia into Yugoslavia's most industrialized republic, leaving a legacy of industrial gigantism with attendant debt and employment woes.

As can be seen from Table 8.2, Macedonia's share of total Yugoslav real social product hovered for the last two decades of Yugoslavia's existence at between 5 and 6 percent, while Slovenia's was between 16 and 17 percent. Data on real gross fixed investment tell an almost

TABLE 8.1
Macedonian Macroeconomic Indicators

	Retail Prices[1]	Producer Prices[1]	Industrial Production[2]	Unemployment[3]	Average Wage[4]	Black Market Exchange Rate[5]	M1[1]	M2[1]
December 1991	15.7	19.1	-13.9	166,873	11,974	n.a.	n.a.	n.a.
March 1992	41.1	46.2	-6.4	171,514	27,285	n.a.	19.8	n.a.
April 1992	78.5	103.2	-10.9	172,627	38,412	645.00	73.3	n.a.
May 1992	60.7	59.7	-13.2	172,982	42,858	585.67	13.9	n.a.
June 1992	11.1	7.8	-16.8	171,627	43,268	600.00	6.7	n.a.
July 1992	7.6	3.6	-25.3	171,596	58,058	640.73	25.7	n.a.
August 1992	6.8	5.7	-21.3	172,637	74,316	637.18	15.1	n.a.
September 1992	16.2	7.0	-28.6	173,149	92,779	802.83	11.7	n.a.
October 1992	28.4	17.9	-18.8	172,871	103,497	872.50	12.5	n.a.
November 1992	10.1	13.1	-23.2	172,213	118,064	1,196.17	22.2	n.a.
December 1992	19.8	15.9	-13.6	173,350	133,995	1,595.83	23.9	n.a.
January 1993	15.6	12.0	-30.2	174,022	164,723	1,854.31	7.3	5.2
February 1993	32.5	30.8	-12.7	174,737	203,297	2,203.21	4.3	-0.7
March 1993	8.5	4.3	-15.3	174,367	257,500	2,199.03	10.2	2.8
April 1993	3.4	8.1	-10.4	174,927	294,600	2,036.81	19.8	3.7
May 1993	8.0	1.7	-15.2	175,002	3,229	21.94	15.8	49.7
June 1993	-0.9	1.4	-5.6	174,232	3,487	23.25	5.8	9.3
July 1993	7.7	3.8	-13.9	173,580	3,837	24.98	37.1	13.1
August 1993	9.5	4.8	-3.5	173,798	4,079	25.73	4.6	4.8
September 1993	6.5	3.4	-2.4	175,182	4,659	27.08	-0.2	8.4
October 1993	12.1	10.1	-20.2	175,651	5,156	32.18	5.2	11.9

November 1993	12.1	10.5	−16.7	175,526	5,812	37.46	3.6	10.9
December 1993	13.5	19.2	−10.8	177,156	6,315	44.51	20.2	23.9

Sources: RZS/MSI (1992, 1993); NBRM/B (1992, 1993); some data provided by the NBRM.

Notes:
[1] Percentage rate of change relative to previous month.
[2] Percentage rate of change relative to same month previous year.
[3] Number registered as looking for work.
[4] Denari; average monthly net pay per worker in social sector, including both economic and noneconomic activities.
[5] Denari per U.S. dollar, monthly average of daily rates on Skopje black market as reported in *Nova Makedonija*; daily rates are average of buying and selling rates.

197

identical story. Macedonia produced only a small and declining share of total Yugoslav exports (4.1 percent in 1990 versus 5.5 percent in 1976), while Slovenia's share rose from almost 19 percent to almost 29 percent over this period. The situation is similar for imports, although here Macedonia's contribution rose from just over 5 percent in 1976 to almost 6 percent in 1990; Slovenia accounted for 17 percent of imports in 1976 and 25 percent in 1990.

TABLE 8.2
Macedonia vs. the Rest of Yugoslavia

		Macedonia		Slovenia		
		Absolute Figure	*Percent Yugo. Total*	*Absolute Figure*	*Percent Yugo. Total*	*Yugoslavia*
Population[1]	1970	1,629	8.00	1,718	8.43	20,371
	1980	1,893	8.49	1,885	8.45	22,304
	1990	2,131	9.34	1,953	8.20	23,809
Labor Force[1]	1970	314	7.53	564	13.52	4,169
	1980	545	8.27	806	12.24	6,583
	1990	679	8.51	862	10.81	7,978
Unemployment	1970	17.78		2.97		7.67
Rate[2]	1980	21.51		1.34		11.93
	1990	23.03		5.17		16.40
Real Social	1970	1,220	5.60	3,560	16.33	21,795
Product[3]	1980	2,145	5.63	6,452	16.94	38,086
	1990	2,298	5.77	6,651	16.46	39,850
Real Social Product	1970	748		2,072		1,070
Per Capita[4]	1980	1,133		3,423		1,708
	1990	1,078		3,359		1,674
Real Gross Fixed	1970	416	5.99	914	13.16	6,948
Investment[3]	1980	797	6.60	1,681	13.93	12,072
	1989	374	4.97	1,343	17.85	7,526
Real Gross Fixed	1970	255		532		341
Investment Per	1980	421		892		541
Capita[4]	1990	177		689		318
Real Net Personal	1970	989		1,376		1,173
Income Per	1980	981		1,465		1,337
Worker[5]	1990	665		1,076		955
Exports[6]	1975	7,304	5.49	24,832	18.65	133,168
	1980	11,428	4.66	50,133	20.46	245,086
	1990	6,555	4.05	46,681	2.81	162,043

		Macedonia		Slovenia		
		Absolute Figure	Percent Yugo. Total	Absolute Figure	Percent Yugo. Total	Yugoslavia
Imports[6]	1975	10,308	5.12	34,351	17.08	201,109
	1980	21,149	5.14	67,235	16.35	411,257
	1990	12,601	5.95	53,017	25.05	211,611
Population per	1970	40		11		28
Passenger Car	1980	11		5		9
	1990	9		3		7
Population per	1970	1,015		707		917
Doctor and	1980	634		486		583
Dentist	1990	398		380		417
Infant Mortality	1970	88.0		24.5		55.5
Rate	1980	54.2		15.3		31.4
	1990	35.3		8.9		20.2

Sources: RZS/SG (1991, pp. 551–554, 556, 563, 568–569, 616); SZS (various issues).

Notes:

[1]Thousands.

[2]Number of unemployed divided by sum of this number and number of workers; percent.

[3]In 1972 prices; thousand dinari.

[4]In 1972 prices; dinari.

[5]In 1970 prices; dinari.

[6]In current prices; million dinari.

In per capita terms, Macedonia's real social product fell from 70 percent of the national figure in 1970 to 64 percent in 1990, while Slovenia's went from 194 percent in 1970 to 201 percent in 1990. However, the picture is not totally dark. Macedonia enjoyed the fastest growth of industrial production over 1965–87 of all eight Yugoslav regions, resulting in its having the highest share of industry in social product of all regions (51.5 percent in 1987 versus 47 percent in Slovenia). Total factor productivity grew faster in Macedonia than in the other three LDRs (Kraft, 1992, p. 26).

It is difficult to come up with reliable absolute figures on output per capita according to Western definitions. The World Bank (1992, p. 12) reports a debt-to-GNP ratio implying a GNP per capita of $1,157.

Physical indicators of the standard of living often reveal a large gap between Macedonia and the more prosperous parts of Yugoslavia. Even though Macedonia's infant mortality rate fell by 60 percent between 1970 and 1990, the national average fell by 64 percent over this period, and the Macedonian rate was fully 75 percent higher than the national average in 1990 (versus only 59 percent in 1970). However, such other indicators as the number of persons per passenger car and the number of persons per doctor and dentist show Macedonia improving its relative position over time.

As one of Yugoslavia's LDRs, Macedonia was the recipient of various forms of transfers over the years, with monetary/credit policy being the largest source of such flows. Although disbursements from the so-called Federal Fund amounted to only 4.1 percent of Macedonian gross social product (GSP) during 1984–88, net subsidies of various forms came to 35 percent of GSP (Kraft, 1992, p. 15). The net subsidy figure includes formal taxes and subsidies, as well as quasi-subsidies and quasi-taxes, and losses and gains on money.

These transfers have left a harsh legacy for post-Yugoslav and post-communist independence. Although such funds no doubt contributed to Macedonia's relatively rapid industrialization, they left it with a number of heavily indebted — to both domestic commercial banks and foreign creditors — capital-intensive monstrosities with traditional markets only in the former Yugoslavia (largely in Serbia). Some 43 percent of the country's foreign debt is owed by five large industrial enterprises; over 20 percent ($182 million) is owed by the large ferro-nickel plan "Fenimak" alone (World Bank, 1992, pp. 11–12).

External Economic Activity

Macedonian external economic relations during the postwar period were characterized by persistent trade deficits, small trade volumes compared to other republics, and the strongest orientation toward the socialist world of all republics. It inherited debt-service obligations on a par with those of "moderately indebted middle-income countries" (World Bank, 1992, p. 12) and next to nothing in foreign exchange reserves.

Macedonia's trade balance was in the red every year after 1962, although trade surpluses were registered in 1958–60 and 1962 (RZS/NT, 1991, p. 10). Foreign trade traditionally accounted for only 7 percent of national product, versus 27 percent for trade with other former Yugoslav republics (World Bank, 1992, p. 10). In contrast, Slovenia exported about a third of its production beyond the borders of Yugoslavia (Bookman, 1990, p. 99), while the comparable figure for Croatia was approximately 11 percent (Bićanić, 1993, p. 34). In 1990, 36 percent of Macedonian exports went to and 38 percent of its imports came from socialist countries; the figures for the developed capitalist countries were

53 and 54 percent, respectively (RZS/NT, 1991, p. 12). For comparison purposes, during 1990 Slovenia conducted only 20.5 percent of its export trade, and 13.5 percent of its import trade, with the socialist world (BS, June–August 1992, pp. 21–22).

MONETARY INDEPENDENCE AND MACROECONOMIC STABILIZATION

Macedonian monetary independence has been sufficiently successful to vindicate the decision to leave the Yugoslav dinar zone; monthly inflation, while high by most standards, has been well below that in hyperinflationary Yugoslavia. Macedonia also outperformed Croatia in this respect through October 1993, when that more developed but war-torn land experienced a major decline in monthly inflation rates under its own stabilization program.

Macroeconomic stabilization in Macedonia can be divided into three stages: (1) the formal and only partially successful effort that began with the introduction of the denar and the promulgation of a heterodox stabilization program (Petkovski, Petreski, and Slaveski, 1992) on April 26, 1992; (2) the first Crvenkovski government's less formal, initial attempts to stabilize the economy, which began in October 1992 (although by mid-1993 these efforts had showed some success in reducing inflation and stabilizing the exchange rate, the fall of the year revealed that they too were far from sufficient to deal with the country's macroeconomic imbalances); and (3) a more formal stabilization package introduced in early December 1993, toward the close of the period covered by this chapter. This program has the advantage over its predecessors of enjoying the support of the international financial community (World Bank, 1994) and more than a year later it continued to provide the country with a respectable level of macroeconomic stability.

The initial stabilization program emphasized tight monetary policy, fiscal restraint, incomes policy, and price controls on a small number of necessities. This program at first scored some success in reducing inflation and stabilizing the black market exchange rate. However, the maintenance of a dual exchange rate mechanism, the absence of an incomes policy, the persistence of muddled Yugoslav budgetary accounting, and the provision of selective credits to agriculture from the primary emission all contributed to the program's undoing.

The only slightly revised stabilization program of October 1992 initially did little to improve the situation. Nonetheless, in the spring and early summer of 1993 improvements in the external environment and new legislation governing the foreign ex-change market and foreign trade led to improved economic performance. The monthly rate of retail price change fell from 32.5 percent in February 1993 to an improbable −0.9 percent in June 1993 and the exchange rate was more or less stable from February through May.

Unfortunately, the country still lacked a comprehensive stabilization program backed by the international financial institutions, dealing with the various macroeconomic imbalances, a real wage considerably higher than in neighboring postsocialist countries, parafiscal deficits, and low foreign exchange reserves. By October, inflation returned to double-digit territory, and the denar depreciated against the dollar by roughly 50 percent between May and December.

The reform program launched in December 1993 stresses restoring wage discipline, focusing monetary policy on its proper role as a foundation of macroeconomic stability and away from selectively crediting individual sectors, and fiscal sector reform to reduce the budget deficit and shift spending from entitlements to measures supportive of structural reform (Government, 1994). This program deserves praise for its clear-headed focus on the most important macroeconomic problems that have eluded solution in the past. Nonetheless, the government must still reckon with a low level of foreign exchange reserves — a significant proportion of which were used in the arrears-clearing exercise with the World Bank — and an extremely harsh and unpredictable external environment, both of which may detract from exchange rate stability in the future. Still, more than a year after introduction, the program had produced relatively low inflation, a small budget deficit, and a stable currency.

Background Information on the Domestic and External Economies

Partly as a result of the restrictive policies described below and partly as a result of exogenous shocks related to the Wars of Yugoslav Succession, the UN embargoes, and border problems caused by Greece, Macedonia is in a deep depression. Industrial production fell by 8.8 percent in 1990, 17.4 percent in 1991, 16 percent in 1992 (RZS/MSI, no. 6, 1993, p. 8), 15 percent during 1993 (MR, 1993, p. 2), and 15 percent in 1994, a cumulative decline over 1990–94 of almost 54 percent. By the beginning of 1992 the standard of living is said to have fallen to the level of 1962 (*Nova Makedonija*, December 6, 1992, p. 2); estimates of GDP per capita in 1993 run as low as $687 (MIC, February 4, 1994).[5]

As for the balance of payments, Macedonia has been running small trade, current account, and overall imbalances. Table 8.3 provides some idea of the order of magnitude of these deficits. The data presented in the table are from official sources and deviate somewhat from those reported by the IMF, especially for 1991, although the underlying trends described below are present in both data sets.

Note that the chief method of closing the financing gaps posed by the overall deficits has been via increases in payments arrears with international financial institutions and the London and Paris Clubs. There has been precious little in foreign exchange reserves to deplete. Additional methods of keeping payments imbalances under control have been cutting back on imports, especially from countries other than former Yugoslav republics and former CMEA member-states, and a sharp reduction in the net outflow of short-term capital on the part of commercial banks. In 1994 Macedonia received slightly less than $100 million from international financial institutions, compared with virtually nothing in earlier years. Another $222 million worth of international assistance went to settle arrears and to make current payments to these same institutions (MR, 1993, p. 4).

Maintaining trade links with other former Yugoslav republics has been extremely difficult given the payments difficulties that have arisen now that they all use different currencies and the wars in Croatia and Bosnia-Herzegovina. Despite the distance and the wars between them, Slovenia is Macedonia's largest trading partner among the former republics. In 1992, Macedonia imported $133 million worth of goods from that country and exported $78 million to it; the trade deficit widened during 1993, when Slovenian exports increased to $198 million, while Macedonian exports grew to only $89 million (BS, no. 2, 1994, p. 23). Through 1993, trade between Croatia and Macedonia also showed imbalances in Croatia's favor, although trade volumes were smaller than in the Slovenian case and were falling over time. In 1993 Croatia had a trade surplus with Macedonia of $17 million, compared with $31 million in 1992 (RHDZS, no. 2, 1994, p. 36).

In the meantime, trade with Macedonia's eastern and western neighbors, Albania and Bulgaria, respectively, has increased considerably, although no data exist allowing comparison of such activity before and after independence. Macedonian trade with Bulgaria was highly unbalanced in the latter's favor in 1992 and 1993. According to Official Bulgarian data — which likely substantially underestimate these flows — Macedonian imports from Bulgaria were $158.51 million in 1992 and $224.7 million in 1993, while its exports to that country

TABLE 8.3
Macedonian Balance of Payments (million U.S. $)

	1990	1991	1992	1993
Current Account	−409	−259	−19	−8
Trade Balance	−418	−225	−7	−144
Exports	1,113	1,150	1,199	1,055
Imports	1,531	1,375	1,206	1,199
Services, Net	−75	−6	−42	−11
Non-interest, net	−20	23	30	45
Interest, net	−55	−29	−72	−56
Transfers, Net	84	−28	30	147
Private	84	−28	30	119
Official	0	0	0	28
Capital Account	−51	−206	−162	−62
Medium- and Long-term Capital, Net	−61	−107	−96	−79
Received	60	14	9	0
Repaid	121	121	105	−79
Short-term Capital, Net	10	−99	−66	17
Trade credit, net	21	38	15	40
Commercial banks, net	0	−118	−64	−17
Other short-term, net	−11	−19	−17	−6
Errors and Omissions	444	424	87	5
Change in Net Official Reserves	0	0	−61	−66
Change in Cumulative Arrears/Ex Ante Financing Gap	16	41	155	131

Source: *NBRM/B* (1994, p. 79).

amounted to only $34.88 million and $73.17 million, respectively (NSI, 1993, p. 6).

On September 30, 1993, before the arrears to the World Bank were settled, Macedonia's foreign debt in convertible currencies came to $836 million, not including its share of the debt contracted by the erstwhile federal government, which amounts to $3.1 billion. The $836 million broke down as follows: $350 million was owed to commercial banks, $208 million to official creditors, $260 million to international financial organizations (including $161 million to the World Bank), and $17 million in "other credits" (NBRM/B, no. 3, 1993, pp. 43–44).

The Introduction of the Denar

The new currency, in the form of temporary coupons whose replacement with permanent notes and coins began in May 1993, was introduced in an abrupt fashion.[6] The denar — equal to 100 deni — became legal tender during April 27–29, 1992, at which time physical persons could engage in a one-time exchange of their Yugoslav dinari for denari at a rate of 1:1 at banks, post offices, and the Social Accounting Service (SAS). Citizens could have bank accounts converted into denari in amounts of up to 50,000 dinari, also at 1:1. Dinari in excess of this sum were to be deposited in a special savings account at the bank or post office. After that, deposits in dinari would no longer be accepted (*Nova Makedonija*, April 28, 1992, p. 3).

During the exchange of dinari for denari, citizens were allowed to withdraw from their accounts up to 100,000 denari for cash payments and an unlimited amount for noncash payments. There were restrictions on the amounts that physical persons who had exchanged more than 50,000 denari could withdraw from their accounts (*Nova Makedonija*, April 28, 1992, p. 3). Banks and money changers were allowed to sell foreign currency only for denari. Legal persons had to deposit all their cash in their giro accounts at the SAS by April 27. The balance in those accounts on March 31 could be spent, but anything above that sum was to be deposited in a special account. The source of the funds in that account had to be declared to the SAS (*Nova Makedonija*, April 28, 1992, p. 3).

The dinari obtained through the monetary reform were transferred to the NBY, which had been informed in advance of the date and method of the denar's introduction. At the same time, the Yugoslav government agreed not to block trade and payments once the two countries began using different currencies (Grličkov, 1992).

The Content of the April 1992 Anti-Inflation Program

The authors of the anti-inflation program introduced on April 26, 1992, chose to implement a "heterodox" stabilization program, that is, one that includes incomes policy and some price controls, along with the traditional monetary and fiscal measures included in "orthodox" programs. The authors selected monetary, fiscal, and incomes policies as the program's nominal anchors. They did not choose the nominal exchange rate as an anchor, although they decided to maintain a fixed official exchange rate (Petkovski, Petreski, and Slaveski, 1992, pp. 1–2).

With respect to targets in the monetary/credit sphere, the growth of M1 and net domestic assets was to be kept below the rate of price increase. The growth of credit granted by commercial banks and the NBRM was also a nominal indicator. Positive real interest rates were introduced. Such measures as increasing commercial banks' required reserves and raising the discount rate from 60 percent to 170 percent were sufficient to cut the (nominal) liquidity in the banking system by 57 percent between April 30 and May 10 (NBRM/IOM, 1992, p. 3).

On the fiscal side, the program noted that although the state budget was nominally balanced, there were a number of "parafiscal" deficits that had arisen in the extrabudgetary Pension and Disability Fund, Health Care Fund, Employment Fund, and Goods Reserve Fund. Taking these funds into account, the general government cash budget deficit was 3.6 percent of GDP in 1991 (Government, 1994, p. 4). Public consumption was to fall from 38 to 35 percent of national product (Petkovski, Petreski, and Slaveski, 1993, p. 35), largely via eliminating subsidies, which accounted for a third of the budget.

The exchange rate was not to be a nominal anchor because of the lack of foreign currency reserves. A dual exchange rate mechanism was selected, whereby most transactions would take place at a freely floating ("black market") rate, while foreign debt repayment and imports of oil and medicine would take place at the fixed rate of 360 denari to the Deutsche mark (DM) (Petkovski, Petreski, and Slaveski, 1992, p. 4).[7] It was hoped to receive $200 million in foreign financial support to build up the foreign exchange reserves (Petkovski, Petreski, and Slaveski, 1992, p. 4).

With respect to incomes policy, individual wages could be increased by 30 or 25 percent (depending on the sector), while the minimum wage would be set according to a social compact among the three "social partners": the government, the Syndicate of Trade Unions, and the Chamber of Commerce. Those wages that were subject to existing legal regulation would be frozen at 125 percent of their March level. These measures were to stay in place for at least six months, after which there would be partial indexation of wages to monthly inflation, with a tax on wage increases in excess of the percentage allowed (Petkovski, Petreski, and Slaveski, 1992, p. 5). The prices of a number of staple foods, electrical energy, oil derivatives, and communal services would be increased and then frozen for six months (*Nova Makedonija*, April 28, 1992, p. 2).

Results of the April 1992 Anti-Inflation Program

The program had some initial success in reducing inflation and stabilizing the black market exchange rate, but macroeconomic performance subsequently deteriorated as the program's lacunae with respect to foreign exchange, incomes, fiscal, and monetary policy became apparent.

During the six months after the inception of the program and the introduction of the denar, inflation and the decline in the black market exchange rate were far below what prevailed in the rump Yugoslavia. Nonetheless, inflation accelerated to a monthly rate of over 28 percent by October, after falling to below 7 percent in August. Following an initial period of rough equality between the black market and official exchange rates, the gap between them reached 70 percent by October, when the government (officially) devalued the denar.

Perhaps the most important cause of the deterioration in price performance was the collapse of the black market exchange rate (Wyzan, 1993). There was also the breakdown in wage discipline that occurred when the Assembly in July, in the interregnum between governments, increased wages (Cvetkovska, 1992a), sending the real dollar monthly wage from a little over $70 during May and June to almost $119 in October. Additional factors are the parafiscal deficits and the failure to receive the anticipated level of international financial assistance. Finally, the growth rate of M1 was very rapid from July onward, largely the result of the selective credits out of the primary emission to the agricultural sector (Dičevska, 1992).

The biggest failings of Macedonia's first anti-inflation program were as follows: failure to create a unified, market-determined exchange rate; chaos in incomes policy; delay in adopting budgetary accounting that clarifies the government's fiscal stance; and monetary policy subject to hijacking by individual sectors.

The Revamped Stabilization Program of October 1992

Content of the Revamped Program

Macroeconomic policy during Crvenkovski's first term can be divided into two periods. The first, the subject of this subsection, begins with the promulgation of a slightly revised version of the anti-inflation program on October 9, 1992, and runs through December 1993.

With inflation taking off again and the discrepancy between the official and black market exchange rates becoming enormous, the new government revamped its predecessor's anti-inflation program on October 9. Money/credit policy remained a nominal anchor, with control once again exercised over M1, the growth of domestic assets, and credits provided by commercial banks. Credit policy would be tied more closely than previously to the structure of industry, to the seasonal needs of agriculture, and to promoting activities that increase exports (Crvenkovski, 1992). The denar was (officially) devalued to 600 to the DM and its value tied to a basket of currencies rather than just the Deutsche mark. As the second nominal anchor, public consumption was again to be no higher than 35 percent of social product.

The revitalized program maintained the heterodox character of the original by emphasizing control over prices and wages. A new tax on pensions and wages that exceeded twice their respective averages for the republic was proposed (Crvenkovski, 1992). After a one-time increase, wages could be raised further only if actual price inflation exceeded its predicted level (Cvetkovska, 1992b). A minimum wage was set, although organizations without sufficient funds to pay it could pay up to 20 percent less. The prices of various public utilities and communal services would be increased and then frozen, while price controls remained on bread, milk, and flour (*Nova Makedonija*, October 10, 1992, pp. 1–2).

Success of the Revamped Program

There was little improvement in economic performance in the first months after the adjustments to the stabilization program, as rapid monetary growth was accompanied by high inflation, a collapsing exchange rate, and enormous increases in real wages. The downward spiral of the denar on the black market continued: on December 7, by which point the official rate deviated form the black market rate by 80 percent, the denar was again devalued. Although dollar real wages had fallen to $84 in December, without a new collective contract or any other wage regulation mechanism, this figure had increased to almost $145 by May 1993. How was such an increase possible? Cvetkovska (1993a, p. 2) notes that "in order to purchase social peace a large number of enterprises take out expensive bank credits, [and] eat up the social capital, [so that] wages are covered by expensive state money rather than by production."

Nonetheless, by the middle of 1993 there were improvements on a number of fronts: the monthly rates of both retail and producer price inflation remained in the single digits from March through October — including to that point postcommunist Eastern Europe's largest monthly deflation, –0.9 percent in June — and the black market exchange rate was more or less the same in June as it was in February (see Table 8.1).

These developments resulted form the coincidence of a number of circumstances that put downward pressure on prices: a supposedly restrictive monetary policy;[8] long delays by many enterprises in the payment of wages, and by the government in the payment of pensions; a healthy supply of agricultural products resulting from a freer import regime and the inability to place traditional agricultural exports on foreign markets; and the supply-side effects of various forms of international assistance (Anastasova, 1993b).[9] Credit is also due to legal changes (discussed below), including a liberalized foreign trade regime for agricultural imports and the creation of a unified market-determined exchange rate.

However, the country still lacked a systematic stabilization program supported by the international financial community and dealing with all sources of macroeconomic instability. Particularly worrisome were the very high and rising — if more slowly toward the end of the year — dollar real wage, the expansionary fiscal stance, and the low level of foreign exchange reserves (which by the end of 1993 had risen to about $120 million, from only $4.2 million at the end of 1991) (NBRM/IOM, 1992, p. 17).[10]

Furthermore, fiscal imbalances continued to plague the economy. The budget deficit of the general government — including the parafiscal deficits — rose from about 6 percent of GDP in 1992 to 10.1 percent of GDP in 1993 (Government, 1994, p. 4). The low degree of compliance with tax and customs duty obligations, especially on the part of the growing private sector (Cvetkovska, 1993b), along with the depressed state of the economy, and sloth in passing new tax legislation, had led to a downward spiral in real budgetary revenue.

The Stabilization Program of December 1993

Toward the end of the period covered by this chapter, the government promulgated Macedonia's third stabilization program since independence. This time around there were two distinct advantages over previous attempts. The program directly addressed the problems that have eluded solution to date and it had financial, technical, and moral support from the IMF, World Bank, and European Bank for Reconstruction and Development (EBRD) (Crvenkovski, 1993; *Nova Makedonija*, December 21, 1993, p. 3).

The stabilization program has enjoyed considerable initial success because of the government's ability to honor the ambitious policy intentions that the program contains. Its ultimate fate will depend at least as much upon such exogenous circumstances as the permeability of the southern border and the longevity of the UN sanctions against the rump Yugoslavia (and that country's attitude toward Macedonia when the sanctions are lifted).

The program, which was presented to the assembly on December 20, is based on the (correct) assumption that these sanctions would continue throughout 1994. The main goal was to fight hyperinflation through measures in three chief directions: (1) restoration of wage discipline by means of the enforcement of a new law on wage control; (2) refocusing monetary policy away from supporting economic sectors to fighting inflation; and (3) a series of measures on both sides of the government ledger to reduce the budget deficit. Quantitatively, the goal was to reduce monthly inflation to 10 percent early in the year, 5 percent by the middle of 1994, and 2–3 percent by the end of the year. GSP was expected to fall by a further 8 percent in 1994.

Turning first to wage control, the law on this subject passed on December 22 specified limits on benefits and payments in kind for social sector enterprises. For enterprises in the economic sector, net personal income payments per worker during January would be limited to 95 percent of the average such payments in these enterprises during August–September 1993, corrected by an adjustment for inflation during October–December. For the remainder of the year, economic sector wage growth would be limited to 1.5 percentage points below actual monthly price inflation up to the monthly inflation target and to one-half of any inflation above that target. In the noneconomic sector — where wages had increased by 25 percent relative to the economic sector since 1990 — the measures were similar, except that 92 percent replaces 95 percent, and 2.5 percentage points replaces 1.5 percentage points. An adjustment to the August–September wage base would be made for enterprises that paid less than 75 percent of the average economic sector wage (Government, 1994, pp. 1–2).

In the realm of monetary policy, the growth of reserve money was to be limited to 17 percent during the first quarter of 1994 and 12 percent during the second quarter. The phasing out of selective credits out of the primary emission for the agricultural sector was to be completed by the end of March 1994. New rediscounting by the NBRM of commercial bank agricultural credits fell markedly in the final quarter of 1993 and would be limited to 140 million denari in the first quarter of 1994.[11]

Similar to Bulgarian practice until August 1994, credit ceilings would now be imposed on the lending and borrowing (from the NBRM) activity of individual commercial banks. The auctioning of NBRM credits as a substitute for selective credit provision began in November 1993. Once this practice was sufficiently established to determine a reliable market-based interest rate, the NBRM's discount rate would be adjusted in line with that rate; in the meantime, the discount rate was set at the annualized average inflation rate during the past two months plus a 5 percent "real interest rate component" (Government, 1994, p. 3). Quantitative targets were set for net domestic assets, credit to the central government, the NBRM's net foreign reserves, new nonconcessional external medium- and long-term debt, and new external short-term debt (Government, 1994, pp. 2–4, 11–12).

A host of measures in the fiscal sphere are planned so as to bring some order to that particularly troubled realm. The government program observed that the general government budget deficit would reach 13.5 percent of GSP in the absence of such measures; the steps taken were said to be consistent with a deficit of 6.7 percent of GSP. The goal was to cut central government expenditures by an amount equal to 5.4 percent of GSP, provide additional funding for social programs, unemployment compensation, and bank rehabilitation worth 2.5 percent of GSP, and come up with additional revenue in the amount of 4 percent of GSP.

Central government expenditure cuts encompassed such items as agricultural subsidies, wages in the noneconomic sector, interest payments, and expenditures on certain social programs. Measures to accelerate structural reform included targeting social assistance on low-income households (replacing the previous bread subsidy), increasing payroll contributions to the unemployment compensation fund, and allocating funds for bank rehabilitation. Steps to increase revenue encompassed reducing the number of sales tax rates and requiring paying of import tax at the time of entry; increasing excise taxes on oil derivatives, alcohol, cigarettes, and cars; centralizing a number of functions previously split up among institutions under a new Office of Public Revenue within the Ministry of Finance; and reforming the personal income tax, so as to create a unified tax with progressive rates and to eliminate several exemptions (Government, 1994, pp. 4–5).

Special attention was devoted to the problems of the pension fund, whose deficit in the absence of corrective measures would reach 5.9 percent of GSP in 1994. Steps to be taken included reducing the ratio of the average pension to the average wage from 82 percent to 74 percent by the end of 1994, abolishing existing schemes for early retirement, increasing payroll contributions, increasing the retirement ages for both sexes, changing the base for pension calculation so that it is no longer tied to the ten-year period with the highest income, and measures to increase participation of the private sector in the pension scheme (Government, 1994, p. 6).

As mentioned above, this package of measures obtained the support of the international financial community. A big hurdle was overcome on February 8, 1994, when with the help of a group of donor countries the country settled its approximately $107 million arrears with the World Bank. The sources of the funds for this settlement were as follows: $26.5 million from donor countries (including $10 million from the Netherlands and $5 million from the U.S.), $9 million from George Soros, $32 million in credits from the World Bank and International Development Association (IDA), $17.5 from the IMF (the first payment under a $35 million structural transformation facility), and $22.5 million from the country's own reserves (MIC, February 9, 1994). After this settlement, the intention was to meet all obligations to multilateral creditors as they fall due and to begin rescheduling negotiations with the Paris Club.

The arrears settlement with the World Bank unlocked a $40 million loan from that institution and a further credit of the same size from the IDA. The government hoped that by the end of June 1994 the IMF would be sufficiently pleased with the performance of the economy to agree to a standby arrangement, on top of the aforementioned $35 million (Government, 1994, p. 10). The EBRD has agreed to lend $33 million for construction of a long-distance power line (MIC, February 9, 1994).

By the end of 1994, it was clear that this latest set of measures would be more successful than its predecessors. It is difficult to disagree with the choice of measures as the most appropriate ones for dealing with the country's macroeconomic imbalances.

The important questions at the outset were, first, whether these steps were likely to be implemented as outlined in the program, and, second, whether they might be derailed by circumstances beyond the authorities' control. As to the first concern, the issue was whether the interest groups affected by tighter wage control, the elimination of easy money for agriculture, and tougher pension rules would be able to mobilize themselves either to get these measures weakened or to find ingenious ways to get around them.

One who has watched the events of recent years was inclined at the outset to be optimistic about those steps that were under the direct control of the national bank. However, with a population well practiced since Yugoslav times in the art of evading the government's intentions and a legislature prone to populistic influences, there was concern that the fiscal measures contained in the program would not live up to expectations. Nonetheless, the authorities deserve a great deal of credit — in both the literal and figurative senses of the word — for their diagnosis of the problems and the progress made in solving them.

The unpredictability of the behavior of Greece, as evidenced by its effective blockade of the border as of February 16, 1994, and of the wars to the north makes this tiny country especially vulnerable to exogenous shocks. Moreover, the foreign exchange reserves have remained disconcertingly small. Indeed, as noted above, the first $17.5 million received from the IMF went entirely to pay off the arrears with the World Bank, and $22.5 million worth of pre-existing reserves were used in the same operation. Thus, the reserves fell during early 1994 below $100 million, a dangerously low level.

Looking briefly at economic performance just before and just after the promulgation of the stabilization program, inflation was extremely high from October 1993 through January 1994 (see Table 8.1 for data through the end of 1993). This can be attributed to the rapid depreciation of the denar through mid-December, adjustment of controlled prices, and increases in bank credit and wages in anticipation of the controls on these variables under the program. However, through the fall of 1994, monthly inflation had fallen back into the low single digits — indeed, it was –0.6 percent in July — and, supported by the $40 million from the World Bank, the denar has been stable for more than a year.

LEGAL AND STRUCTURAL CHANGE

For most of the time since Macedonia's declaration of independence, little in the way of structural reform has taken place, an important exception being a 1991 law on the independence of the NBRM (Cohen and Stamkoski, 1992, p. 18). However, May 1993 proved a banner month for new economic legislation, with the passage of laws on foreign investment, foreign trade, the foreign exchange market, and foreign credit relations. June 1993 saw the enactment of the law governing the privatization process. Important laws on the budget and on various forms of taxation were passed in late December 1993.

Foreign Economic Relations

The important changes in this sphere encompass new laws — all passed on May 12, 1993 — on the foreign exchange market, foreign investment, foreign trade, and foreign credit relations. Foreign exchange operations are now governed by a fairly simple regime in the mold of the Bulgarian and Slovenian laws. The foreign investment law is extremely liberal, with no requirement for permission to invest, no restrictions on repatriation of profit or on the activities in which one may invest, and tax breaks promised to foreign investors. The law on foreign trade creates a liberalized regime.

From its declaration of independence in November 1991 until May 1993, Macedonia employed a highly dysfunctional "tripartite" exchange rate mechanism. This entailed an overvalued official exchange rate that applied to only a very limited number of transactions, a black market rate valid for most transactions involving physical persons, and a third rate determined via a so-called *šticung* (a sort of interenterprise market).

On May 12, the Assembly passed a law on foreign exchange operations that put an end to this system and created a new one.[12] The law establishes a fluctuating exchange rate for the denar through the organization of a foreign exchange market, in which enterprises and other legal persons, commercial banks authorized to participate in that market, and the NBRM freely buy and sell foreign currency. It allows physical persons to buy and sell foreign exchange at exchange offices (*menuvačnici*).

Exchange offices may operate independently, on behalf of commercial banks, or on behalf of the NBRM; their manner of operation determines their obligation to sell or return certain portions of their foreign exchange to the entity on whose behalf they work. Exchange offices may sell up to one-half of the foreign currency that they obtain on a given day to physical persons. The NBRM, on the basis of the activity in the foreign exchange market during a given day, determines an "average" exchange rate, which becomes a reference point for transactions on the following day, and which must be accepted by exchange offices working on the account of the NBRM.

The regime, although quite liberal, entails a number of restrictions. Enterprises that have obtained foreign exchange via their export activity may keep it in their accounts for up to ninety days, after which they must sell it at the going rate. The law gives the government the right to introduce compulsory purchase of denari by foreigners upon entering the country. The NBRM may, in cases where its foreign currency reserves or the foreign exchange liquidity in the country fall dangerously low, institute compulsory sales to it of up to 30 percent of the foreign exchange purchased by exchange offices.

Mid-May 1993 provided some interesting drama as the law went into effect. Although on the first day of operation of the foreign exchange market not a single transaction took place, by early June both the market and the exchange offices were in full swing. Since the introduction of the new system, exchange rates on the black market — to the extent that such still exists — have been virtually identical to those determined by the NBRM. Moreover, from June to December 1993, the real value of the denar remained largely unchanged: retail price inflation ran at 91.73 percent and the currency depreciated against the dollar by 91.42 percent (see Table 8.1).[13]

Turning next to foreign investment — the level of which has dwindled to almost nothing since the beginning of 1991 (Cohen and Stamkoski, 1992, p. 3) — the new law is brief and to the point.[14] Foreign investors are allowed to invest in domestic enterprises, to form joint ventures, and to open their own wholly owned enterprises in the country under the same conditions as domestic persons. Such investors have the right to participate in profit and to transfer that profit abroad, to the return of objects and funds invested in enterprises, to a share of the property of a joint venture that has ceased operation, and to participate in the management of the enterprise. Foreign investors — including foreign banks and insurance companies — may invest in enterprises, banks, savings institutions (štedilnici), insurance companies, and cooperatives.

Enterprises that have received foreign investment have the same rights and responsibilities as wholly domestic enterprises. Special reduced tax rates on profit and on re-invested funds, as well as reduced rates of customs duty, may be offered during an initial period of operation of an entity created wholly or partly through foreign investment; the specificities of this matter are, however, left to separate legislation.

The law on foreign investment is the most liberal in Eastern Europe, going even beyond the January 1992 Bulgarian law, previously considered worthy of this distinction (Wyzan, 1992). Like the Bulgarian law, the Macedonian legislation sets no upper or lower limits on foreign investments and extends foreign investors national treatment. It goes further than the Bulgarian law in not requiring permission for investing in any particular sphere of activity and not putting any restrictions on the repatriation of foreign workers' earnings. It resembles the Polish and Hungarian laws, and differs form the Bulgarian law, in mentioning tax breaks for foreign investors. It is, perhaps, too early for there to be any visible effects of the law on foreign investment, which in any case should not be expected until the international climate improves.

Other laws passed on May 12 deal with foreign credit relations and foreign trade.[15] The latter provides for a more liberal regime than previous legislation, allowing, for example, all physical and legal persons to engage in foreign trade activity and liberalizing the importation of certain goods, so that 90 percent of goods may be imported without customs duty.[16]

Privatization of Industrial Enterprises

This all-important aspect of the transition to a market economy is still at an early stage in Macedonia, since the law governing the process was passed only on June 14, 1993.[17] The method called for by the law does not entail mass privatization as practiced in the Czech Republic, Slovakia, or Russia. Nor does it rely entirely upon buyers being found who can pay for assets outright, as in the so-called "market" methods practiced in Hungary and Bulgaria.[18]

The Macedonian approach proposes a large number of methods of privatizing enterprises of various sizes, with the biggest novelty being a form of leveraged buyout. The government successfully held the line against pressure from the trade unions to provide free shares to present and past workers in those enterprises, although the trade unions opposed the law. The approach may not, however, result in profit-minded noninsiders coming to power in enterprises, since managers and workers are the likely actors to take advantage of the various methods.

Macedonia was the only Yugoslav republic where a large number of enterprises participated in privatization according to the law on the subject promulgated by the federal government of Ante Marković in 1990. Shares in a total of 249 enterprises — and 100 of the 135 enterprises with more than 250 workers — were partially transformed by means of what amounted to giveaways of shares to workers (Veljanovski, 1992). Another 1990 law that allowed enterprises technically under a wage freeze to issue internal shares in lieu of wages had a similar effect. The new law contains detailed provisions for auditing the enterprises that have undergone these procedures in preparation for privatizing them in a more transparent manner.

The enterprises to be privatized under the law number 1,468, or 79.1 percent of all social sector enterprises, with 77.8 percent of all those employed in enterprises with social or mixed capital. The firms excluded are in the spheres of public utilities, public works, social services, natural monopolies, and agriculture (Šukarov and Hadži Vasileva-Markovska, 1993, pp. 2–3).

The method enshrined in the new law provides for a variety of methods of privatization for enterprises of various sizes.[19] For small enterprises — those with fewer than 50 employees or meeting various other criteria — allowable techniques include sale of the entire enterprise to its workers (who must buy at least 51 percent of its value) and the sale of shares through public tenders and via a contractual arrangement with a buyer. For medium-sized enterprises — those with between 50 and 250 workers or meeting various other criteria — approved methods include sale of shares, direct purchase of 51 percent of the enterprise, the receipt of shares by virtue of additional investment, and transformation of a debt obligation into an ownership interest in the firm.

There is also a unique "leveraged buyout" method. The firm may be sold to a person who upon presenting an acceptable program for the development of that firm buys at least 20 percent of it and who agrees to buy no less than 51 percent over no more than five years. Dividends must be plowed back into the firm until the 51 percent level is reached. Large enterprises are subject to the same provisions as medium-sized ones, except that buyers under the leveraged method need not put more than 10 percent down, and that large enterprises are to form special councils to manage the process. Other allowable methods include purchase of an enterprise via leasing it over a period of not more than seven years, sell-off of all of an enterprise's assets, and transformation of an enterprise through bankruptcy. Small and medium-sized enterprises must make a decision on the preferred method of transformation within a year of the passage of the law, large enterprises within two years.

The biggest controversy surrounding the privatization law concerned the privileges allowed to workers, former workers, and pensioners. Individuals empowered to do so may purchase at most a total of 30 percent of the value of the shares at a general discount of 30 percent of the shares' value, increased by 1 percent for every full year of work at the enterprise; no one person may obtain more than 25,000 DM worth of shares in this manner.

An Agency for the Transformation of Enterprises with Social Capital was created that will oversee the entire process and hold nonvoting shares in transformed enterprises. The agency would not receive support from the budget but be funded by proceeds from the sale of enterprises. The agency has decided against the pre-privatization restructuring of enterprises in the near future. This is because it wishes to avoid raising the price of these enterprises before their privatization, because it doubts that the government or the agency would be able to come up with a better restructuring plan than a new private owner, and because of the shortage of investment capital in the country (Šukarov and Hadži Vasileva-Markovska, 1993, p. 12).

As might be expected, given the slow pace of institutional change in Macedonia and the complexity of the privatization process enshrined in the law, implementation got off to a slow start. Although the new agency for the Transformation of Enterprises with Social Capital was to be founded within 15 days of the law's passage, this did not happen until October 21 (Šukarov and Hadži Vasileva-Markovska, 1993, p. 1). A methodology for evaluating firms with social capital was adopted by the government on November 30.[20]

The elaborate methodology has a number of strengths, especially the great variety of methods on offer, the rejection of free share giveaways, and the innovative recourse to leveraged buyouts. The fact that unions initially vowed to wage a campaign of civil disobedience against the law's implementation (Kiridžievska, 1993) shows that the government and Assembly had the strength to resist pressure from special-interest groups. The agency's aversion to restructuring before privatization seems quite sensible.

On the other hand, it seems likely that it will be managers and workers who will avail themselves of the various methods available for purchasing enterprises. One may thus question whether the chosen method makes it sufficiently likely that noninsiders interested in profit and enterprise growth, rather than job retention and receiving subsidies, will have an important role in corporate governance.[21] It is also unclear whether privatized firms will be sufficiently profitable in the early years to pay out the dividends that are to be used to purchase a controlling interest in those firms (Poulton, 1993, pp. 28–29).

The expectation that the agency will be self-supporting seems unrealistic in view of the experience of other transforming countries. A more straightforward form of mass privatization might have had a larger impact and have been more likely to get outsiders involved, as Bulgaria and Hungary seem to be in the process of discovering.[22]

Budget and Tax Policy

While mid-May 1993 saw the rapid-fire enactment of many important pieces of legislation on foreign economic relations, late December of that year was similarly fruitful with respect to fiscal legislation. A law on the budget process of the Republic and of the units of local self-government — that is, the communes (*opštini*) and the city of Skopje — was passed on December 21, along with the budget for 1994. The law assigned to the Republic government all revenues from the profit tax, personal income tax, and sales tax on goods and services (and excise taxes), as well as tariffs and customs fees. Local governments are financed by the property tax, inheritance and gift tax, and sales tax on immovables and property rights, along with transfers from the Republic government (to be governed by a separate law). This legislation clearly describes the preparation, enactment, and execution of the annual budgets of the various levels of government; it appears to be one of the better constructed laws on this subject in Eastern Europe.[23]

On December 24, laws on the personal income tax (which is progressive with marginal rates of 23, 27, and 35 percent), profits tax (which has a flat 30 percent rate), and property tax were passed, along with much other fiscal legislation.[24]

CONCLUSIONS

In concluding this chapter, I briefly discuss the following two questions: (1) how are the costs and benefits of separation from Yugoslavia affected by Macedonia's special circumstances as a poor and ethnically diverse part of the former Yugoslavia; (2) is Macedonia economically viable?

As to the first query, it is clear that many of the advantages of independence enjoyed by such breakaway states as the Czech Republic, Estonia, Latvia, or Slovenia will not be enjoyed by Macedonia. As a former recipient of federal subsidies, Macedonia does not benefit directly from their elimination. It is far from obvious that it will be more likely to be able to join the EC or attract foreign investment as an independent state — especially in the face of Greek objections — than it would have been as a part of Yugoslavia.

The average level of technical skills and knowledge of the outside world is probably lower than that which prevailed in the former Yugoslavia. Moreover, as an ethnically divided state, it is not clear that policy making will benefit from the end of the rivalries between distributional coalitions that characterized Yugoslavia.

By the same token, all the costs of separation, including trade reorientation, lost scale economies, enhanced autarkic tendencies, potential foreign domination, and a flow of refugees, apply at least as much to a poor republic as to a rich one (see Chapter 6 in this volume).

It is unlikely that a cost-benefit analysis of Macedonia's separation from Yugoslavia would yield a positive net benefit. On the other hand, no such analysis has been or is likely to be performed by the people of the country in question or their leadership. As is often true in such cases, Macedonia's motivation for secession was not primarily economic; in any event there was no strategic decision maker in a position to make such a calculation. For Macedonia the main question was instead whether it could get away with secession and hence escape paying for and participating in Serbia's aggressive military designs. The answer to this all-important question appears to be positive. Moreover, the alternative to secession posed by a cost-benefit analysis — remaining in a peaceful, decentralized Yugoslavia — is simply unavailable.

I turn now to the second question, that of economic viability. As argued in the Introduction to this volume, such viability is more closely related to its government's ability to deal with prevailing problems than to the nature of those problems. Problems certainly abound. Indeed, Macedonia's domestic and external political situations are among the most disadvantageous in Eastern Europe.

Dissatisfaction abounds among the ethnic Albanian minority and occasional violent incidents have occurred involving both the Albanian and Serbian minorities. Moreover, the split of the leading ethnic Albanian political party into hard-line and moderate factions, and the arrests in November 1993 of a number of Albanian politicians (including two deputy ministers in the government), charged with forming an armed "All-Albanian Army" with alleged plans to overthrow the state (Troebst, 1994, p. 38), are nothing if not alarming.

Nonetheless, one's worst fears concerning the country's ethnic tensions have so far proved unfounded. In the long run, the integration of ethnic Albanians into the mainstream of political and economic life is a key prerequisite for Macedonia's ability to survive as a state and an issue to which the government and the international community must devote considerable attention.

Externally, the UN embargo against the rump Yugoslavia and the actions of Greece have taken an enormous toll on the economy. Even though the embargo will certainly be temporary, Greek hostility will likely not be. Moreover, Macedonians cannot be certain of Serbia's attitude toward them once the embargo is lifted and the U.S. troops currently stationed in Macedonia go home.

Everything considered, however, the common view of journalists and others that Macedonia is somehow precariously perched on the brink of extinction is wildly exaggerated. In a thoughtful recent paper, Troebst (1994) considers six alternative scenarios posing threats to Macedonia's existence as a separate state. These include Serbian military agression, spillover of an ethnic civil war in Kosovo, partition by neighboring countries, unification with Bulgaria based on a recognition of a common ethnic identity with that country, domestic ethnic conflict between Slavs and Albanians, and a voluntary return to the rump Yugoslavia. His conclusion, with which this author largely concurs, is that none of these scenarios is especially likely, and indeed that they have become less probable over time.

In the end, Macedonia's economic viability is not a question of physical survivability, but rather of its leadership's ability to conduct competent economic policy and demonstrate to the international community that the country is worthy of support. From this standpoint, the Macedonian experience provides considerable scope for optimism. A new currency far more stable than that of the former federation has been introduced, minorities have been brought into the government, commendable economic legislation has been passed in a variety of spheres from international trade to budget policy, interest-group pressure for giveaways in the privatization process has been resisted, new trading opportunities and partners have been found, and successful application for membership in international organizations has been made. Serious problems remain, of course, especially with respect to restructuring a very poor and distorted economy, a direction in which less progress has been made than perhaps anywhere else in Central and Eastern Europe. Everything considered, however, the Macedonian experience is surprisingly encouraging.

NOTES

The author thanks Anders Åslund, Gligor Bišev, Ilze Brands, Patrick J. Conway, Ardo H. Hansson, Simon Johnson, Jane Miljovski, Gary O'Callaghan, Mihail Petkovski, Goce Petreski, Trajko Slaveski, Sofija Todorova, Stefan Troebst, Ljube

Trpeski, Vančo Uzunov, and Milan Vodopivec for comments and assistance. He is grateful to the Zavod za meģunarodna naučno-tehnička sorabotka na Makedonija for making the arrangements for two visits to Skopje. None of the above is responsible for the methods or conclusions herein.

1.   The Macedonian Chamber of Commerce estimates that the various UN resolutions have cost the country about $200 million. Greece objects to Macedonia's name, state symbols, and certain features of its constitution. The flag contains the sixteen-ray "Sun of Vergina," a symbol found in the tomb of Philip of Macedon when it was discovered at Vergina (in Greece) in 1977. The objectionable feature of the 1991 constitution is contained in Article 49, which states that the "Republic cares for the status and rights of those persons belonging to the Macedonian people in neighboring countries. . . ."

2.   The Clinton administration announced a decision to recognize Macedonia on February 9, 1994, but a month later elected to delay implementation of that decision. This irresolution is ironic in the light of the stationing of some 300 U.S. troops under the aegis of the UN in Macedonia in July 1993. The Australian and Canadian governments have also found policy making toward the new state extremely difficult in the face of the pressure that they face from their sizable ethnic Greek (and Macedonian) populations.

3.   The census of April 1991, boycotted by the Albanians, showed them to have only 21 percent of the population; ethnic Albanian sources, however, claim a figure as high as 40 percent. A special, EC-funded population census under international supervision took place in June and July 1994 and came up with a figure of 22 percent. Oe seemingly reliable estimate is that of Magnusson (1993, pp. 10–11), who applied the population growth rate of the Albanian population in Kosovo during 1981–91 to their ethnic compatriots in Macedonia over this period and came up with a figure of 27 percent.

4.   The figure for Slovenia applies to November 1991–May 1993, and that for Croatia to January 1992–July 1993. In each case, the period covered begins in the second month after monetary independence and runs for 19 months. This measure understates the extent to which Slovenia has gotten inflation under control: the monthly inflation rate there has been under 2 percent every month since February 1993, with the exception of October of that year.

5.   Newspaper articles without attribution are treated in this chapter as in this citation of *Nova Makedonija*; attributed newspaper articles are found in the References. "MIC" refers to the Macedonian Information Centre, a news service.

6.   A more detailed discussion of the introduction of the denar and of macroeconomic policy through the end of 1992 is contained in Wyzan (1993). The discussion of this and the following two sections relies heavily on that paper.

7.   The system actually involved three distinct exchange rates, as discussed below.

8.   That monetary policy had been restrictive and was frequently asserted by cabinet members (see, e.g., Anastasova, 1993b) as one reason for the improved performance on the inflation front. However, as seen in Table 8.1, the growth of M1 was not especially slow during the spring of 1993. M2 growth may in fact be more indicative of the state of monetary policy. During February, March, and April, M2 grew

by −0.7, 2.8, and 3.7 percent, respectively, making tighter control of M2 a potential contributing factor to the slower inflation, although M2 growth picked up again after April.

9. This assistance includes a $25 million revolving credit received in January 1993 from George Soros, which was used to purchase 80,000 tons of crude oil and to provide 38 exporting enterprises with short-term credit through two local commercial banks (Anastasova, 1993c), 40,000 tons of wheat donated by the U.S., and medicine provided by the EC (Anastasova, 1993b).

10. Another source of inflation was the selective crediting of agricultural activities using the primary emission, which continued on a reduced basis throughout 1993 and the first quarter of 1994 (see below).

11. Another unfortunate practice was the provision of credit by the commercial banks to 25 large loss-making enterprises that accounted for 90 percent of the total losses in the economy. Under pressure from the IMF, the authorities agreed in January 1994 to switch to a more restrictive practice after June 30 (MIC, January 31, 1994). During 1994 a program was drawn up to deal with this problem.

12. The law appeared in *Služben vesnik*, 49, no. 30, May 14, 1993, pp. 673–687. *Služben vesnik* is the official state legal digest.

13. Whether such virtual constancy of the real exchange rate is desirable depends on one's view of the appropriateness of that rate before the introduction of the new system. Given that the dollar wage was over $147 in May, one might argue in favor of a real depreciation. In any case, in early 1994 high inflation — especially in January — was accompanied by an unchanged nominal exchange rate, seemingly setting the stage for further currency instability down the road, especially in the light of the low level of foreign reserves; this fear proved unfounded, however.

14. The law appeared in *Služben vesnik*, 49, no. 31, May 20, 1993, pp. 732–734.

15. The law on foreign credit relations appeared in *Služben vesnik*, 49, no. 31, May 20, 1993, pp. 716–719, and the one on foreign trade in the same issue, pp. 719–732.

16. In the sphere of monetary policy, a law on the conversion of short-term credits out of the primary emission — which were discussed above — into long-term credits was passed by the Assembly on May 7 and appeared in *Služben vesnik* 49, no. 29, May 10, 1993, pp. 658–660.

17. The law, which appeared in *Služben vesnik*, 49, no. 38, June 21, 1993, pp. 881–892, is the brainchild of then Minister Without Portfolio Jane Miljovski, who discusses it in Anastasova (1993a).

18. In fact, those countries that initially insisted that enterprises and their assets be sold off and that no one be allowed to obtain anything for free are now moving in the direction of adopting some form of mass privatization. The Videnov government in Bulgaria is now considering a mass privatization scheme; Okolicsanyi (in Slay, 1993, p. 53) reports a "growing political trend toward mass privatization" in Hungary.

19. For a quantitative description of the enterprises included under the privatization program, broken down by size category, see Šukarov and Hadži Vasileva-Markovska, 1993, p. 4.

20. The methodology for evaluating enterprises appeared in *Služben vesnik*, 49, no. 74, December 3, 1993, pp. 1669–1673.

21. For an examination of potential conflicts between insider and outsider owners of privatized firms viewed through the lens of noncooperative game theory, see Abdalla and Wyzan (1994).

22. By mid-March 1994, 60 enterprises had applied to be among the first 20 firms to be privatized. The agency has decided that in order to be selected for privatization an enterprise must not be operating at a loss or be majority socially owned, and must not be undergoing ownership problems, among other criteria (MIC, March 16, 1994).

23. The law on the budget process appeared in *Služben vesnik*, 49, no. 79, December 28, 1993, pp. 1887–1892.

24. All three tax laws appeared in *Služben vesnik*, 49, no. 80, December 30, 1993 (on the personal income tax, pp. 1951–1963; on the profits tax, pp. 1967–1970; and on property taxes, pp. 1976–1980).

REFERENCES

Abdalla, Adil E.A., and Michael L. Wyzan. "Privatization and Performance in Postcommunist Economies: Insights from Noncooperative Game Theory." Stockholm Institute of East European Economics, 1994 (mimeo).

Anastasova, Maja. "(R)evolucija vo mozokot." *Nova Makedonija*, July 24, 1993a, p. 13.

Anastasova, Maja. "Koj ja kontrolira inflacija." *Nova Makedonija*, July 20, 1993b, pp. 1, 3.

Anastasova, Maja. "Prvata rata — 2,5 milioni dolari." *Nova Makedonija*, July 24, 1993c, p. 3.

Bićanić, Ivo. "The Croatian Economy: Achievements and Prospects." *RFE/RL Research Report* 2, 26 (June 25, 1993): 33–38.

Bookman, Milica Zarkovic. "The Economic Basis for Regional Autarchy in Yugoslavia." *Soviet Studies* 42, 1 (January 1990): 93–109.

[BS.] *Monthly Bulletin*. Ljubljana: Banka Slovenije, various 1992 and 1994 issues.

Čangova, Katica. "Najmnogu Makedonici bez rabota." *Nova Makedonija*, April 17, 1993, p. 5.

Cohen, Ben, and George Stamkoski. *Euromoney Supplement: Macedonia, Ready for Recognition?* 1992.

Crvenkovski, Branko. "Problemite gi nametnuvaat prioritetite (Ekspose na Branko Crvenkovski)." *Nova Makedonija*, October 9, 1992, p. 2.

Crvenkovski, Branko. "Nudime merki so svetska verifikacija (Ekspose na Premierot Branko Crvenkovski)." *Nova Makedonija*, December 21, 1993, p. 3.

Cvetkovska, Violeta. "Ke se deli samo zarabotenoto." *Nova Makedonija*, October 3, 1992a, pp. 1–2.

Cvetkovska, Violeta. "Nema razlika za juli i avgust." *Nova Makedonija*, October 27, 1992b, pp. 1–2.

Cvetkovska, Violeta. "Platite rastat — standardot opaǵa." *Nova Makedonija*, July 29, 1993a, pp. 1–3.

Cvetkovska, Violeta. "Pretprijatijata se borat za opstanok." *Nova Makedonija*, August 7, 1993b, pp. 1–2.

Dičevska, Borjana. "Gorčlivite plodovi na bogata berba." *Nova Makedonija*, October 10, 1992, p. 13.

[Government.] "Policy Statement of the Government of the Republic of Macedonia." Skopje: Government of the Republic of Macedonia, January 14, 1994 (mimeo).

Grličkov, Vladimir. "Ograničenja s novim novcem." *Ekonomska politika*, May 11, 1992, p. 14.

Kiridžievska, Sonja. "Rapuštanje na parlamentot i novi izbori." *Nova Makedonija*, June 16, 1993, pp. 1, 3.

Kraft, Evan. "Evaluating Regional Policy in Yugoslavia, 1966–1990." *Comparative Economic Studies* 34, 3–4 (Fall–Winter 1992): 11–33.

Magnusson, Kjell. "Den makedonska frågan." *Internationella Studier*, no. 1 (Spring 1993): 7–12.

[MR.] "Dokumentacija kon Stabilizacionata programa na Vladata na Republika Makedonija." Skopje: Ministerstvo za razvoj, December 3, 1993 (mimeo).

[NBRM/B.] Bulletin. Skopje: Narodna banka na Republika Makedonija, various 1992, 1993, and 1994 issues.

[NBRM/IOM.] "Izveštaj za ostvaruvanjeto na monetarno-kreditnata politika i ekonomsko-finansiskite odnosi so stranstvo vo prvoto polugodie od 1992 godina." Skopje: Narodna banka na Republika Makedonija, August 1992 (mimeo).

[NSI.] *Iznos i vnos*. Sofia: Natsionalen statisticheski institut, no. 4, 1993.

Petkovski, Mihail, Goce Petreski, and Trajko Slaveski. *Antiinflation Programme*. Skopje: Government of the Republic of Macedonia, April 1992.

Petkovski, Mihil, Goce Petreski, and Trajko Slaveski. "Stabilization Efforts in the Republic of Macedonia." *RFE/RL Research Report* 2, 3 (January 15, 1993): 34–37.

Poulton, Hugh. "The Republic of Macedonia after UN Recognition." *RFE/RL Research Report* 2, 23 (June 4, 1993): 22–30.

[RHDZS.] *Mjesečno statističko izvješće*. Zagreb: Republička Hrvatska Državni zavod za statistiku, no. 4, 1994.

[RZS/MSI.] *Mesečen statistički izveštaj*. Skopje: Republički zavod za statistika, various 1992 and 1993 issues.

[RZS/NT.] *Nadvorešna trgovina na Republika Makedonija 1987–1990 godina*. Skopje: Republički zavod za statistika, 1991.

[RZS/SG.] *Statistički godišnik na Republika Makedonija*. Skopje: Republički zavod za statistika, 1991.

Slay, Benjamin (ed.). "Roundtable: Privatization in Eastern Europe." *RFE/RL Research Report* 2, 32 (August 13, 1993): 47–57.

Šukarov, Miroljub, and Verica Hadži Vasileva-Markovska. "Privatization Report: Republic of Macedonia." Skopje: Agency of the Republic of Macedonia for Transformation of Enterprises with Social Capital, November 1993 (mimeo).

[SZS.] *Statistički godišnjak Jugoslavije*. Belgrade: Savezni zavod za statistiku, various years.

Troebst, Stefan. "Macedonia: Powder Keg Defused?" *RFE/RL Research Report* 3, 4 (January 28, 1994): 33–41.

Veljanovski, Čento. "Privatising Socialist Industry: A Programme for the Republic of Macedonia." In *Privatisation: An International Symposium*, pp. 37–56. London: Centre for Research into Communist Economies, August 1992.

[World Bank.] "The Challenge of Economic Recovery and Social Harmony in the Former Yugoslav Republic of Macedonia." Central Europe Department, Europe and Central Asia Region, World Bank, August 1992.

[World Bank.] "Former Yugoslav Republic of Macedonia Reforms Against All Odds, Receives First World Bank Assistance." World Bank News 8, 6 (February 10, 1994): 1, 3–4.

Wyzan, Michael L. "Bulgarian Law Lowers Investment Barriers." *RFE/RL Research Report* 1, 13 (March 27, 1992): 41–43.

Wyzan, Michael L. "Monetary Independence and Macroeconomic Stabilisation in Macedonia: An Initial Assessment." *Communist Economies and Economic Transformation* 5, 3 (1993): 351–368.

III

OTHER CASES

9

Slovakia

Herta Gabrielová, Egon Hlavatý, Adela Hošková,
Zora Komínková, Milan Kurucz, and
Brigita Schmögnerová

INTRODUCTION

After the dissolution of the Czech and Slovak Federal Republic (CSFR) at the beginning of 1993, two independent states — the Czech Republic and the Slovak Republic — came into existence. The dissolution of the former CSFR and the creation of an independent Slovakia are part of the process of the disintegration of the multinational states of Central and Eastern Europe. They are the result of a complicated interaction of external and internal conditions. They are not only the outcome of the disintegrative tendencies of the former communist states, and of the nationalist aspirations of certain political groups, but also of an important national and democratic movement that forms part of the democratization of society. For the first time in modern history, an independent, democratic state has come into being on the territory of Slovakia.

Slovakia has committed itself to proceeding with the political, social, and economic transformation which had commenced in the former federal state. Slovakia's economic transformation consists of two processes: first, transition from a centrally planned to a market economy; and, second, transformation of an unwieldy economic structure based on the inter-republic and international division of labor that prevailed within the CMEA into one more consistent with the country's comparative advantages on the world market.

The results so far of Slovakia's economic transformation depend to some extent on its initial economic situation. Therefore, to analyze the present situation, and to predict the future development of the Slovak economy, an international comparison of Slovakia with the Czech Republic, Hungary, and Poland, as shown in Table 9.1, may be instructive.

POLITICAL AND SOCIAL ASPECTS OF SLOVAKIA'S INDEPENDENCE AND THEIR ECONOMIC IMPACT

Slovakia's geopolitical situation has been fundamentally changed by independence. The Slovak Republic is now the smallest state in Central Europe. It is surrounded by countries all of which are larger both in territory and number of inhabitants. Except for Austria, all of its neighbors are postcommunist states. Slovakia's frontiers with Poland, Ukraine, Hungary, and Austria, which are identical to those of the former Czechoslovak state, were set by the Trianon Treaty of 1920, as partially modified by the Paris Peace Treaty of 1947. Slovakia has had no territorial disputes with Poland, Austria, or Ukraine — existing frontiers have never been questioned by any side.

However, tension has lately been observed in Slovakia's relations with Hungary. The two states have different opinions concerning the construction of the dam and hydroelectric power station at Gabčíkovo on the Danube, which forms the border between the two countries. One of Hungary's objections to the dam has a territorial background.[1]

The two countries' assessments of the situation of the Hungarian minority in Slovakia, which lives along the Slovak-Hungarian frontier, are also divergent. A negative Hungarian attitude toward the Trianon Treaty, which determines Slovakia's southern frontier, has been observed, although officially the existing border has never been questioned. The two sides disagree over whether an interstate treaty should guarantee the common frontier. The Slovak government has suggested that an article stating that neither country has or will have any territorial claims against the other should be included in such a treaty. However, Hungary considers such a pledge superfluous, since both countries have signed the Final Statement of the Conference on the Security and Cooperation in Europe (CSCE; the Helsinki Accords),[2] which contains an article on the inadmissibility of any forcible change of frontiers.[3]

Diplomatic Recognition and Association to International Political and Economic Institutions

The fact that Slovakia's separation from the Czech Republic was entirely peaceful contributed to quick diplomatic recognition by its

TABLE 9.1

A Comparison of Macroeconomic Indicators for Slovakia, the Czech Republic, Hungary, and Poland

	1990				1991				1992			
	Slo.	Cze.	Hun.	Pol.	Slo.	Cze.	Hun.	Pol.	Slo.	Cze.	Hun.	Pol.
GDP[1]	97.5	98.8	96.5	88.4	88.2	85.8	88.1	92.4	93.0	92.9	95.5	98.5
Industrial production[1]	95.2	96.6	90.4	75.8	82.2	75.6	81.2	88.1	86.2	86.3	89.9	104.2
Industrial producer prices[1,3]	104.8	102.5	124.2	722.4	168.9	170.4	131.9	148.1	105.3	109.9	109.7	128.5
Consumer prices[1]	110.4	109.7	128.9	685.8	161.2	152.0	134.0	160.0	110.0	112.7	122.0	144.0
Unemployment[4,5]	39.6	39.4	79.5	1,126.0	302.0	221.7	406.1	2,156.0	260.3	134.8	663.0	2,509.0
Unemployment rate[4,6]	1.6	0.8	1.7[2]	6.3	11.8	4.1	8.5[2]	11.8	10.4	2.6	12.3[2]	13.6

Source: ČSÚ (1993a; 1993b); FSÚ/SR (1992); FSÚ/GUS/KSH (1992); SŠÚ (1992a); ŠÚSR (1993a); WIIW (1993).

Notes:

[1]Index with previous year set equal to 100.

[2]Figure applies to December of previous year.

[3]Data apply to firms employing more than 100 persons in 1991 and more than 25 persons in 1992.

[4]At end of period.

[5]Thousands.

[6]Percent.

closest neighbors, as well as by geographically more distant countries. The two former Czechoslovak republics were accepted as members of the United Nations less than three weeks after they had become independent. Within a short time, Slovakia acquired membership in such other organizations and institutions as the CSCE (from January 1, 1993), UNESCO (from February 9, 1993), and the International Labor Organization (from January 22, 1993).

Slovakia's admission to the Council of Europe was delayed by Hungary, which raised the issue of the treatment of ethnic minorities, especially ethnic Hungarians. The two successor states of the CSFR were finally accepted as members of the Council of Europe on June 30, 1993, after a half-year of their existence. By becoming a member of the Council of Europe and acceptance of the Additional Register to the European Agreement on Human Rights of Ethnic Minorities, Slovakia confirmed its commitments to develop a democratic society and to honor the rights of its national minorities.

As one of the successor states of the former CSFR, Slovakia has been trying to achieve quick succession to the international economic treaties which had been concluded between the CSFR and the EC (the so-called Europe Agreement), EFTA, and the GATT. As for the last of these, both Slovakia and the Czech Republic have taken over the stringent obligations on international trade policy agreed to by the former CSFR at the Tokyo round; these include the fact that 97 percent of trade concessions are to be binding commitments, an average tariff incidence of 5.7 percent, and restricted resort to nontariff measures. The acceptance of these stipulations sped up the process substantially and no prolonged negotiations over trade policy were necessary. Slovakia's succession to the Central European Agreement on Free Trade (CEFTA) among the CSFR, Hungary, and Poland took place on December 21, 1992. A protocol with EFTA was signed on April 19, 1993.

Slovakia has also tried to achieve succession to the Association Agreement with the EC that had been signed by the former CSFR. The fact that this agreement was not ratified before the split of the CSFR, as well as the division of the common state into two, necessitated new negotiations. Thus, Slovakia's association with the EC was delayed until February 1, 1995. Nevertheless, thanks to a prolongation of the Interim Agreement concluded between the EC and the former CSFR, which went into effect on January 1, 1993, and which divided the quotas between the successor states, the postponement of the Association Agreement brought no losses to Slovakia.

Succession to the IMF was accompanied by the division of the member quota of the former CSFR. The final division of the quota, 2.29:1, did not correspond to the principle governing the division of the IMF loans to the successor states, which was 2:1. On the other hand, capital assets and obligations vis-à-vis the World Bank were divided according to the ratio 2:1.

From the above analysis the following conclusions can be drawn:

- From the beginning of its existence, Slovakia has declared its commitment to its integration into the political and economic structures of Europe and the world; it has carried out the most important steps leading to such integration. The goals were to avoid peripherization and to create the international conditions necessary for its transformation into a modern, developed, democratic state.

- In general, international institutions did not raise any obstacles to Slovakia's becoming a member of or being associated with them. The applications of the two successor states of the former CSFR for admission to these institutions were not always sufficiently coordinated. Nonetheless, in many cases, such as entry to the Council of Europe and association with the EC, they had common interests and cooperation prevailed. In an effort to avoid bilateral misunderstandings, their agreements with international institutions were concluded in parallel.

Ethnic Minorities — Social and Economic Issues

In our view, nationalism and isolationism are characteristic features of neither Slovakia's economic nor its foreign policy. This is a result, first and foremost, of its geopolitical situation and small economic dimensions, which make economic and political integration inevitable. Moreover, we do not see the Slovak population as inclined to nationalistic extremes and, as confirmed by opinion polls, even the breakup of Czechoslovakia was not met by nationalistic euphoria (Bútorová, 1993).

The fact that Slovakia is not an ethnically homogeneous state represents an important factor for its future development and international status. In present-day Slovakia the most numerous ethnic minorities are the Hungarians, Gypsies, Czechs, Ruthenians/Ukrainians, Poles, and Germans. According to the latest census — taken on March 1, 1991 — the number of inhabitants was 5,268,935, of whom 757,256 (14.37 percent) claimed to belong to a nationality other than Slovak.

From the point of view of their numbers, ethnic self-consciousness, and political activity, the strongest among the minorities are the Hungarians, who numbered 566,741. The Hungarian minority lives in a relatively compact region in the southern and southeastern part of

Slovakia. In most cases these are districts with favorable conditions for agriculture, where the standard of living rose during communism's final 20 years, due largely to the increasing prosperity of agricultural producers. The economic transformation process that began in 1989 has dramatically changed this situation. Because of the ongoing agricultural crisis, these districts are among the most economically depressed in Slovakia, having, for example, a higher rate of unemployment than the Slovak average (SŠÚ, 1991, p. 2). It is apparent, however, that this economic deterioration has a regional or sectoral basis, rather than an ethnic one.[4]

This contention is supported by the fact that the economic programs of the Hungarian political parties in Slovakia are in most cases of a macroeconomic character and are not ethnically based. One exception to this rule is the question of restitution. The Hungarian political parties support the extension of the restitution cut-off date from 1948 back to 1945. The consequence of such an extension would be an immense increase in restituted property, since in 1945 former Czechoslovak President Beneš signed decrees confiscating and putting under national control the property of Germans and Hungarians living on Czechoslovak territory. These parties also favor amendment of the Act on Land and Other Agricultural Property of 1991 in such a way that agricultural land exceeding 50 hectares would be restituted, a move that would particularly benefit ethnic Hungarians.[5]

The second most numerous ethnic minority in Slovakia are the Gypsies. According to the latest census, they numbered 80,627 (only 1.5 percent of the population), but according to data from the state administration their real numbers are considerably larger (approximately 5 percent).[6] The greatest concentration of Gypsies is found in Eastern Slovakia, where their proportion of the population is between 2.5 and 8 percent (SŠÚ, 1992b, pp. 1–3). The social and economic situation of the Gypsies is characterized by a low standard of living, a low educational level, considerable social isolation, and rapid population growth, all of which worsen their social conditions.

In spite of considerable government expenditures, all efforts to solve the problems of the Gypsies over the last 50 years have failed. The main reason for this is the state's paternalistic approach, which did not take into account the minority's specific features. There is a real danger that the Czech Republic will expel from its territory some 150,000 Gypsies who "emigrated" there from Slovakia in the past. Such a step would have very unfavorable consequences for Slovakia, including the necessity to increase budgetary social expenditures, growing criminality, and so on.

Slovakia is also inhabited by approximately 50,000 citizens of Czech nationality, and by about 30,000 Ruthenians and Ukrainians.

The individual and collective rights of ethnic minorities are safeguarded by Slovakia's constitution. The constitution guarantees that all citizens, irrespective of nationality or social status, have equal rights, including the right to freely determine their own nationality. With respect to the rights of ethnic minorities, the constitution complies with such international documents as the International Covenant on Civic and Political Rights, the Document of the Copenhagen Meeting of the Conference on the Human Dimension of the CSCE of 1990, and the Final Statement of the Helsinki Follow-Up Meeting of the CSCE in 1992. Nevertheless, it is necessary to refine the details of the general formulations contained in the constitution, and to enact a number of related laws concerning ethnic minorities that would precisely define the manner in which existing laws will be enforced in practice.[7] This is important not only from the point of view of Slovakia's international obligations, but also for internal reasons, so that ethnic conflict does not threaten the transformation process that the Slovak society and economy is currently undergoing.

Political Relations with the Czech Republic and
Their Economic Consequences

By the end of June 1993, the Czech Republic and Slovakia had concluded 41 interstate agreements, the most important of which in the political sphere is the Treaty on Good-Neighborliness, Friendly Relations, and Cooperation concluded in November 1992, and ratified on January 1, 1993. The speed with which these agreements were concluded — and the fact that mutual recognition and diplomatic relations were established from the first day of the two states' existence — prove that mutual relations are considered important and that there is an interest in developing them. There is certainly no shortage of political, economic, cultural, or historical reasons for this cooperative attitude.

This does not mean, however, that mutual relations are without tension. The frontier regime, the division of the property of the former federation, and citizenship are among the most controversial issues. The Asylum Act passed by Germany and the increasing threat of a mass inflow of emigrants through the Slovak-Czech frontier have compelled the Czech Republic to normalize the frontier regime in accordance with prevailing international standards. Unfortunately, Slovakia will face serious political, economic, and security problems until bilateral agreements on the return of asylum seekers to the first nation to which they migrated are signed with Poland, Hungary, and Ukraine.

As a consequence of the dissolution of the former CSFR, a sizable Slovak minority has come into existence in the Czech Republic: 308,000 people, or 3 percent of the population. These Slovaks — unless they receive Czech citizenship — become foreigners with potentially negative consequences for their economic and social life. With this in mind, Slovakia has been trying, as of this writing without success, to conclude an agreement on double citizenship with the Czech Republic.

According to the Law on the Division of the Property, the property of the former CSFR was divided on the basis of two principles: the territorial principle and the proportional principle, the latter taking into account the relative number of inhabitants of the two new states.[8] According to the proportional principle, the property in question was divided in a 2:1 proportion.

The process of property division was characterized by numerous bones of contention: examples include the use of the federal trademarks ČSAD (Czechoslovak Automobile Transport), Čedok (the Czechoslovak Travel Agency), and ČSA (Czechoslovak Airlines); the temporary freezing of the distribution of shares in Czech enterprises to Slovak individual investors under voucher privatization;[9] and the dispute over the return of Slovak gold kept in Czech banks. As of August 1993, approximately 5 percent of the property of the former CSFR had yet to be divided, the most important of which are the assets of the former federal Czechoslovak State Bank (SBČS).

TOWARD THE MONETARY AND FINANCIAL INDEPENDENCE OF SLOVAKIA

According to the division of powers between the federal and the republic governments, the federal government was responsible for macroeconomic policy. This had several important consequences:

- Opportunities for the Slovak government to modify or even to participate in the preparation of macroeconomic policy were strictly limited.
- In the prevailing Slovak view, the transformation program and attendant economic policy corresponded more or less to the interests of the Czech economy and did not take into account conditions in the Slovak economy. One example is the overly expensive federal social policy financed partly by the Slovak budget.

- Since the Slovaks participated in the federal decision-making process only to a very limited extent, a lack of experience in Slovakia in such fields as monetary policy, and to a lesser extent financial and foreign trade policy and the compilation and analysis of statistics, is apparent. There is a shortage of adequately trained experts and professionals in the government bureaucracy and the banking sector.

Thus, the need to prepare macroeconomic policy from scratch and to set up new institutions represented an important comparative disadvantage for Slovakia in comparison with the Czech Republic. The fact that the leading economic officials have remained in their positions in the Czech (formerly, federal) government for the entire period since 1989 has ensured economic and political continuity in the Czech Republic. At the same time the Czech Republic benefited from a more stable and therefore more experienced government bureaucracy.

The Monetary Independence of Slovakia

From Monetary Union to Own Currency

It was intended that monetary union would be preserved for the first six months of the existence of the independent states. According to agreement, there was supposed to be a common currency, coordination authority — that is, the board of the national bank — and monetary policy during this period. Each member of the union was entitled to leave the union if any of the following held:

- the state budget deficit surpassed 10 percent of GDP;
- foreign exchange reserves dropped beneath the monthly import volume;
- capital transfers between the republics were higher than 5 percent of total deposits; or
- there was principal disagreement over monetary policy.

As of January 1, 1993, the hard currency reserves of the CSFR, which amounted to $1.231 billion, were divided between the Czech Republic and Slovakia according to the ratio 2:1.[10] On that date, the National Bank of Slovakia (NBS) came into existence as a successor to the previous Czech and Slovak State Bank's Center for the Slovak Republic. For the first time in postwar history, responsibility for monetary and exchange rate policy, money circulation, and banking supervision was transferred to Slovakia. Even so, monetary and exchange rate policy during the period of the monetary union was to be decided by a coordinating body.

A sharp decrease in hard currency reserves served to speed up the annulment of the Monetary Agreement, which was broken as early as February 2, 1993. Despite some technical complications, the currency "divorce" was implemented unexpectedly smoothly and without particular problems with respect to the monetary circulation. Thus, the Slovak currency — the Slovak koruna (SK) divided into 100 heller — came into existence.

Immediately after the breakup of the monetary union, a payments agreement was concluded between the two countries so as to ensure that mutual economic relations remained on the highest possible level. This agreement, based on bilateral clearing, solved payments questions and determined the two states' mutual obligations. Payments relations and arrangements for the settlement of mutual obligations were distinguished on the basis of whether they had arisen before or after the date of currency separation. Obligations that had been incurred before February 2, 1993, were recalculated at the fixed exchange rate between the koruna and the ecu (European currency unit) valid on the date of currency separation; the purpose of this step was to prevent any difficulties that might arise due to exchange rate fluctuations.

The starting exchange rate for both new currencies on February 8, 1993, was the same — 34.48 Czech koruna and 34.48 Slovak koruna were set equal to one ecu. From that date the exchange rates of the two currencies have been fixed by the countries' respective national banks independently. New obligations arising after the currency separation are calculated in so-called "clearing ecu." In addition, both national banks are supposed to maintain the difference between the exchange rate for ecu within a 5 percent corridor. Obligations larger than 130 million ecu are to be paid by the fifteenth day of the next month in convertible currency. The interest rate is 10 percent before this date and 15 percent thereafter.[11]

From a Common to an Independent Monetary Policy

The NBS's monetary policy has been developed gradually. During the period of monetary union, continuity with the monetary policy of the former CSFR was ensured. From February 8, 1993, the new priorities and objectives of Slovakia's monetary policy come to the fore. The NBS's monetary policy aims in particular to stabilize the Slovak koruna, to minimize inflation, to maintain equilibrium in the balance of payments, and to increase the hard currency reserves. The overriding objective is to maintain the internal convertibility of the koruna.[12] The NBS has implemented several measures in order to realize these goals, such as administrative steps for controlling exports, introduction of import surcharges (20 percent), and a 10 percent devaluation of the koruna. The goal of these measures is said not to be to increase protection or to isolate the domestic market, but to ensure the new state's macroeconomic stability. The NBS also intends to undertake certain medium-term steps designed to bring about economic recovery in the next few years.

The monetary projection for 1993, based on assumptions of a 4 percent decline in GDP and 17 percent inflation, forecasted growth of M2 of 12 percent and a 14 percent increase in credit granted to the enterprise and household sectors. Nevertheless, preliminary results have been less favorable. In comparison to 1992, when inflation in the CSFR reached 12 percent, the introduction of new taxes in Slovakia (especially the VAT) has had unexpectedly negative effects. These tax reforms engendered an 8.9 percent price jump in January 1993; consumer price inflation gradually stabilized at a monthly rate of 1–1.5 percent. This represents an average annual price increase of 19±1 percent. The devaluation of the koruna in July and the introduction of an additional import surcharge probably added another 6–8 percentage points to inflation in 1993, which came to 25.1 percent.

Development of Financial Infrastructure

The gradual development of financial infrastructure represents an important part of the economic transformation process. After the NBS came into existence the process of creating new commercial banks accelerated as well. Although the oligopolistic position of three large commercial banks (General Credit Bank, Slovak Savings Bank, and Investment and Development Bank) persists, the numbers of other financial and banking institutions, as well as those of specialized banks (e.g., Guarantee Bank, Building Savings Bank, Post Bank), have been growing. The total number of banks in Slovakia in July 1993 was 26. Legislation governing the entry of foreign banks is simultaneously being developed. Unfortunately, the steep growth in the numbers of financial institutions has further deepened the shortage of qualified banking experts.

The Financial Independence of Slovakia

From Three Budgets to the Slovak State Budget

In the former CSFR there were three budgets: the federal budget and two republic budgets. The coordination of financial and budgetary policies was ensured by the Financial Board, on which both the federal and republic representatives sat.

In the course of 1991 and 1992, financial and budgetary policy underwent a gradual process of disintegration. Priority was increasingly given to management of the resources collected in republics separately. At that time the major part of budgetary resources included a turnover tax, a corporate profit tax, and an import tax, all concentrated in a single basket and subsequently divided between the federal and republic budgets. In 1992 the proportions were 35 percent for the federal budget, 41.5 percent for the Czech budget, and 23.5 percent for the Slovak budget. The process of making the budgetary policy of the two republics more independent increased the transparency of the financial links between them. In any case, during 1991 and 1992, transfers from the federal budget helped to alleviate the republic budgets' paucity of resources.

Despite the fact that the 1991 Slovak budgetary program expected a surplus, there was a deficit of 10.2 billion CSK (3.5 percent GDP), and in 1992, instead of the projected balanced budget, a deficit of 7.9 billion CSK (2.8 percent GDP) was recorded. After the decision to dissolve the CSFR, the republic budgets for 1993 were elaborated separately. Although Slovakia's state budget for 1993 was programmed as balanced in the first months of independence, revenue proved inadequate, and the budget deficit in the first quarter reached 11 billion SK.[13] For all of 1993, the budget deficit was 23 billion SK, 6.8 percent of GDP.

One of the main reasons for the state budget deficit in 1993 was the very deep recession. Furthermore, the dissolution of the CSFR necessitated extra expenditures for financing the costs of running the new state, including those of setting up new institutions. The cutoff of transfers from the federal to the republic budgets, and the negative impact of the new tax reform, should also be mentioned.

The main objective of the budgetary policy of the former CSFR during 1991 and 1992 was to maintain macroeconomic stability. Budgetary policy in Slovakia has also adopted this policy guideline, albeit in the face of considerable difficulties. This is why the Slovak government, taking into consideration the recommendations of the IMF, adopted the unavoidable measures to prevent an even larger state budget deficit in 1993.

The Transformation of State Finance

The transition from a planned to a market economy requires a rapid transformation of the state budget and its functions. The extent of centralization of financial resources — that is, the share of the state budget in GDP — was reduced, as was resort to the budget for redistributive purposes. Subsidies to enterprises were greatly reduced and the budget's importance for the implementation of social policy increased. The most important change on the income side — tax reform — was prepared and implemented in a relatively short time span.

The tax policy of the federal government up until 1993 provided little opportunity for the republic governments to pursue independent tax policies. These governments were allowed to make only small modifications to certain tax instruments (e.g., tax cuts for promoting new small and medium-sized enterprises). From 1990 to 1992 some corrections were introduced to the tax policy inherited from the command economy. The rate schedules of various direct and indirect taxes, first and foremost the turnover tax, were simplified. The share of indirect taxes rose and income tax rates were unified.

A new tax system was implemented on January 1, 1993. The system included a value-added tax (VAT) with two rates — 5 percent and 23 percent — a consumption tax, and a road tax. A corporate tax rate of 40 percent of profit and social taxes of 38 percent of the wage bill were introduced. The tax laws allow for tax allowances and tax "holidays" for promoting certain economic policy aims, such as the attraction of foreign direct investment and the encouragement of regional development.

The planned shares of the various taxes in state budget revenue for 1993 were as follows: income taxes represented 23.9 percent (of which corporate taxation made up 20.5 percent); social taxes, such as pension, sickness, and health insurance fees, came to 32.2 percent; and taxes on goods and services accounted for 32.2 percent (of which the VAT accounted for 19.3 percent and consumption taxes 12.7 percent).

ECONOMIC TRANSITION ISSUES IN SLOVAKIA

Economic Transition Program

From Federal to Slovak Economic Transition Policy

The tendency of growing disparities between the main economic indicators for the Czech Republic and Slovakia in 1991 persisted through June 1992, when elections were held, as can be seen from Table 9.2. An exception was the trend in construction activity, which was in Slovakia's favor. On the other hand, the large disparity between the unemployment rates remained more or less unchanged.[14]

TABLE 9.2

Comparative Indicators for Slovakia and the Czech Republic

	1991		1992	
	Slovakia	*Czech R.*	*Slovakia*	*Czech R.*
Consumer prices[1]	161.2	152.0	110.0	112.7
GDP[1]	88.2	85.8	93.0	92.9
Unemployment rate[2]	11.8	4.1	10.4	2.6
Budget balance[3]	−10.8	−8.3	−9.3	−1.7
Industrial production[1]	82.2	75.6	86.2	86.3
Construction[1]	68.0	67.6	106.4	104.8

Source: ČSÚ/ŠÚSR (1993, pp. 65, 68–69); WIIW (1993).

Notes:
[1]Previous year is set equal to 100.
[2]Percent.
[3]Billion Slovak koruna.

The fact that the impact of the federal economic transition program was more severe on the Slovak economy led to a call for the elaboration and implementation of a specifically Slovak transition policy. The political party that expressed this view in the most convincing way won the elections in June 1992. The program of Valdimír Mečiar's victorious Movement for a Democratic Slovakia promised to consider the social aspects of the transition through a less tough fiscal policy and an increasing role of the government in industrial restructuring.[15]

The dissolution of Czechoslovakia raised the hypothetical possibility of independent policy making by Slovakia. However, it very quickly became obvious that such policy independence is subject to strict limitation.

Possibilities for and Limitations on Independent Transition and Economic Policy in Slovakia

The new Slovak government proclaimed its full commitment to the process of economic transition. On the other hand, in contrast to federal transition "orthodoxy," it was proclaimed that the Slovak approach would be based more on Keynesian philosophy than on Milton Friedman's. However, internal and external barriers to a transition program based on this "new" philosophy emerged in a very short time. It was pointed out that some steps in the federal transition program were irreversible; furthermore, the costs of certain of these steps had already been incurred. Moreover, the growing budget deficit narrowed — at least in the short term — the possibilities for a "more socially oriented" policy. Indeed, compared with the previous period, the government's social policy had to become even more restrictive.

There were also many external factors that constrained Slovakia's ability to change course. First, Slovakia had to take into account the IMF's and World Bank's orthodox transition model, on the basis of which these organizations provide credit necessary for the stabilization, restructuring, and recovery of the Slovak economy. Further limitations on independent economic policy making are created by agreements between the Slovak and Czech governments, especially by the Monetary Agreement and Customs Union Agreement, which presuppose common monetary and foreign trade policies. Indeed, the Customs Union Agreement continues to be the most important determinant of Slovakia's foreign trade policy.

Economic Results in the First Months of Independence and the Macroeconomic Stabilization Program

After the dissolution of the CSFR, the first critical moments for Slovak economic policy were represented by the two rounds of negotiations with the IMF in February and May–June 1993. After the Slovak government committed itself to implementing a so-called economic policy memorandum, an IMF stabilization loan was granted.[16]

An assessment of economic developments in Slovakia in 1993 must consider numerous factors: the persistent recession; the economic consequences of the dissolution of the CSFR (the reduction in inter-republic trade was projected to reduce GDP by some 5 percent); the high costs of creating the institutions of a sovereign state; and the introduction of the new tax system on January 1, 1993, which has been accompanied by serious difficulties in its initial phase.

Macroeconomic indicators for the Slovak economy in 1993 were as follows: a 4.1 percent decrease in GDP and a 13.5 percent decrease in industrial production; 25.1 percent inflation; a 14.4 percent unemployment rate; a negative foreign trade balance of $900 million; a nominal wage index of 190.5; and a 23 billion SK (6.8 percent of GDP) state budget deficit.

A tendency toward chronic budget deficits has been observed: the monthly budget deficits in the first three months moved between 11 and 14 billion SK, approaching the IMF's limit of 16 billion SK for all of 1993. With the aim of eliminating the risk of exceeding this deficit limit, the Slovak government — taking into account IMF recommendations — committed itself to implementing several measures on both the revenue and expenditure sides of the budget. To increase state budget revenues, on August 1, 1993, the two VAT rates were raised from 5 to 6 percent, and from 23 to 25 percent, respectively.

At the same time, certain consumption tax rates and the property tax were increased. In addition, measures for improving tax collection were implemented. The estimated increase in budget revenue as a result of these steps was 3.4 billion SK. Simultaneously, investment and noninvestment expenditures and subsidies to education, health care, administration, and enterprises, as well as social allowances, were cut. These measures were expected to save from 4.5 to 5 billion SK.

Nonetheless, certain positive economic tendencies were observed during the first months of independence. These included the favorable development of the export-import ratio and relatively low rate of price increase.

Slovakia's macroeconomic stabilization program included a tougher monetary policy for the second half of 1993. On the basis of pessimistic estimates showing a decrease in GDP of 7–8 percent and 30.4 percent inflation, M2 was projected to increase by 19 percent and the annual growth of net domestic assets not to exceed 20 percent. The growth of net credit to the government was projected at 51.3 percent, while the growth of credit to the enterprise and household sectors was to be 13.6 percent. To maintain internal currency convertibility — on top of the aforementioned administrative measures introduced in the first months of 1993 — the NBS devalued the koruna by about 10 percent in June

(NBS, 1993, p. 30). The introduction of a 20 percent import surcharge on consumer goods was another measure intended to help stabilize the economy.

Restructuring the Slovak Economy

Industrial Restructuring

Slovakia's sectoral and industrial structure — inherited from central planning and the old model of the interrepublic division of labor — is one of the main reasons why the nation's economic prospects are poorer than the Czech Republic's. In Slovakia the primary and secondary sectors remained predominant. In 1989, the employment shares of these two sectors came to 17.1 and 44.8 percent, respectively, while the share of the tertiary sector was 38.1 percent (FSÚ/SI, various years). With respect to the industrial structure, the shares of metallurgy and the chemical industry were particularly high: in 1990 their respective shares of industrial production were 10.3 and 15.8 percent (ŠÚSR, 1993c).

The consequences of the dependence of the Slovak economy on heavy industry include high energy consumption, serious environmental disruption, and a high dependence on oil and ores imported from the former Soviet Union. At the same time, Slovak industry faces decreasing external demand for such traditional products as iron, steel, textiles, and cement, along with substantial import barriers raised by the market economies.

These factors make restructuring the Slovak economy unavoidable. The most important aspect of industrial restructuring is undoubtedly conversion of the military industry. The major part of the Slovak military industry developed in the postwar period as the product of two factors: the geographic location of Slovakia within the Warsaw Pact; and the nature of the program for industrializing the Slovak economy in the context of the prevailing model of inter-republic economic links. At the end of the 1980s the share of the Slovak military industry in total Czechoslovak military production came to 65 percent.

Within the branch structure of the military-industrial complex, the dominant industry was machine building (86.1 percent). In 1987, the share of military production in the output of the machine building sector was 32 percent. During 1975–88 the products of the Slovak military industry were predominantly sold to the Czechoslovak army and to the armies of other Warsaw pact members. The political changes of 1988 and 1989 obviously necessitated conversion of the military industry to civilian production. Nevertheless, the federal government's decision to reduce military-industrial production in Slovakia to barely 10 percent of its 1988 level within two or three years has had very serious economic, social, and political consequences. Undoubtedly, these consequences helped to speed up the dissolution of the CSFR.

Any assessment of structural developments during 1990–92 would not be very positive, since the shares of the energy industry and iron and steel increased, while those of light industry and engineering decreased. Less sophisticated products are more easily tradable on the Western markets, toward which Slovak exports were reoriented after the collapse of the CMEA, than more sophisticated ones. Other than the military industry, the most troubled industries are electronics, construction materials, textiles and clothing, and nonferrous metals.

The most significant structural change that occurred was a decline in agriculture from 13.2 percent in 1990 to 8.5 percent in 1991 in terms of production, and from 14.2 percent in 1990 to 11.7 percent in 1991 in terms of employment (FSÚ/SI, various years). During 1989–92, gross agricultural production declined by 26.5 percent. At the same time, the profitability of agricultural enterprises has deteriorated, so that more than 90 percent of them have become loss-making. Among the factors contributing to this situation are the large spread between buying and selling prices, the decline in the demand for foodstuffs, a sharp reduction in food subsidies, and competition from Czech and Western food products.

The sectoral and industrial restructuring of the Slovak economy clearly represents a complicated aspect of the transformation that requires time and vast capital investment. Government involvement in this restructuring by means of efficient policies on export promotion, imports, and taxation seems to us to be unavoidable.

Progress on Privatization

By the summer of 1993, small-scale privatization in Slovakia was almost complete. The number of units sold via auctions from February 1991 to December 31, 1992, amounted to 9,676, and the proceeds from small-scale privatization reached 14.5 billion SK. It is thus clear that obtaining the proceeds from privatization was not the major objective of small-scale privatization. The sectoral structure of privatized small enterprises, rounded off, is as follows: trade and catering, 73.4; services, 13.5; industry, 8.2; and construction, 4.4.

The first phase of large-scale privatization was nearly completed in the first half of 1993. The number of state-owned enterprises (SOEs) subject to such privatization included 503 joint stock companies privatized in the first phase of voucher privatization, 180 firms sold in direct sales to predetermined owners, and 170 instances of sales of shares in state-owned joint stock companies. An analysis of the purchase price/book value ratio in cases of sales of shares and sales of property to domestic and foreign buyers shows that there is a tendency to "give away" state assets to domestic investors (the ratios are very close to unity).

Sales of shares to foreign investors proved more successful in bringing revenue to the state budget, as the corresponding ratio was 3.157:1. With respect to sales of property to foreigners, the ratio 1.47:1 had earlier provoked accusations that the government was "selling the country short" (Schmögnerová, 1993, p. 34). As in the case of small-scale privatization, revenue from the sale of property was not the primary objective, and an even smaller amount — 13.85 billion SK — was obtained for the budget than from small-scale privatization.

In the voucher privatization of 503 joint stock companies, 98 such companies were completely sold. The distribution of shares between investment funds and individual investors was according to the ratio 56.4:43.6, so that the dominant new owners of the former SOEs will be investment funds. The ownership structure of privatized enterprises as of the end of 1992 was as follows: 77 percent institutional and individual share ownership generated by voucher privatization, 11 percent permanent ownership by the state, 6 percent temporary ownership by the state, 3 percent ownership generated by restitution, and 3 percent ownership generated by restitution.

As of the end of 1992, the results of privatization were encouraging as regards the share of private organizations in the total number of economic organizations, which reached 77.3 percent and the increasing share of the private sector in the economy. The sectoral shares of the private sector were as follows: trade (59.3 percent), services (45.1 percent), road transport (36.6 percent), construction (32 percent), agriculture (21.3 percent), and industry (9.5 percent) (ŠÚSR, 1993b).

In any event, the manner in which the behavior of newly privatized enterprises will be affected by the nature of their ownership structure — that is, whether it is dominated by institutional or individual share owners — is far from clear. Accordingly, it is unlikely that the efficiency of these enterprises will increase in the short run.

Although before 1989 the industrial and construction sectors were over 90 percent in state ownership, in agriculture cooperative ownership prevailed. In the course of 1992 the so-called "transformation of the former socialist cooperatives into cooperatives of owners" occurred. Ownership shares depended on the work and property contributions of the cooperatives' members (and affiliated nonmembers).

Restitution of the property claimed by former land owners preceded the transformation of the cooperatives. At the beginning of 1993 over 100,000 individuals raised restitution claims, of which 67.7 percent were claims for the land belonging to the cooperatives; altogether these claims did not exceed 6.7 percent of the total agricultural land. The average claim was 1.34 hectares per client. The number of new proprietors who must be paid rent amount to over 350,000. At the moment, one-third of all agricultural land is burdened by the payment of such rent, which varies from 104 to 833 SK per hectare. This additional cost has caused a further deterioration in the already poor financial situation of the agricultural cooperatives.

The privatization policy of the two Mečiar governments (the one elected in June 1992 and that elected in September 1994) has differed from those of the federal and Czech governments. The major differences include divergence in view as to the overriding priority of privatization (speed versus efficiency); as to the weights to be given to the methods to be employed (i.e., the voucher method versus more standard, market-oriented approaches); and with respect to certain branch- and sector-specific issues.

While the first Mečiar government proclaimed its strong commitment to privatization, the speed of the process slowed under it. This can be explained by many factors: unlike in the Czech Republic, speed was not considered the number one priority; more emphasis was put on traditional privatization methods which are more time consuming; and legislation had to be amended. Although that government claimed to be interested in speeding up privatization and intended to take measures to encourage the participation of more domestic and foreign investors, in reality, the process slowed considerably during its tenure (which ended in March 1994).

Slovakia's External Sector

Export and Import Trends

As a product of the interrepublic division of labor of the past 40 years, Slovakia's external sector in the second half of the 1980s was characterized as follows:

- A greater import and a lesser export orientation in comparison with the Czech Republic.
- Less sophisticated export products compared to those of the Czech Republic. Heavy machinery — including military products — iron, steel, and chemicals held the dominant export shares.
- Raw materials, oil, and fuels predominated among imports.
- In the territorial structure of exports and imports, the share of nonmarket economies was higher than in the Czech Republic.

Accordingly, it is not surprising that the rapid trade liberalization of 1991 and the sharp devaluation of Czechoslovak koruna (an 86.6 percent devaluation at the end of 1990) more severely affected Slovakia's external sector than that of the Czech Republic. At the same time, the collapse of CMEA trade has had a disastrous impact on the Slovak economy, since until 1989 such trade dominated the territorial structure of Slovak exports.

Despite its less favorable starting position, however, the Slovak external sector has partially succeeded in adjusting to the new situation. In 1991 and 1992, two important trends in the Slovak export appeared:

- A territorial restructuring of exports in favor of the market economies. During 1989–92, the share of the former CMEA countries in Slovakia's exports decreased from 57 to 30 percent, and the share of EC and EFTA (European Free Trade Association) countries increased from 27 to 52 percent. Similar, although not identical, trends appeared in the territorial structure of Slovak imports.
- An increase in the share of exports in GDP from 21.3 percent in 1990 to 33.2 percent in 1991, and to 35 percent in 1992.

In addition, considerable success has been achieved in establishing new forms of economic links with the advanced market economies, and in the process in incorporating Slovakia into European economic structures. By virtue of free trade agreements concluded with EFTA, CEFTA (Central European Free Trade Association), and the EC, a successive liberalization of mutual trade has taken place. The asymmetry of some of these agreements — such as those with EFTA and with the EC, although in the latter instance the Europe Agreement is considered in Slovakia not to go far enough — provides an adjustment period thought necessary for the integration of a less-advanced economy with more advanced ones.

The negative impact of the "external shock" from the collapse of CMEA trade and the devaluation in 1991 on the import-dependent

Slovak economy contributed to Slovakia's negative trade balance that year, when the trade deficit amounted to $343.3 million. In 1992, the trade deficit decreased, unfortunately not so much due to an increase in exports (+1.9 percent) as to a decrease in imports (–5.3 percent). This trade deficit is largely explained by Slovakia's dependence on fuel imports from the former USSR. The trade deficit with the former Soviet Union in 1992 reached $700 million. An increase in exports to its successor states is highly unlikely in the short- to medium-term, in view of the insolvency of most importers there.

A more significant improvement in the performance of Slovakia's external sector would require deeper changes in the structure of production and exports. The present achievements in exports are largely connected to increases in exports of such primary products as steel and chemicals, while exports of machinery and transport vehicles are lagging considerably.

One positive side of the former communist regime in Czechoslovakia was that it did not resort to foreign borrowing to the same extent as Bulgaria, Hungary, or Poland. By the beginning of the transition, the foreign debt of Czechoslovakia had reached around $8 billion (OECD, 1991, p. 33) — substantially less per capita than in these other nations. In the course of 1991–92, the external debt of the federal government expanded to $9.36 billion, of which Slovakia's share came to one-third, or $3.2 billion, representing 32.7 percent of 1992 GDP.[17] Although it is safe to assume that the external debt will increase further, the expected debt burden should not reach the range of the more heavily indebted states in the region.

Economic Links with the Czech Republic

Interrepublic trade links are more or less the product of the division of labor between the Czech and Slovak economies as it developed over the postwar period. Slovakia's postwar industrialization resulted in a branch structure based on heavy industry which was complementary to the structure of Czech industry. Slovak exports to the Czech Republic consisted primarily of raw materials, semi-finished products, and heavy machinery, while Czech exports to Slovakia were dominated by finished products and means of transportation: cars, trucks, and locomotives. Many products were exclusively produced either in the Czech Republic or in Slovakia. In 1989, the list of goods produced only in the Czech Republic included the following: lead, hard coal, cars, motorcycles over 50 cubic centimeters, and certain labor-saving devices, while the equivalent list for Slovakia included aluminum, nickel, refrigerators, and television sets.

In the course of the last 40 years a strong economic interdependence developed between the Czech Republic and Slovakia. The reliance of the Slovak economy on its Czech counterpart is more significant than vice versa. In 1992 Slovakia's trade with the Czech Republic represented more than 48 percent of the former's "foreign trade," while in the opposite direction this share did not exceed 28 percent.

In many industrial branches imports from the Czech Republic to Slovakia and vice versa are indispensable for production. A significant share of consumer products are imported into Slovakia from the Czech Republic; this is also the case in the other direction. The replacement of these imports by imports from third countries would generate shortages of hard currency in both countries. Accordingly, the two nations will undoubtedly endeavor to keep inter-republic trade at an adequate level.

On the other hand, the present economic links between the two republics may be considered temporary. Even in the course of the first two years of the transition, as a consequence of the sharp decline in internal demand and an increasing preference for exports to the market economies, inter-republic trade fell by 50 percent. At the end of the 1980s Slovakia exported 28 percent of its industrial production to the Czech Republic; by 1992 this figure had fallen to 21 percent. At the same time, the share of Slovak industrial exports going to the third countries increased from 17.5 percent in 1989 to 23 percent in 1992. Similar trends are visible in the Czech economy: Industrial exports to Slovakia declined from 13.5 percent of total exports at the end of the 1980s to 9 percent in 1992, while exports to the third countries increased from 16.5 to 18.8 percent. This reorientation of the direction of Slovakia's trade may be expected to persist in the long run.

The development of mutual trade in the first months after the dissolution of the CSFR was rather unfavorable; it decreased to an estimated 50 percent of the level of the previous year. By the winter of 1994, mutual trade had fallen by about 30 percent since the break up of the federation (Cook, 1994).

In an effort to keep mutual trade as large as possible, the Czech Republic and Slovakia concluded several economic agreements prior to the dissolution of the CSFR. Among the most important are the Customs Union Agreement, the Monetary Agreement, the Employment Agreement, the Investment Protection Agreement, the Social Agreement, the Environment Agreement, and the Agreement on Avoidance of Double Taxation. In addition, the unexpectedly short existence of the monetary union necessitated the conclusion of the Payments Agreement, which makes possible payments in national currencies, thereby promoting inter-republic trade.

Two forms of trade agreement — a free trade agreement and a customs union agreement — were under discussion at the end of 1992. A free trade agreement would have made it possible for Slovakia to pursue an independent trade policy and to protect its more vulnerable economy (Okáli, 1993). Nevertheless, such external factors as a less complicated and more rapid succession to agreements with the EC, to GATT, and to other international economic organizations ultimately led the parties to select a customs union, the more advanced form of cooperation.

Foreign Aid and Foreign Direct Investment in Slovakia

After the dissolution of the CSFR, the foreign aid previously granted to the federation was given directly either to the Czech Republic or to Slovakia. Aid granted but not dispersed by the end of 1992 was either divided according to the 2:1 principle or directed to a "common package," from which it would fund projects depending on their required level of funding. In Slovakia this makes it possible, for instance, to receive a larger share of the capital provided by the former Czechoslovak-American Enterprise Fund, the aim of which is to support small and medium-sized enterprises. Foreign aid includes nonrepayable and repayable contributions by governments and international institutions, oriented most of all to supporting the transformation of the Slovak economy. The most important is that granted by the EC, which during 1993 provided 1.4 billion SK for the development of the private sector, human resources, and infrastructure, and for technical assistance.

As for foreign direct investment, as of the end of 1992 the inflow of such investment into Slovakia was less than 10 percent of that obtained by the Czech Republic. There are a number of explanations for this imbalance, including the proximity of the Czech Republic to the largest exporter of foreign capital (Germany), and the fact that the Czech economy is more advanced, thus offering better infrastructure and higher efficiency. Another reason for the disparity is beyond doubt the information asymmetry in favor of the Czech Republic. The CSFR's diplomatic offices and trade representatives mostly employed Czech employees, who provided more information about the Czech economy than about its Slovak counterpart.

Political developments after the elections held in June 1992 — which led to the dissolution of the CSFR — had a highly negative impact on the flow of foreign direct investment into Slovakia.[18] This reflected fear and uncertainty concerning Slovakia's future political and economic development. It was not until the first quarter of 1993 that confidence was at least partially restored and foreign direct investment increased by 14.2 percent relative to December 31, 1992.

Foreign investors on the Slovak market, whose comparative advantages include qualified, but cheap labor — even cheaper than in the Czech Republic — and closeness to and knowledge of Eastern markets, have generally made relatively small investments. This can be seen from figures on the average investment per foreign organization or joint venture: $80,650 as of December 31, 1992; and $82,600 as of March 31, 1993. That the typical investment is minuscule becomes even clearer when it is realized that such large investments as Volkswagen's into the automobile industry, Henkel's into the chemical industry, and Samsung's into the production of refrigerators have been included in the average. In terms of country of origin, the largest foreign investors in Slovakia as of March 31, 1993, were Austria ($80.8 million or 30.5 percent of the total), Germany ($57.4 million or 21.6 percent), and the U.S. ($43.8 million or 16.5 percent).

Just as foreign direct investment in the Czech Republic has mostly been concentrated in Prague and a few other cities, the highest concentration of such investment in Slovakia has been in Bratislava and several other regional centers: Košice, Martin, Poprad, and Nitra. The main reason for this concentration is that these cities have a relatively highly developed infrastructure, qualified labor, and, in the case of Bratislava, the advantages of being the legal and administrative center. The proximity of Bratislava to Vienna and Budapest also plays a decisive role. Other, less favored regions, such as the southern and eastern parts of the country, have a very low share of total foreign investment.

Although many obstacles preventing an increased inflow of foreign investment have already been removed, foreign investors are still discouraged by Slovakia's insufficiently stable economic and political situation, its inadequate infrastructure and capital market, gaps in legislation, administrative obstacles, and, arguably, by the low degree of protection afforded the domestic market. In our view, however, in the long run, a respectable inflow of foreign direct investment may be generated by Slovakia's advantageous geopolitical situation, provided that economic policies are devised that strongly emphasize international economic cooperation.

CONCLUSIONS: AN ASSESSMENT OF
SLOVAKIA'S FIRST STEPS TOWARD
ECONOMIC INDEPENDENCE

(1) The disparities between the Czech and Slovak economies, which grew during 1991 and the first half of 1992, have since gradually been reduced. By the end of 1992, there appeared to be no important factors that would predetermine great differences in the level of economic development of the republics after the dissolution of the CSFR.

Nevertheless, the impact of the breakup of Czechoslovakia on the Slovak economy, due to such short-term negative factors as the high cost of creating the new institutions of an independent state and the cutoff of federal budgetary transfers, are greater than those faced by the Czech economy. The same may be said of such longer-term phenomena as a smaller internal market, a less adequate industrial structure, lower competitiveness, and greater dependence on Eastern markets. In 1993, the Slovak economy experienced negative growth of GDP of 4.1 percent, inflation of 25.1 percent, a budget deficit of 6.8 percent of GDP, and ended the year with an unemployment rate of 14.4 percent. In contrast, the Czech Republic in 1993 saw GDP decline by –0.3 percent, inflation of 18.2 percent (the lowest of all economies in transition), a virtually balanced budget, and an unemployment rate of 3.5 percent (the lowest in the region, other than former Soviet republics) at year's end.[19]

(2) One alleged benefit to Slovakia of the dissolution of the CSFR was to be the opportunities that dissolution afforded to create a transition program adapted to the particularities of the Slovak economy. In the end, however, the economic stabilization program first adopted by the Mečiar government turned out to be an orthodox one of the sort prescribed by the IMF and the World Bank.

(3) The list of problems that the Slovak government had to face in 1993 is rather long: a large state budget deficit; a sharp increase in prices; a growing state debt; a swelling external debt; a low level of hard currency reserves; and a fall in the government's credibility. The disintegration of the CSFR, the new tax system, and the EC's protective policies may prove to have still further negative side effects. A breaking of the "social contract" with the population would be one of the most dangerous side effects. Efforts must be made to distribute more evenly the negative side effects of the ongoing economic and political transition and to protect the neediest elements of the population.

NOTES

1.   The joint project for the construction of the dam was based on a bilateral intergovernment treaty from 1977, which at present Hungary refuses to recognize. The two countries have agreed to submit the dispute to the International Court of Justice in the Hague.

2.   Slovakia has assumed all relevant contractual obligations of the former Czechoslovakia.

3.   However, the possibility is allowed for that they may be modified in a peaceful manner.

4.   In many districts with a high proportion of Hungarians, there is a considerable degree of entrepreneurial activity supported by an inflow of capital from Hungary. This may become an important dynamizing factor in the near future.

5.   This would mean that more than half of the woodlands and a great part of the agricultural land would become the property of ethnic Hungarians.

6.   A low level of ethnic self-consciousness and self-identification problems that cause Gypsies to consider themselves members of other minorities are among the main reasons for the differences in the statistics.

7.   Amendment of the language law is urgently needed, so as to settle the issue of the use of first and family names written in the minority's own language. The same applies to the question of the inscription of place names in both languages.

8.   The Law on the Division of the Property of the former CSFR between the Czech Republic and the Slovak Republic was enacted on November 13, 1992.

9.   The Czech government had argued that since more shares of the Czech enterprises were sold in Slovakia than vice versa, compensation of 19 billion Czech koruna should be paid to the Czech government by the Slovak government. Reaction from abroad forced the Czech government to change its mind.

10.   In June 1992, the hard currency reserves of the CSFR came to $4.89 billion. In the course of the second half of 1992, Czech commercial banks bought up a considerable part of these reserves. At the same time, Czech imports increased considerably. The Czech trade deficit that year reached 22.6 billion CSK, while the equivalent figure for Slovakia was only 2.1 billion CSK.

11.   This difference is flexible. During the period from February to April 1993, the NBS made use of the entire corridor and devalued the Slovak koruna by ten percent relative to the Czech currency unit. The Czech national bank revalued at the same time in such way that the difference between Slovak koruna and Czech koruna came to 7 percent. After Slovakia had by the late fall run up a clearing deficit with the Czech Republic that threatened to exceed the limit of 130 million ecu, the Slovak koruna was devalued by a further 8 percent relative to the ecu on December 7 (Cook, 1994).

12.   Internal convertibility gives enterprises and organizations the right to buy foreign currencies in commercial banks at the official exchange rate for financing imports. At the same time these actors are obligated to offer foreign currency acquired via exports at the same official exchange rate to the commercial banks. Every citizen over 15 years of age may buy a limited amount of foreign currency at a commercial bank (in 1993 this amounted to 7,000 SK).

13.   In the first quarter of the year, revenue represented 16 percent (25 billion SK), and expenditures 23 percent (36 billion SK), of the annual budget. The highest degree

of underpayment occurred for the VAT (65.8 percent of the expected level of revenue), the income tax (62 percent), and social taxes (52 percent).

14.   This can be explained by various factors: a greater degree of overemployment in Slovakia prior to 1989; demographic factors; faster development of the private sector in the Czech Republic; and perhaps by more "socially oriented" behavior on the part of Czech enterprises.

15.   The election program of the winning party was not based on the disintegration of the CSFR but in fact called for the formation of a confederation between the two states.

16.   Slovakia received a new kind of loan from the IMF, a so-called "systemic transformation facility" (STF) designed to provide funding to countries with severe balance of payments problems due to disruption of their traditional trade and payments arrangments. An STF is to be granted in instances where conditions are not yet met for the provision of a conventional standby arrangement. The first tranche of the loan totaled $90 million.

17.   In 1989 the Hungarian external debt amounted to 70.8 percent of GDP.

18.   As much as 75 percent of foreign direct investment received in 1992 entered Slovakia during the first half of the year.

19.   The figures for 1993 cited here for Slovakia and the Czech Republic were collected from official sources — and in certain instances are projections based on information found in those sources — by Sten Luthman of the Stockholm Institute of East European Economics. See also ÚET (1993, p. 7).

REFERENCES

Bútorová, Zora. "Premyslené 'áno' zániku ČSFR? Image strán a rozpad Česko-Slovenska očami občanov Slovenska." *Sociologický časopis* 29, 1 (1993): 88–103.

Cook, Joe. "Let's Stay Friends." *Business Central Europe*, February 1994, p. 19.

[ČSÚ.] *Číselné zrcadlo české ekonomiky*. Prague: Český statistický úřad, 1993a.

[ČSÚ.] *Přehled ukazatelů sociálního a ekonomického rozvoje ČR*, 1993/1. Prague: Český statistický úřad, 1993b.

[ČSÚ/ŠÚSR.] *Statistické přehledy*, no. 3. Prague: Český statisticky úřad/Štatistický úřad Slovenskej republiky, 1993.

[FSÚ/SI.] *Statistické informace*. Prague: Federálni statistický úřad, various years.

[FSÚ/SR.] *Statistická ročenka ČSFR*. Prague: Federálni statistický úřad, 1992.

[FSÚ/GUS/KSH.] *Statistical Bulletin*, no. 3. Warsaw: Federálni statistický úřad, Główny urząd statystyczny, and Központi statisztikai hivatal, 1992.

[NBS.] *Správa o národnohospodárskom a menovom vyvoji v SR v 1. štvrťroku 1993*. Bratislava: Národná banka Slovenska, 1993.

[OECD.] *OECD Economic Surveys: Czech and Slovak Federal Republic*. Paris: Organisation for Economic Co-operation and Development, 1991.

Okáli, I. *Stratégia oživenia alebo prežitia?* Bratislava: ELITA, 1993.

Schmögnerová, Brigita. "Privatization in Transition: Some Lessons from the Slovak Republic." Geneva: UNCTAD, May 1993 (mimeo).

[ŠÚSR.] *Medzinárodné porovanie Slovenska s ČSFR, Maďarskou a Poľskou republikou, no. IV/1992.* Bratislava: Štatistický úrad Slovenskej republiky, 1993a.

[ŠÚSR.] *Štatistické analýzy a informácie.* Bratislava: Štatistický úrad Slovenskej republiky, May 1993b.

[ŠÚSR.] *Štatistická správa o hlavných tendenciách vývoja národného hospodárstva SR v roku 1992 a odhad vývoja na I. polrok 1993.* Bratislava: Štatistický úrad Slovenskej republiky, 1993c.

[SŠÚ.] *Medziokresné porovnania v SR za rok 1991.* Bratislava: Slovenský štatistický úrad, 1991.

[SŠÚ.] *Buletin*, nos. 1–10. Bratislava: Slovenský štatistický úrad, 1992a.

[SŠÚ.] *Národnostná štruktúra, obyvateľstva SR (predbežné výsledky sčítania 1991).* Bratislava: Slovenský štatistický úrad, 1992b.

[ÚET.] "Trh práce v Slovenskej republike: Analýze a projekcia na rok 1993." Bratislava: Ústav ekonomickej teórie, Slovenska akadémia vied, 1993 (mimeo).

[WIIW.] "Slovakia: comprehensive statistical data for the first time." *Mitgliederinformation* 10, pp. 28–31. Vienna: Wiener Institut für internationale Wirstschaftsvergleiche, 1993.

Index

successor state, 43; tax policy by,
239, 241; trade by, 20, 248–50;
transition limitations and, 242
Slovenia: autarkic tendencies by,
156–57; banking reform in,
152–53; capital accumulation
and, 159–60; Croatian trade with,
171, 181; European Community
and, 139, 157, 158, 160–61;
exchange rate policy and,
148–49; fiscal reform by, 146–47;
generalization of experience by,
161–62; germanization and, 157;
independence achievement by,
139–40; inflation in, 140–41,
147; labor market and, 16,
153–54, 159; leadership quality
and, 3; Macedonia compared
with, 195, 198–99, 200;
Macedonia's trade with, 203;
macroeconomic background of,
140–41; monetary independence
by, 141, 145–46, 159; monetary
policy by, 16, 144, 147–48;
performance improvement by,
15–16; price stabilization by, 144;
privatization and, 16, 141,
149–52, 160; refugee problem
and, 157; risk perception about,
157, 158; secession costs/benefits
and, 16–17, 155–61; trade
reorientation by, 155–56;
unemployment in, 141; Yugoslav
pre-independence relations with,
155
Social Accounting Service: in
Croatia, 17, 174; in Macedonia,
205; in Slovenia, 151
Social Agreement (former
Czechoslovakia), 251
Social Democratic Alliance
(Macedonia), 194
Socialist Party (Kazakhstan), 103
Solidarity, 76
Soros, George, 212
Soviet republics. *See*
Commonwealth of Independent
States (CIS)

Soviet Union: debt of, Estonia and,
43; disintegration of, 1–2;
Georgia and collapse of, 115,
116, 126; power collapse of,
26–27; Ukrainian production for,
54
Srijem, Croatia, 182
State Committee on Privatization
(Kazakhstan), 92
Sukhumi, Georgia, 118
Sweden, 44
Swiss Bank KAM, 102
Syndicate of Trade Unions, 206
Systemic Transformation Facility
(STF), 101

Taagepera, Rein, 30
Tadzhikistan, 98
Taiwan, 71
Tallinn, Estonia, 29, 36
Tbilisi, Georgia, 133
Temirmunay, Kazakhstan, 84
Tengiz, Kazakhstan, 84
Tereshchenko, Sergey, 93
Thessaloniki, Greece, 194
Treaty on Good-Neighborliness,
Friendly Relations, and
Cooperation (former
Czechoslovakia), 235
Trianon Treaty, 230
Troebst, Stefan, 221
Tudman, Franjo, 191 n.51
Turkey: broad money-to-GPD ratio
in, 63: Central Asian ties by, 102;
exports by, 55; Georgian trade
with, 127; Kazakhstan and, 104;
Muslim ex-Soviet republics and,
44; pipeline construction and,
100; regional cooperation and,
106; Ukraine and, 71
Turkmenistan, 98, 127

Ukraine: agricultural sector and, 72;
banking sector and, 72; budget
deficit of, 62–63; energy supply
and, 56; food prices/supply and,
58–62, 64–65, 67–68, 69;
geographical area of, 54;

About the Editor and Contributors

IVO BIĆANIĆ is Professor, Department of Macroeconomics and Economic Policy, Economics Faculty, University of Zagreb.

PATRICK J. CONWAY is Associate Professor, Department of Economics, University of North Carolina at Chapel Hill.

MILAN CVIKL is Economist, Central Europe Department, World Bank.

HERTA GABRIELOVÁ is Senior Research Fellow, Institute of Economic, Slovak Academy of Sciences.

ARDO H. HANSSON is Research Fellow, Stockholm Institute of East European Economics, Economic Advisor to the Government of Estonia, and Board Member, Bank of Estonia. He has also served as an economic advisor to the Ukrainian government.

EGON HLAVATÝ is Senior Research Fellow, Institute of Economics, Slovak Academy of Sciences.

ADELA HOŠKOVÁ is Senior Research Fellow, Institute of Economics, Slovak Academy of Sciences.

TIMUR R. ISATAEV is Graduate Student, Department of Economics, Johns Hopkins University, and Assistant to the Executive Director, World Bank.

SIMON JOHNSON is Assistant Professor, Fuqua School of Business, Duke University; he has served as an economic advisor to the Ukrainian government.

ZORA KOMÍNKOVÁ is Senior Research Fellow, Institute of Economics, Slovak Academy of Sciences.

EVAN KRAFT is Assistant Professor, Department of Economics and Finance, Salisbury State University, and Fulbright scholar, Ekonomski Institut, Zagreb.

MILAN KURUCZ is Associate Professor, Department of Business, Economic University of Bratislava.

CHANDRASHEKAR PANT is Economist, Country Operations Division, World Bank.

PETER RUTLAND is Associate Professor, Department of Government, Wesleyan University, and Assistant Director for Research, Open Media Research Institute, Prague.

BRIGITA SCHMÖGNEROVÁ is Senior Research Fellow, Institute of Economics, Slovak Academy of Sciences, and a former deputy prime minister of Slovakia.

OLEG USTENKO is Lecturer, Kiev State Economic University.

MILAN VODOPIVEC is Economist, Transition Economies Division, World Bank, and Advisor to the Prime Minister of Slovenia.

MICHAEL L. WYZAN is Associate Professor, Stockholm School of Economics, and Senior Research Analyst, Open Media Research Institute, Prague.

ISBN 0-275-94717-3

EAN

9 780275 947170

90000>